The Green Guide to
Germany

KIEL
Schleswig-Holstein

HAMBURG
Mecklenburg-Vorpommern
SCHWERIN

BREMEN

Niedersachsen

HANNOVER
POTSDAM
BERLIN

MAGDEBURG
Brandenburg

Nordrhein-Westfalen
Sachsen-Anhalt

DÜSSELDORF
LEIPZIG
Sachsen

KÖLN
ERFURT
DRESDEN

BONN
Thüringen

Hessen

WIESBADEN
Rheinland-Pfalz
FRANKFURT
MAINZ

Saarland
SAARBRÜCKEN

Bayern

STUTTGART

MÜNCHEN

Baden-Württemberg

0   50 100 150 200 250km

The Green Guide to
Germany _____

Fleur & Colin Speakman

**GREEN
PRINT**

Also in this series

Green Guide to England
Green Guide to Scotland
Green Guide to Wales
Green Guide to France

First published in 1992 by
Green Print
an imprint of the Merlin Press
10 Malden Road, London NW5 3HR

© Fleur and Colin Speakman
The right of Fleur and Colin Speakman to be identified as authors of this work has been
asserted in accordance with the Copyright, Design and Patents Act 1988.

ISBN 1 85425 070 1
Phototypeset by Computerset, Harmondsworth, Middlesex

Printed in England by Biddles Ltd., Guildford, Surrey
on recycled paper

Contents

To our many friends in the recently reunited Germany

ACKNOWLEDGEMENTS

We would like to thank the many people in both England and Germany who helped us to create this book, including a number of professional and voluntary organisations, who provided detailed information so freely and readily.

We would like to express special gratitude to the following without whose help this book would not have been possible. Needless to say, any mistakes and misinterpretations are entirely our own.

In Germany: Patricia Bergholz (Hamburg), Jürgen Brunsing (Dortmund), Wolfgang & Gaby Buchenau (Erfurt), Herbert Hamele (Starnberg), Herr Jorbandt (Lübben), Hans Dieter Knapp (Rügen), Gisela and Rolf Nowtny (Niedersachswerfen), Eva Pongratz (Grafenau), Hans Schneider (Nordhausen), Hubert Zierl (Berchtesgaden).

In England: Lothar Vogel and Catherine Peters (Deutsche Bundesbahn), Rupert Brown (BR International), Arthur Howcroft (Vice President, European Ramblers' Association), Russell Hafter, Roger Henderson.

And especial thanks to our copy editor, Annemarie Weitzel.

Vorwort

Weltweit hat der Tourismus in den letzten Jahrzehnten starke Zuwachsraten zu verzeichnen. Dabei ist insbesondere das touristische Interesse an der Natur enorm gestiegen. Dies ist mit einer an die Substanz gehenden Belastung der wertvoller Natur- und Kulturlandschaften verbunden. Um sie vor Über-Nutzung und Zerstörung zu bewahren, müssen naturschonende Formen des Tourismus entwickelt werden. 'Sanfter Tourismus' darf nicht nur ein Schlagwort bleiben! Der *Green Guide to Germany* leistet dazu einen bemerkenswerten Beitrag. Er ist ein exzellentes Beispiel dafür, wie der naturorientierte Tourist heute ein Land und sein Volk unter Beachtung naturverträglicher und sozialverantwortlicher Spielregeln erleben und kennenlernen kann.

Auch die Federation der Natur- und Nationalparke Europas hat sich die Förderung naturschonender Formen des Bildungs- und Erlebnistourismus in Europäischen Schutzgebieten zur Aufgabe gemacht. Sie gratuliert den englischen Autoren zu diesem hochinteressanten und rundum gelungenen Werk. Der *Green Guide to Germany* sollte zum Reisegepäck aller Besucher gehören, die künftig von der 'Insel' in das gute, alte Germany kommen.

Eva Pongratz

Foreword

Worldwide, tourism has grown very rapidly in recent years. This has been matched by increased interest in the natural world by tourists, which has resulted in an additional pressure on valuable natural and cultural landscapes. Responsible forms of tourism must therefore be developed in order to protect such areas from damage and exploitation, so that 'green tourism' does not just remain an empty slogan.

The Green Guide to Germany gives a substantial impetus to that movement. It is an excellent example of how today's environmentally aware tourist can experience and get to know a country and its people while following environmentally and socially responsible guidelines.

The Federation of European Nature and National Parks has conceived its task as promoting environmentally friendly forms of tourism, including educational holidays and related activities in Europe's protected areas. It congratulates the English authors on this extremely interesting and successful work. *The Green Guide to Germany* should become part of the luggage of every potential traveller from the British Isles who would like to come to 'good old Germany'.

Eva Pongratz
Executive Director of the Federation
of Nature and National Parks of Europe

Why a Green Guide to Germany?

This isn't an ordinary guide book. A Green Guide differs from ordinary guide books in a number of important ways.

First and foremost, the term 'green' reflects what might loosely be described as green principles, namely that the earth is a small, fragile ecological system whose resources are finite and that all human activity has to be judged against the effect that activity has on both the immediate and the global environment.

Secondly, you'll find little in these pages about 'tourist attractions' as such, or 'sights'. You'll search hard to find a system of stars to tell you what you must see or can't really afford to miss. There's nothing about night life, or fashionable places to be seen. Luxury hotels and gourmet restaurants are also given a miss. The guide totally ignores motorway routes and you'll find nothing about scenic drives, winter sports or leisure centres.

So what is it about?

It is a guide book to some of the greenest things in Germany: its countryside, its wildlife, its national parks, its protected areas, its unique culture. The focus is on what you can see on foot, by cycle, by bus, by train and tram, and occasionally by boat. Hopefully there will also be a few signposts for appreciative travellers to help them share a little of our pleasure in and enjoyment of one of Europe's most fascinating countries and cultures.

Of course tourist areas are included in this book, because to omit some of the most famous and beautiful areas of Germany would be self-defeating, a form of inverted snobbery, but such places are there not as jewels floating in a disembodied vacuum but as an integral part of the region and culture which has produced them.

We have to confess at the outset that people planning a purely motoring holiday may not find much comfort in this book. As the average car contributes up to four times its own weight in carbon dioxide – the principal cause of the greenhouse effect – each year, not to mention huge quantities of pollutants leading to acid rain and toxic smogs, a guide book which encourages people in however small a way to add to those forces which threaten our very existence on this planet is the opposite of green.

Not that we suggest that a car doesn't have an important part to play in discovering a country as vast as Germany. But as we hope to demonstrate, it is perfectly possible to get around Germany without being dependent on a car and rather than being disadvantaged, the non-motorised traveller can enjoy a richer and deeper experience of even quite remote parts of the countryside.

Most other guide books are written with the automatic assumption that a car is available and will be used for most of the time. It is therefore no coincidence that motor traffic is the single most socially disruptive and environmentally damaging feature of late twentieth-century tourism. Tourism that doesn't rely on a personal automobile is very much less damaging to local environments and local communities.

Germany is one of Europe's most complex, fascinating, rewarding, contradictory and delightful countries. It is also one of the largest and most economically successful of European nations, a fact which creates an ambivalent reaction among its neighbours. Yet the inevitable moves towards a much more closely integrated and united group of nations, together with the improvement in transport, mean that it will be increasingly important to remove not only tariff and trade barriers, but some of the often highly artificial political and cultural blockades which, over the centuries, have divided people.

Scholars, clerics and missionaries could travel throughout medieval Europe in comparative ease, communicating with each other not in the locally distinctive dialects of the dominant Germanic or Romance languages, but in Latin. Perhaps a form of English has now replaced Latin as the *lingua franca*, as a language of travel and commerce.

It was a young English Benedictine monk, Winfrith of Crediton in south Devon, who in the early eighth century evangelised Germany, 'the land of our fathers whose inhabitants are our own blood', becoming Boniface, Archbishop of Mainz on the Rhine, and founder of the German Christian church. Is it naïve to imagine that the coming together of European peoples, with or without formal political or federal links, will recall not so much our early Christian church fathers, but a shared human concern for a threatened planet, an ecosystem which, unless we dramatically change our ways, cannot survive more than a few more decades in the form that we know it?

Nothing for us has brought home the realities of our common European and human predicament more than the North Sea, whose waters link so many North European lands, including our own and Germany. We have seen the superbly beautiful seascapes of the Schleswig-Holstein and the Niedersächsisches Wattenmeer national parks and have begun to understand how these fragile ecosystems, upon which we and our children depend, are now close to collapse thanks to the ignorance, greed and arrogance of modern industrial civilisations.

Yet at the same time it is in Germany, a rich consumerist society whose activities have done as much as anyone's to endanger our environment, including the North Sea and the Central European forests, where we have discovered so much hope, a highly developed awareness of how things can be changed not just at the level of national and international parliamentary democracy and effective legislation, but locally, through community action and initiative, through individual responsibility, through joint action whether by recycling waste, reducing energy consumption, campaigning to reopen a railway line, protecting an ancient woodland, or 'renaturing' derelict land.

Not all of course is good. Germany too has nightmarish problems of gargantuan cities, a motorway culture and especially in the East, horrendous problems of soil and air pollution almost too enormous to grasp. But our own travel even through some of these areas has convinced us that if the Green Revolution has started anywhere, it has already started in Germany, and for that reason alone it's a country and a people who are going to be making a major contribution to our collective efforts to ensure that human civilisation, our natural environment and our very planet survive the coming century.

This book is primarily intended for people who will be travelling through Germany to see and discover these things for themselves. We imagine most readers will be actual or potential visitors to the country. But hopefully some may be English-speaking residents wanting to know more about their temporary or even permanently adopted home. And it is nice to imagine that a few may even be German themselves.

Naturally this short book can barely penetrate the surface. We had only minimal time at our disposal to explore some parts of a vast and complex country. We have had to take much advice from other sources. We can only apologise in advance for any shortcomings. But we hope that nevertheless it will provide a practical and useful introduction, a few important indicators to what makes Germany so fascinating, and for the environmentally aware visitor, so very rewarding.

The green traveller and responsible tourism

Sustainable or responsible?

It is fashionable to speak of 'green' or 'sustainable' tourism in the countryside. Neither word is quite accurate and 'sustainable' in particular begs a number of key questions. The concept of sustainability has come into use through the Brundtland Report and refers to sustainable development or a sustainable economy. Tourism by its nature is a short-term activity which may reflect or support a sustainable or a non-sustainable local economy. Highly exploitative forms of tourism can be sustainable over a long period if they are underwritten by economic or political might, as too often happens in the Third World as well as in many parts of Europe.

The concept of forms of tourism which are not exploitative, now being enthusiastically taken up in Britain by a variety of organisations, not all of them with genuine green credentials, actually originated in the Alpine countries, most particularly in Switzerland and Austria where the development of ski resorts in Alpine valleys was threatening entire fragile ecosystems. These same valleys have been dominated by vast holiday villages, leading to a loss of cultural identity and domination of host communities by a huge seasonal influx of visitors with little or no concern for the unique qualities of the area or the local community.

Just as obnoxious but perhaps even better recognised has been the impact of vast concrete conurbations along the Mediterranean and Adriatic coasts, with tower block hotels and apartments destroying all local character and appearance and imposing a huge pressure on the environment. Such forms of mass, exploitative tourism have been described by the Swiss writer Krippendorf and others as 'hard' tourism. Krippendorf and his colleagues, aware that tourism also has vital economic benefits, especially for rural communities, which cannot be ignored, have sought to develop more environmentally and socially acceptable forms of tourism, which they have described as 'Sanfter Tourismus', meaning soft or gentle tourism in contrast to 'hard' tourism. Unfortunately the word 'Sanfter' does not translate easily into English, although 'gentle' is perhaps a particularly appropriate word to use for a form of tourism which intends, at least, not to destroy or damage fragile systems.

On balance we prefer the term 'responsible' tourism, implying as it does consideration for one's actions and behaviour and literally a response to an awareness of the effect that behaviour will have on the environment and on host communities. This responsibility extends equally to the provider of accommodation or visitor facilities in town or countryside and to the visitor and the user of those facilities.

Responsible tourism therefore respects a local environment and, just as significantly, a local culture. Activities which permanently destroy that environment by whatever means, be it by pollution, degradation, erosion, or urbanisation, have no place in it. Equally, responsible tourism maximises local economic benefit, by using local produce and local labour, wherever possible patronising locally owned business, by avoiding the most crowded places and responding to the wishes of local people in terms of appropriate activities. It respects difference, variety, uniqueness, above all that subtle and complex 'sense of place' which is so difficult to define and yet so vital in keeping the wild, beautiful and ancient places of the world as part of our common civilisation and culture.

The Starnberg-based group Studienkreis für Tourismus have developed what is a useful set of 'Principles of Responsible Tourism' to be adopted by the green traveller. We reproduce them here.

The five key principles of responsible tourism

1. *Be prepared to make use of less comfortable accommodation.*
Responsible or green tourism means using fewer raw materials, less energy and fewer consumer goods, combined with a lower standard of comfort, such as being more economical with water in hotter countries.

2. *Be prepared to use public transport.*
A great deal of pollution is caused by the use of individual private cars, which can also cause social problems. Responsible tourists are ready to use public transport, especially to help such services improve.

3. *Be prepared to make the most of your available leisure time.*
Tourism should not cause unnecessary stress and inconvenience to either visitor or host. Care should be taken so that neither the countryside not its people suffer

from easily avoidable problems. It takes time to get to know another culture and environment. Rushing round the sights is not part of green tourism.

4. *Be prepared to show consideration towards the daily routine of the local inhabitants.*
The lifestyle and culture of the host country shouldn't be falsified through tourism. Customs and traditions should be respected. The green tourist can get to know the special features of a country better by understanding its daily life.

5. *Be prepared to take positive steps towards environmental protection.*
Everybody disturbs the environment by their activities in some way. These disturbances must not in the long term lead to outright damage, particularly in regard to leisure activities. The concerned and responsible tourist sees his or her free time as an opportunity to help with the upkeep or conservation of the environment and the natural world.

These are all principles that we would thoroughly endorse; indeed this book does, we hope, consciously reflect them. Ultimately it is a question of attitude. It is, after all, a privilege to experience and enjoy landscapes different from our own, and share, however briefly, in a different culture.

But of all the five principles outlined above, the one which perhaps causes greatest difficulty even to the green traveller is the second – using public transport.

Cars and pollution

When it comes to personal transport, the temptation to compromise is strong. The car is so convenient, useful and comfortable that it takes unusual willpower and self denial to leave the car and travel by bus, train, boat, cycle or on foot.

But the case against the car, and perhaps even more so the motorised caravan or trailer caravan, couldn't be more damning. A vast consumer of the earth's resources in its manufacture and servicing, it requires huge quantities of a finite resource, fossil fuel, which both in its refining and transportation, as well as its actual usage, is a major source of environmental pollution.

Yet the psychology of the car is a subtle one. Whilst we deplore the effects of roads and road traffic, we are usually able to isolate our own actions from any responsibility for the situation out there. Because the decision to drive or take the car will produce no perceptible difference to the situation, we assume it doesn't really matter and take what appears to be a pragmatic and self-interested decision.

But it does matter. Every car journey adds to the total burden on an already severely strained environment, adding to the total emissions of dangerous exhaust gases and acid rain. Road traffic is now the fastest growing source of additional greenhouse gases from Europe. Long touring trips by car are therefore particularly harmful in terms of overall pollution. In the words of Edward Burke, 'Nobody made a greater mistake than he who did nothing because he himself could do only little'. So the less you use your car the better. Best of all leave the car at home and learn how to make use of public transport.

Using public transport

Not that public transport doesn't cause pollution, whether it is electric or diesel-powered. But the amount of pollution per passenger kilometre is in fact only a fraction of that caused by even the best maintained private car, and, more fundamentally, when the traveller uses existing public transport rather than his or her own transport they are simply using a facility which is already provided, thus adding no additional burden to the environment or increasing energy consumption by more than an immeasurable amount. Furthermore, a fact largely ignored by conventional transport economists, the payment of a fare recycles resources into local or national economies, reducing the need for subsidy and avoiding the importation and costs of additional fuel. Travelling by public transport therefore benefits a region's economy far more than private travel.

First and foremost, especially if you plan it well, travelling by public transport can be fun, particularly by surface transport. You see a lot more of the countryside and the cities, and you meet many more people. Secondly, you have, paradoxically, a greater flexibility to get away from the invisible umbilical cord of the car and travel by different modes – train, bus, ship, walking, cycling; a whole range of different kinds of experiences. Thirdly, the actual means of travel – branch line railways, the occasional narrow gauge steam railway, canal boats, flat-bottomed ferries to islands over shallow coastal seas, bikes along a cycle trail, have an intrinsic interest linked to engineering, architecture and transport geography. Nor is speed an advantage when you are experiencing a landscape; in green travel terms slow is beautiful. Walking and cycling are unbeatable ways of discovering what's around you.

Speaking German

One particular problem for an English-speaking visitor to Germany is invariably that of language. If responsible tourism is a question of responding to local culture, communication with local people is vital. You will be involved much more in meeting people, reading notices and timetables, and generally being 'exposed'. To what extent is it necessary, therefore, to be able to speak German to be a green traveller in Germany?

It would be wrong to deny the fact that the visitor who can speak German with a reasonable degree of fluency does enjoy very considerable advantages over the person to whom the language is a totally closed book. Having said that, most professional people in the larger towns and cities and most young Germans, at least in the former West Germany, speak competent and sometimes fluent English and are usually delighted to try it out on the receptive visitor. Even in remoter areas, fragments of school English will be remembered.

If you are able to match this with at least a smattering of common German words and phrases (particularly for those all-important timetables and notices), you will cope surprisingly well, especially when you discover those many common words which English and German share, albeit with differences of meaning and intonation.

Life can, however, be more difficult in remoter rural areas, and in the former DDR (East Germany) where until very recently Russian, not English, was the main foreign language, lack of German can be a problem. A language is part of a culture and the green traveller needs to make at least some effort to have that basic vocabulary for some common needs, even if longer conversations with local people, often the real essence of green travelling, may be impossible.

On the other hand, if your preparations for a trip to Germany have included time to achieve even only a very modest grasp of the language, you can enjoy delightful evenings with a people whose warmth and enthusiasm can be truly infectious, and discover how, beneath superficial differences of culture and experience, so much that really matters, above all about environmental issues, is shared. Conversations at least initiated in German are often much more rewarding that those started with the inevitable discourtesy of assuming a stranger knows your language.

Regarding place names, with rare exceptions, such as where the English name has become a household word (e.g. the Rhine, the Baltic), we have used German names throughout, except for the first appearance in the text where, if there is a common English translation, it is given. There is a good practical reason for this; unless the visitor is familiar with such names, he or she will be looking in vain on road signs or in timetables for names like Cologne or Munich, let alone Bavaria and Saxony.

Further reading

Jost Krippendorf, *The Holiday Makers* (Heinemann, 1987).

Germany, its people and its land

As William Rees-Mogg declared in *The Independent* in November 1989 after the Berlin Wall had been breached: 'It will be a German Age'.

The 1990s are an exciting decade for Germany, a period of dramatic change following the reunification of a divided land. Problems of all kinds still abound, but if ever a nation was able to resolve them, then Germany is the most likely with a long history of overcoming sometimes overwhelming odds.

Who are the Germans and what exactly is the country we call Germany?

Germany is certainly not a geographical entity as such. It is largely land-locked, without much in the way of natural features for frontiers except on its northern coast. It shares its borders with no less than nine other countries and over the centuries these borders have fluctuated to no little degree.

German economic and cultural influence has always gone well beyond its political boundaries. Its northern frontier with Denmark for example has resulted in close links with Scandinavia, which can also be easily reached from the North Sea or Baltic ports. To the west lie the Netherlands, Belgium and Luxemburg, again producing close cultural ties. The British Isles are a comparatively short distance away over the common frontier of the North Sea and again cultural links are fairly strong. To the southwest is France with the river

Rhine as the boundary; much of the border regions have had a long history of belonging to one or other country.

Switzerland along the shared Bodensee (Lake Constance) and Austria form Germany's southern perimeter, where the gentle foothills rise to the towering crags and peaks of the Alps. To the east is Czechoslovakia, where the great Bavarian and Bohemian forests form a natural barrier once crossed by the barbed wire fences of the Iron Curtain. To the northeast lies Poland, with the rivers Oder and Neiße forming since World War Two the boundary which places the former German territories of Silesia, Pomerania and East Prussia within Poland and Russia.

Now Berlin has been chosen as the capital of the reunified federal republic, it is hoped that Germany will play an increasingly significant role with both its newly enfranchised East European neighbours and its existing allies and partners in the EC; a strong, stabilising force in the heartland of central Europe.

Physically, modern Germany offers remarkable contrasts in landscape and scenery, not entirely surprising in a country which lies on a north/south axis extending well over 800 kilometres from the Baltic to the Alps. For simplicity, it can be divided into three main east-west bands of landscape type – the great North German plain and coast, the central uplands, and the Alps, including the Alpine forelands.

The great North German plain, with its landforms smoothed out by Ice Age glaciers, is characterised by areas of rich agricultural land, fertile reclaimed marshland, and the great mud flats or Watten on the North Sea. From at least as early as 800 AD farmers along the North Sea and Baltic coasts were building dykes to reclaim or protect their land from the ever threatening sea. Some of the often rigorous obligations governing this protection were laid down in the thirteenth-century *Sachsenspiegel*, an early law book.

The virtually tideless Baltic has impressive chalk cliffs along part of its coastline, as on the island of Rügen, where the superb wooded coastlines are now protected as a national park.

The central uplands enjoy a much more undulating terrain, making a landscape of fairly gentle hills, moors and lakes, rising to modest ranges of wooded hills (Mittelgebirge) such as the Harz mountains. Much of Germany's industrial heartland is clustered round the valleys of the Rhine-Ruhr region in the north of the central uplands.

Further south into Baden-Württemberg and Bayern (Bavaria) are the deeper valleys, thicker forests and fast flowing streams of the Schwarzwald (Black Forest), the Schwäbische Alb, the Alpine foreland which finally yields to the dramatic peaks of the high Alpine regions which occupy the country's southeast corner.

Most major German rivers, including the Rhine and its tributaries, flow from south to north into the North Sea, the exception being the Danube which heads through Austria, Hungary and Romania to the Black Sea.

A feature about Germany worth remembering is that more than a third of its land surface is thickly forested. These forests have a deep spiritual, cultural and emotional significance for German people – the 'Wald' of folklore and legend – as well as being favoured recreation areas. This explains why forests dying of pollution and acid rain are of more than just ecological significance.

In terms of climate, the maritime north contrasts with the typically more continental heartlands and the highland south. July is usually the hottest month everywhere, but winter temperatures can actually be lower in the south than in the north as the area is further from the sea and altitudes are a good deal higher.

If what makes a nation is a common language, history and culture, then some of these elements must be outlined in order to understand its people.

The modern German language is derived from what used to be known as High German, though regional dialects remain a strong and positive feature. Politicians for example will demonstrate how much they identify with their constituents by showing themselves to be fully conversant dialect speakers in political speeches in their home town. In the north, 'Plattdeutsch' is still spoken in rural areas and differs from High German with many English-sounding words, as does Frisian which is still spoken in small pockets in the North Sea coastal areas.

But then modern English and German have a common ancestor. The Germanic languages, as distinct from German, are a branch of the Indo-European family and are divided into East Germanic (Gothic, now extinct), North Germanic (Scandinavian) and West Germanic, which evolved into German, Dutch, Frisian and English. English and German still have many words in common – though others, looking or sounding similar, may have changed their meaning.

High German became the language we know today. Low German or Niederdeutsch is the name Germans use for Dutch. Plattdeutsch is a dialect of German, its name implying its use by 'unlettered' peasants. Regional dialects, like the dialects of any other country, are local variations of the standard form of German.

Frisian, however, evolved many centuries ago into a quite separate language. It is more closely related to English than to German or Dutch, due to the fact that Frisians (and Jutes) were part of the Anglo-Saxon invasion of England, whilst those remaining tended to live in areas where no one else wanted to be so that they kept themselves fairly isolated.

High German only came into general use as a literary language to replace Latin or French after about 1500. This formal language became standardised and popularised by Martin Luther's great translation of the Bible, which was a seminal influence on written and eventually spoken formal German.

A more widely spoken mother tongue than English in Europe, and the second language of many Eastern European countries, German has also sustained a major literature, including some of the greatest poets, dramatists, novelists and philosophers of western civilisation – Goethe, Schiller, Heine, Hegel, Schopenhauer, Kant, Klopstock, Leibniz, Lessing, Mörike, Nietzsche, Storm, Heinrich and Thomas Mann, Marx, Brecht and many others.

The language which has proved such an effective medium for philosophy can also produce lucid words and phrases for concepts and experiences for which often there is no real English equivalent. A marvellous, often poetic concision can telescope a wealth of meaning into a single word or phrase. But the Germans have a habit, too, of joining words to produce often ponderous pantechnic words of quite amazing length, sometimes also leaving foreigners to lose their way in the excesses of a string of Latinate dependent clauses. Yet it is a language capable of expressing the finest nuances and shades of feeling; at other times it has a refreshing vigour and earthiness almost lost in modern English (though not in dialect or regional English).

But more than most other people in Europe, the Germans are prisoners of their history, most particularly their recent history, which has experienced not only triumphs and success, but the blackest nightmares of despair.

Perhaps the most important clue to modern Germany is an awareness that only for a relatively short period of its history, from the second half of the nineteenth to the middle of the twentieth century, was it the kind of highly centralised state that Britain, or even France, are. Since the collapse of the Third Reich in 1945, Germany has become a federal republic consisting of what are now sixteen regional states or Länder, each with their own separate identity and a degree of autonomy within an overall co-ordinated and balanced federal structure, based on partnership, rather than domination by a single power-base. Its constitution is enshrined in a written basic law, the Grundgesetz, and its parliament or Bundestag has an additional legislative assembly, the Bundesrat, which has representatives from the various Länder parliaments, which operate at a more local level.

Though this federal constitution was in fact drawn up by the victorious Allies after World War II (partly to avoid the risk of any highly centralised military super-state from ever again emerging), it reflects a far older tradition of independent states among German-speaking peoples living and working in co-operation.

As early as 89AD, the Roman historian Tacitus wrote that the Germani tribes liked to consult together over major affairs, and this tradition is still proudly upheld.

The great Völkerwanderung in early European history had caused the Franks and the Alemanni to cross into the Rhineland by the fifth century AD. The Franks had conquered northern Gaul and overcome the Roman Empire and the 'Limes', the central European equivalent of Britain's Hadrian's Wall across what is now central Germany, was breached in many places. The Frisians had already established themselves from Roman times in the marshlands and islands off the northern coast to the west of Schleswig-Holstein, and the Thuringians at an early stage in Thüringen. Pressure from the east from the Germanic tribes of Saxons, Bavarians, Thuringians and the Slavs caused the emperor Charlemagne to build frontier defences against them in the ninth century which also helped to make a cultural and ethnic divide between Germans and Slavs till about 1200. Many of these ancient tribes are the ancestors of various ethnic groupings which still exist in present day Germany, though the picture was of course complicated by the mass movements of the various peoples through the exigencies of war, famine and resettlement over the centuries.

The Franks, who had conquered the Alemanni in the sixth century, established their capital at what is now Frankfurt on a river crossing. By the late eighth century the Frankish kings finally vanquished the Saxons and Charlemagne was able to unite all Germanic tribes. He was buried at Aachen, where his crown can still be seen in the cathedral.

After his death, Charlemagne's Germanic empire was divided, the west becoming France in due course and the east largely modern Germany. After the Carolingian dynasty died out, the monarchy increasingly had to depend on the consensus of its peers for election to that office, as in the case of Duke Conrad I, now considered to be the first German king. Otto I, who had even greater ambitions, had himself crowned Emperor at Rome by the Pope. For about 300 years the emperors allowed themselves to be preoccupied with Italy rather than Germany, so that the various princes were able to consolidate their powers. A bitter power struggle between Heinrich IV and the papacy in the eleventh century ended in Heinrich's excommunication, only lifted after his penance at Canossa, demonstrating thereby that he fully recognised the authority of the church. A walk to Canossa to this day proverbially means 'climbing down' and humiliating oneself. For a time under Friedrich Barbarossa, Germany seemed to be heading for a new golden age under the Hohenstaufen dynasty, but the process of internal disintegration of the old empire steadily gathered momentum.

The Habsburg dynasty claimed the throne in the thirteenth century. With the issue of the 'Golden Bull' or imperial constitution by Karl IV in 1356, seven electors were empowered to select the German king and were given special privileges. Once again the effect was to decentralise at a time when other European monarchs were beginning to consolidate their powers. In time these electors and their fortified towns gained greater influence, especially when they co-operated in some way. The most famous of these confederations was the Hanseatic League which was at its height in the fourteenth century. This had formed itself into a powerful economic force of free city-states along the North Sea and Baltic coasts as well as further inland and it lasted several centuries.

As the spirit of intellectual criticism arose with the Renaissance and the rise of Humanism, attention was turned to church abuses. Martin Luther, a charismatic figure, became an instrument of the Reformation which was to unleash a complex chain of political consequences. Both the Knights' Revolt and that of the Peasants in 1525 were brutally crushed and by the Peace of Augsburg in 1555, each of the princes was given the right to decide on their subjects' religion (*cuius regio, eius religio*), the Protestants now having equal rights with Catholics. Four-fifths of Germany was now Protestant, but the Catholic church was to fight back with the Counter-Reformation and the Thirty Years War which erupted in 1618 was not only to aggravate the bitterness between the two warring religious factions, but also widened to become a deep-seated political clash. After 1648 the actual physical state of Germany was such as to delay her political and economic maturity for some considerable time. Decimated by the conflict with her European neighbours, Germany had lost almost half her population. In addition vast areas of the country had been devastated by war, famine and plague, with the religious divisions deeper and more bitter than ever. The power of the emperor was broken and that of the princes had increased, with Germany now consisting of no less than 1,800 assorted minor free towns and dukedoms.

The years which followed began to see the eventual rise of Brandenburg-Prussia under the Hohenzollern dynasty, which was steadily transformed under the Elector Friedrich Wilhelm with Berlin as his capital. Industry, agriculture and the creation of an efficient fighting force were all encouraged under his rule, while his son gave himself the title of King of Prussia. His grandson further perfected the army and his great-grandson in turn felt able to challenge Austrian supremacy and was later able to add additional territorial possessions to an expanding nation state. With the coming of the French Revolution and the advance of Napoleon, Prussia found herself defeated by the French and forced to pay vast sums in reparation.

Reforms were finally put in hand to break down the feudal barriers in Germany and after the defeat of Napoleon, the map of Europe was redrawn at the Congress of Vienna in 1815. In 1834 the German customs union (Deutscher Zollverein), an early form of common market, was founded which at least helped to unify the disparate states within Germany. In 1835 the first German railway line was built, using the technology which had been developed so successfully in England. Rapid industrialisation began and a new class of factory workers or proletariat emerged to serve this industry. Industrial towns and cities, especially in the north and in the Ruhr area, grew rapidly.

During 1848, the year of revolution in Europe, German workers joined in the struggle for emancipation, but were speedily put down and the Nationalversammlung offered Friedrich Wilhelm of Prussia the hereditary German crown. This was turned down as the king did not wish to be seen to owe his throne to a revolution.

More than twenty years later, after the loss of many lives in two major wars, the same objectives were achieved by Bismarck, the Chancellor of Prussia, in 1871 and King Wilhelm was proclaimed German Emperor or Kaiser. Prussia at this point dominated Germany, with territory stretching from the Danish border in the north to the Netherlands and Belgium in the west and, apart from the various south German territories and some small principalities, to the borders of Russia in the east and the Austrian empire in the southeast.

By now Germany was among the world's greatest and most successful trading industrial nations, its coal, iron and steel, chemicals and heavy engineering rivalling even that of its powerful North Sea neighbour Britain. Both were imperial powers, building up rival empires and vast naval and military resources to defend national interests. Such rivalries led inevitably to political confrontation.

With the outbreak of the First World War in 1914, Germany and Austria found themselves on opposite sides from France, Britain and Russia, and at a later stage the United States. Under the Weimar Republic, Germany struggled with oppressive reparations imposed by the Treaty of Versailles and a humiliated and much weakened country was further aggravated by France's occupation of the key coalfields of the Ruhr, and by horrifying inflation that destroyed savings and made the currency virtually worthless. World recession and mass unemployment in 1929 helped to seal the fragile republic's fate and its weakness encouraged the rise of left and right wing extremists, each offering simplistic solutions to the agonising social and economic problems of the time.

The strongest of such parties, which had extreme anti-democratic tendencies and racialist theories based on half-understood Darwinism, and policies based on anti-semitic scapegoat racialism, was Hitler's National Sozialistische Partei – the Nazis. Supported by powerful financial influences as a means of combating Russian-inspired Bolshevism, and tolerated by other western governments for the same reason, the Nazis were quick to exploit opportunities and were skilful in orchestrating public opinion, using the all-too-familiar modern techniques of mass persuasion, control of the press, propaganda and mass hysteria.

It is difficult even after more than half a century to be objective about the Third Reich, or to explain why a failed Austrian painter, of mediocre intellect but of animal cunning, could within an existing democratic constitution build up such an elaborate and coldblooded machinery of terror and thuggery – symbolised by the Gestapo and the SS – with which he could effectively silence and exterminate any opposition, until he could finally take over as Dictator, totally destroying democracy in the process.

Naturally, millions of Germans were only too ready to support Adolf Hitler and the Nazis' evil policies at that time. Xenophobia and racial hatred were not unique to Germany, and flourished long before the emergence of the Nazis. But in Germany, still bitter after the defeats of World War I, it combined with the brutal Prussian militarism and anti-semitism savagely satirised by Heinrich Mann in his prophetic novel *Der Untertan*, published in 1918 and known in English as *Man of Straw*. It was to allow forces of such terrifying evil to emerge that even now they are almost totally beyond comprehension. Rapid military expansion and invasion of neighbouring states by Nazi Germany made the Second World War inevitable.

An insight into how many ordinary individuals in 1930s Germany were able to identify for so long with such a regime is given by Christabel Bielenberg's moving autobiography *The Past is Myself*. An Englishwoman who married a liberal German lawyer, who was himself one of many German intellectuals who were in the Resistance against Hitler, and who narrowly escaped torture and death, Bielenberg describes how their gardener, a kindly decent man, hit by various blows of fate, saw the National Socialists as his only hope of a better existence. For a time the Nazis seemed to reinvigorate the economy and reduce unemployment, as world depression eased and aggressive foreign policies seemed to succeed. The return of the Saar to Germany in 1935, and the annexation of Austria and the Sudetenland on the Czech border, were positive gains to many. And it was easy to ignore or refuse to believe what was happening to Jewish neighbours as Jewish citizens were systematically being stripped of their rights, abused, imprisoned and tortured. While many escaped abroad, at least six million Jews and other proscribed minorities perished appallingly in the concentration camps of the holocaust in what was chillingly known as 'The Final Solution'. Bielenberg's gardener, by that time a minor Nazi official, was found hanged at a lamp post, probably summarily executed by the invading Russian army.

Germans describe the days after the almost complete physical and moral annihilation of their nation in 1945 as 'Stunde Null' – the point at which time stood still. Had Hitler not been such a criminal megalomaniac such destruction and slaughter could have ceased long before the bitter last ditch resistance against overpowering Allied forces and mass civilian destruction.

So shocked were the Allies at the sight of the notorious concentration camps with their pathetic, skeletal survivors, one of the greatest crimes against humanity ever committed, that many military leaders and civilian Germans were brought to trial at Nuremberg in 1946 with the most notorious criminals suffering execution. Such executions and imprisonments could do nothing to outweigh the overwhelming horror of over six million murdered people, most of them Jewish, who had perished because of an obscene political philosophy.

But the process did not end there. A collective guilt remained. The whole surviving population had to undergo a lengthy process of de-nazification. The nightmare years of the Third Reich are burned into European and German consciousness. Many of the concentration camps have been preserved as memorials to Jewish suffering, and as reminders of collective responsibility. In Berlin by the Wannsee, where the policy of the Final Solution was first articulated, there is a Memorial Museum to Jewish suffering. Not far away in central Berlin the Plötzensee prison, where more than 2,500 Resistance leaders and ordinary people who spoke out against the regime were executed, remains as a grim reminder of human bestiality. In Stuttgart, one of Europe's most prosperous and successful cities, if you walk onto the Birchenkopf, a wooded hillside above the town, a pile of rubble is surmounted by a cross with the simple words 'lest we ever forget'. But such a guilt does not belong alone to the German people. All western nations were to some degree responsible for the catastrophe and all share a responsibility to ensure that nothing like it ever happens again.

Most of the large towns and cities were ruined in the Allied Blitzkrieg, and were little more than huge heaps of rubble. Half the nation's houses were destroyed and the economy and the transport system were smashed. Food, water, gas, electricity and housing were all in short supply. Many Germans were still prisoners, or refugees. Starvation threatened. Allied forces had to rescue and save the lives of shattered people who weeks earlier they had helped to bomb into oblivion.

In Berlin 'Trummerfrauen' – surviving women, most of them recently widowed or separated from their menfolk – stood in long lines handing buckets of bricks and rubble to each other, helping to rebuild the shattered ruins.

Germany was partitioned by the Allies into four zones of occupation – British, French, Russian and American, with Berlin the capital itself divided between the four powers. Berlin was thus isolated far into the Russian zone and was to become an easy hostage to fortune. Poland received the southern part of East Prussia, Silesia and Pomerania but Prussia itself, the embodiment of military expansionism, was completely removed from the map.

In 1947 a physical barrier had appeared across roads into the Russian zone as Russia under its communist political system felt itself increasingly under threat by the Allies under their capitalist system. In 1948 the currency reform deemed necessary to develop industry was not accepted by the Soviets, who also refused to accept Marshall Aid from the United States. It was Marshall Aid – substantial financial help – which enabled Western Germany to make its phenomenal recovery, which came to be known as the Wirtschaftswunder or economic miracle. Much of this so-called miracle was due to unparalleled hard work by the German people helping to erase a nightmarish past, but Marshall Aid was also a significant factor, helping the emerging nation to invest in modern equipment and machinery to compete again in world markets. To physically rebuild shattered cities was itself a superb feat. Many historic German town centres are, when you examine them closely, replicas of what they once were, with whole areas including churches, town halls and streets of medieval houses transformed from burned out shells to at least their original façades (though interiors may be modern), thanks to meticulous research using old photographs, followed by careful restoration. Whether this has destroyed their authenticity is a point we will not pursue here.

But as relations worsened between the Soviet and Allied powers, later to become the Warsaw Pact and NATO, the Cold War finally erupted into a total blockade of all land routes to Berlin for nearly a year in 1948-9 in an effort to stop the escape of people from the Russian zone. This blockade was only relieved by an incredible series of Allied airlifts to Berlin which supplied the city not just with provisions, but also with coal and essential equipment. Relations between the two powers plumbed new depths with the building of the Berlin Wall in 1961 across the very heart of the city.

In 1949 the Federal Republic of Germany (BRD) was born within West Germany, with Konrad Adenauer as its first Chancellor. Its constituent states comprised Schleswig-Holstein, Niedersachsen (Lower Saxony), Nordrhein-Westfalen (North Rhine Westphalia), Hessen, Rheinland-Pfalz (Rhineland Palatinate), Baden-Württemberg, and Bayern (Bavaria), while Hamburg and Bremen became city-states and West Berlin kept a special status. The Bundestag or parliament met at Bonn, which was regarded as the temporary capital till the eventual reunification of Germany. In 1957 Saarland was returned to West Germany, thus comprising eleven states or Länder in all.

The German Democratic Republic (DDR) was also formed in 1949 under its Prime Minister Otto Grotewohl, but its people's parliament or Volkskammer was chosen from a single list of candidates. The DDR also recognised the Oder-Neiße line as Poland's western frontier. A programme of collectivisation was started as part of the process whereby land became state owned and land reforms were introduced. In 1952 it abolished the old Länder in favour of fourteen Bezirke or districts, each with a council under central government control and generally focused around the larger towns.

A revolt by the workforce against economic conditions was put down with the help of Russian aid and the DDR became increasingly allied to the eastern bloc, forming part of the Warsaw Pact as the BRD had become part of Nato. The communist or SED regime saw its priorities as full employment for both men and women, cheap rents and cheap basic foods. In order that women were able to contribute fully to work outside the home, an extensive range of crèches and kindergartens were set up and much legislation discriminated positively in favour of the family. However, there were undoubtedly many problems. The average citizen felt the brunt of mysterious shortages of provisions and consumer goods. Failure to support the Communist Party would damage career prospects. Most citizens suffered a total embargo on travelling to the west, with punitive measures taken against those who sought to emigrate. Perhaps the most sinister of all was a highly complicated spy-network which, as under many authoritarian regimes, was able to infiltrate organisations at all levels and traded on fear and denunciations.

The Iron Curtain which divided Europe and the two Germanies had become increasingly strengthened, taking physical form as a high wire fence running across the open countryside, defended by a no-man's land of trip wires, searchlights, guards, dogs, guns, and a forbidden hinterland where ordinary citizens went at their peril. This nightmarish dividing fence was seen as a vital factor in retaining the DDR's skilled workers, to allow the beleaguered country to turn her attention to improving her industrial output with such success, that she was allegedly able to take her place among the top ten industrialised nations of the world.

Sadly much of this economic might was used to finance military hardware and further defences. In the 1970s after the death of Ulbricht, the then leader of the DDR, there was a definite policy of better relations with the West. This emerged through Ost-Politik under the West German socialist Chancellor Willy Brandt, and gradually some restrictions, including those on travel, were eased between what were now in practice two separate countries.

By the late 1980s, as part of a movement towards perestroika initiated in Russia and spreading throughout Eastern Europe, the people of East Germany were in open revolt. In particular, protest had centred in Leipzig in the Nikolaikirche, where each Monday evening thousands gathered in peaceful protest, the lighting of candles symbolising the struggle for freedom. In the meantime, in despair at the intractability of the Honecker regime, thousands of younger people, especially professionals, were escaping to the west via Hungary and Czechoslovakia.

Protest meetings spread throughout East Germany and in Berlin itself, attracting up to a million people. At one stage it looked as if the army might crack down on the peaceful protesters. But when Gorbachev made it clear to Honecker that there would be no Red Army in support to crush the people's rebellion, the regime began to collapse.

On November 9th 1989 the unimaginable happened. The Berlin Wall was breached and in unforgettable images relayed on television around the world, cheering young men and women attacked the wall with pickaxes, hauled their countrymen to freedom, and began what was reputed to be one of the longest street parties in German history. The walls and fences were breached and throughout the country scenes of celebration took place as long divided families and whole communities were reunited.

Inevitable formal political reunification followed, perhaps most memorably symbolised by the concert of Beethoven's Ninth Symphony on Christmas Day 1989, given by the members of the now united Berlin orchestras and choirs under the baton of the late Leonard Bernstein, with Schiller's 'Ode to Joy' becoming an 'Ode to Freedom'.

So the two Germanies have become once more a single country after more than forty years apart. For the older generation it was an unbelievable victory and vindication of faith, for younger people a discovery of a part of their own land and national identity hitherto inaccessible to them.

Chancellor Kohl and the conservative CDU/CSU coalition were seen as the best chance for the former DDR's quickest entrance into capitalist society once more. Rapid monetary and related social and economic reforms were promised and the first all German free elections for over half a century in 1990 gave the CDU a good majority.

But after the first euphoria, problems have occurred. The two countries, both German, had gone their separate ways for over forty years. Economic systems and ways of thinking had diverged over that period. The DDR had been much celebrated for its own apparent economic success without western capital, its high levels of social welfare and for its prowess at international athletics. Reality gave a somewhat less rosy picture.

As the Soviet Union, the DDR's biggest export customer, became swamped with her own economic problems, and Poland and Hungary followed, and later much of Eastern Europe erupted in a turmoil of anti-communist fervour, much of DDR industry, protected from economic and even technological change for over forty years, was found to be hopelessly outdated and inefficient, and faced collapse, unable to compete with the more technologically advanced and efficient west in free world markets.

Nothing symbolised this change better than the little state-produced Trabbi cars, old fashioned and polluting, which when they first ventured across into western Germany, were seen as a symbol of the new freedom and part of a living folklore. But within weeks the Trabbi factory was closed and its workers unemployed, easterners themselves rejecting the old technology in favour of modern, high speed western cars, cheaply bought on the second hand market.

Today the Bezirke in the former East Germany have been abolished and the old federal states revived – five new Bundesländer which have joined the federal republic: Mecklenburg-Vorpommern in the north, Sachsen-Anhalt, Sachsen, Brandenburg, and Thüringen in the south. Berlin itself has finally become an unshackled, unpartitioned city-state once more. Huge problems remain and the federal government has set up the much criticised Treuhand agency to determine what institutions to privatise, or develop or restructure in some form, or even close down entirely as being totally uneconomic.

Restructuring at all levels is needed to rebuild an economic system which when the books were opened was seen to be in dire straits and could only offer full employment by gross overmanning. The cost of maintaining the social and economic infrastructure has been far higher than even the most pessimistic experts had forecast, threatening even the mighty former BRD economy with high taxes and inflation to pay for it, a fact that many westerners understandably resent. Although one cannot for a moment underestimate the amount of problems, especially unemployment, that reunification brought in its wake, the eastern Länder have a tremendous will to survive and an enormous number of very positive steps have already been taken, much of it with western support, including generous twinning arrangements with western Länder. Nor is this a one-way process. The former BRD has much to learn from the east with its often less materialistic attitudes to life and its deep concern that its unspoiled environment and natural beauty, which has so much to offer the visitor as well as local inhabitant, should not be destroyed under an avalanche of western style commercial development and road traffic. Five newly designated Nationalparke in eastern Germany testify to some of the landscape glories that await discovery.

Germany today

Economically Germany is one of the most successful nations on earth. As well as having a sound agricultural base, being a major exporter of foodstuffs, Germany is a major manufacturer of high technology products. Being relatively poorly supplied in raw materials, a healthy export base is essential to maintain the nation's high standard of living.

German industry excels in quality engineering, in vehicle and heavy machinery and machine tool construction, while chemicals, electrical engineering and data processing equipment are all major international industries. Increasingly consumer goods, textiles, food and drink are taking a large share of the market. Farming, forestry and fishing make obvious use of Germany's natural resources.

Decades of prosperity have produced a society in the former West Germany that some critics will describe as materialistic, enjoying as it does perhaps an excessive share of consumer durables. Middle class Germans live in comfortable spacious homes with a notable shift in recent years away from city apartments to well-appointed villas in the suburbs. They are car and gadget owning, with a love of technology almost for its own sake. At the same time they will be deeply conscious of national and international environmental problems, and into recycling, energy saving and green issues in a big way. They enjoy several holidays a year. Often they are active through various green groups or citizens' groups – Bürgerinitiative – to achieve worthwhile environmental ends, or social support, particularly through the churches, to help less fortunate citizens of their own country, Eastern Europe or the Third World. Clean, well organised German towns or villages are a physical manifestation of an aware and concerned society that other nations have cause to envy.

Germans are great travellers and the tourist industry both within Germany and from Germany to other countries is extremely well developed in almost every facet, including a variety of genuinely 'green' activity based holidays. But in addition to normal family summer holidays there is a great tradition of taking 'the cure' at a spa, perhaps staying at a semi-medical establishment or even a clinic and submitting to a regime of drinking local waters, rich in iron, sulphur or other minerals, and enjoying fresh air, rest and a strictly controlled diet. 'Bad' is the German word for bath or spa, but in fact a German spa is about more than just taking the cure, with numerous forms of treatment available ranging from warm saline baths and various other health-giving mineral baths to mudbaths which are particularly useful for rheumatic complaints. There is a whole culture of listening to concerts either in the Kurpark or Kurhalle, taking refreshment at the nearest coffee house if the medical regime allows it, or ambling round the attractive shopping streets and making excursions to various nearby places of interest. An important part of the treatment is a quiet relaxing atmosphere as well as the skilled medical attention. Medical costs can be offset, if the 'cure' is prescribed by one's doctor, by individual health insurance, as can up to 15% of any additional costs for accommodation and other facilities. In the 1930s the Kneipp regime, a favoured form of treatment, was somewhat harsh, consisting principally of ice cold showers several times daily in water with a suitable mineral content; today the regime is more humane.

Towns which supply such treatment, and have official state approval for their facilities – essentially spa towns – are allowed to use the word 'Bad' as part of their name, hence the proliferation of names of tourist centres prefixed with Bad. Such a practice was common in England in the last century, and a few towns such as Cheltenham Spa in Gloucestershire still retain the 'spa' in their name.

However, not all German families – even in former West German Länder – share in the economic miracle, and there are those who for a variety of reasons suffer deprivation. This applies especially to more recent immigrants from the East, and in particular to the Turks, who often inhabit the more deprived parts of towns and cities, doing the more menial jobs for low pay and suffering a degree of racial discrimination and abuse.

Germans as a whole are cultured people, with a higher percentage of good bookshops per head of the population than almost anywhere else in Europe. Music is also central to life. Germany has a long tradition of great composers such as Bach, Telemann, Händel, Beethoven, Weber, Schumann, Mendelssohn, Wagner, Richard Strauss and Kurt Weill, whose works are still an integral part of any classical music repertoire. Most cities and larger towns have their own opera house and concert hall. Jazz, folk and rock clubs flourish in a variety of venues, including pubs, clubs and cellars. Cabaret is a typical German means of political and social comment.

Theatre is also an essential part of German life, both classical theatre of the great dramatists of the past – Shakespeare is probably performed more often in Germany than in England to a degree that he is a German playwright by adoption – but contemporary and experimental writers not only from Germany but from all over Europe are performed as well. Likewise, not only will civic and private art galleries contain the masters of the past, but exhibitions of contemporary and experimental paintings, ceramics and sculpture. Modern sculpture – without graffiti – is to be seen in town and even village centres as a matter of course.

Quality newspapers and magazines sell well, ensuring that the average German is far better informed about current events than most UK citizens. Examples are the weekly current affairs magazine *Der Spiegel* and the 'weighty' weekly newspaper *Die Zeit*, though as in the UK there is a popular, mainly right wing gutter press presenting their readers with an unadulterated diet of sleaze, sex and scandal mostly focused around the private lives of so-called personalities.

Politically, most Germans are of centre right (CDU) or centre left (SDP) inclination, though there has in recent years been a strong surge of support for the Greens. Indeed the very moderation of mainstream German politics and sense of a need to seek a logical compromise in any situation can be seen to be a reaction against the disasters of the recent past. Talk to any older German (and it is wise not to bring the matter up) and you learn of personal tragedy and upheaval, many personal histories emerging of family bereavement, displacement and often deep emotional scars. Many prosperous families originally arrived in the former BRD as penniless refugees. Most thinking Germans studiously avoid any hint of jingoistic nationalism or self-righteous patriotism. Unlike most other Western European nations, Germans know all too well the price of political extremism. The war memorials crowded with names and sometimes otherwise unmarked roadside military and civilian cemeteries are all too frequent reminders. Not surprisingly most people prefer not to talk about wartime experiences.

There is, sadly, and mainly amongst the semi-literate young, a resurgence of right wing extremism, various groups of mainly urban skinheads rather like the British National Front, who seek notoriety by adopting Nazi insignia. Many of these groups are actually outlawed or inhabit a twilight world of fringe politics, surviving on the 'oxygen of publicity' given to them by a sensationalist press. More disturbing perhaps is the Republikaner Partei whose politics of nostalgia and thinly disguised racialism find a welcome breeding ground among the disaffected unemployed, especially in the old industrial areas of the East, and among more backward and xenophobic rural outposts, where they have made small, but significant, electoral gains. The German proportional representation system, whilst being much more truly democratic, might paradoxically also help such anti-democratic forces achieve influence.

Such groups will remain marginal, at least during periods of prosperity and full employment, but are an ever present cancer in any democratic society should the economic mechanism fail. Such risks are perhaps higher in the former DDR Länder, where mass unemployment is a real threat as old overmanned industries collapse and bureaucracies fail, and former 'Gastarbeiter', workers from Vietnam and Africa, are seen as scapegoats, a target for racial attack.

It is difficult not to feel real sympathy, however, for many East German people, who have grown up in a carefully structured society based on communal values, who have always believed their sacrifice of lower living standards was better than capitalist greed, but who now find that their years of sacrifice simply covered up a corrupt and inefficient regime. Worst, their western neighbours now characterise them as pampered and lazy.

Yet the former East Germany has so much to offer, in spite of the sometimes tatty and tired infrastructure, the holes in the road and the broken cobbles and sandy pavements, the peeling paint and old fashioned facilities, the polluting factories (many now rapidly closing down), the old trains, and lack of eating places. It is less commercially developed than the West, at times quite charmingly old-fashioned; the people are genuinely more polite and concerned with each other; the landscape and especially the old country villages are still totally unspoiled.

Our advice is quite simple – see it whilst you can.

Further reading:

Geoffrey Barraclough, *The Origins of Modern Germany* (Blackwell, new ed. 1988)
Margaret Wightman, *The Faces of Germany* (Harrap, 1971)
John Ardagh, *Germany and the Germans* (Penguin, 1987)
Gordon A. Craig, *The Germans* (Penguin, 1982)
Mary Fulbrook, *A Concise History of Germany* (Cambridge, 1990)
Christine Bielenberg, *The Past is Myself* (Chatto & Windus, 1970)
Heinrich Mann, *Man of Straw* (Hutchinson, 1947)

Green politics in Germany

The rise of the Green Party in Germany has been one of the most interesting political phenomena of our time with an enormous influence not only in Germany but throughout Europe. Its success inspired the formation of other Green parties in Europe, and had a profound impact on the agenda of all major political parties in Europe.

The Greens emerged in the 1970s out of a number of disparate grassroots groups, which were deeply concerned about the environment, and campaigned for peace, promoted women's liberation as a more feminist way of seeing the world, and showed their concern for the Third World. In due course they realised the need to band together in order to have real political muscle and to make their voice heard in parliament. At Karlsruhe in 1980 'Die Grünen' were officially founded as a political party and they were fortunate in having from their early days one or two charismatic spokespersons – such as Petra Kelly, who became known throughout Europe.

Though now a much more mainstream political force, the Greens' current manifesto still echoes the same concerns for the protection of the environment and for the human condition, whether it be the endangered tropical rain forests, acid rain, pollution nearer home caused by emissions from lorries and private cars or by a variety of manufacturing processes. They are against nuclear weapons. They campaign vigorously for women to adopt a far higher profile in both their private and public lives and have distinguished themselves by being the only political party in Germany so far which has women as about a third of its deputies. It is keen to show solidarity with and concern for Third World countries which were suffering exploitation from the developed world and sees itself as a watchdog against the erosion of democracy in the federal republic itself and the rising hostility to foreign workers.

Some brief facts and figures show how the Greens were able to challenge the main political parties of CDU/CSU, SPD and FDP. They seemed to be like a blast of fresh air in the staid and solemn world of established party politics at that time and voicing real concerns and anxieties that many people felt they could identify with.

The Greens first real political breakthrough came in the Baden-Württemberg state parliamentary elections when they obtained 5.3% of the vote in 1980, their foundation year, and later in the same year they reached the Bundestag. In 1981 they were elected to the Berlin senate, and in the following year they also achieved representation in Niedersachsen, Hamburg and Hessen. They again reached the Bundestag in 1983 with 5.6% of the vote in the federal elections and they followed this with perhaps the party's most spectacular electoral success to date, an outstanding performance at the European parliamentary elections with 8.2% of the vote in 1984. In 1987 their share of the vote for the Bundestag was 8.3% and they also achieved significant representation in virtually all federal Länder at the same time.

Other members of parliament were amazed at the air of informality the Greens took with them into the weighty Bundestag sittings and even more astonished at representatives who deliberately waived part of their salary as an article of faith for more essential projects.

But the Greens after their initial success were to have some deep-seated internal problems. A split developed between the two wings of the party, the 'Fundis' who were not keen to make political compromises or overtures to the opposition and the 'Realos' who as their name implies were prepared to take a more pragmatic approach to the political scene.

Far more important than any internal wrangling however was the enormous influence the Greens had on the main political parties and on the electorate in general. It was the Greens who put concern for the environment centre stage, lobbying so effectively that the other parties were then forced to absorb some of the Greens' ideas into their own agendas. The SPD for example took up the suggestion that an additional environmental or 'carbon' tax could be levied on all drivers on behalf of the environment at the petrol and diesel pumps. So successfully has the green message been absorbed in Germany that even major manufacturers such as Volkswagen and BASF feel compelled to point out in numerous advertisements what concerned environmentalists they are and what sort of protective measures they are taking.

Paradoxically the Greens have now become the victims of their own success, in that the other parties have been able to benefit from implementing what the Greens had initiated. The German government has introduced perhaps the most radical legislation in Europe restricting the future output of carbon dioxide and cutting drastically the amount of dangerous waste burned on ships in the North Sea. In a very real sense this represents a major victory and fulfilment of Green objectives, even if electoral reward does not follow. At the present time new 'Red/ Green' coalitions which have emerged in certain Länder between the Greens and the SPD show that the Greens can still wield major influence.

The Greens also campaign in a very car-orientated society against ever increasing car ownership and usage which results in an increasingly damaged environment. They promote cycling and walking, especially the former, as the best modes of transport for all shorter journeys and call for a motorway speed limit. They demand that public transport should be improved and that the various transport authorities should work together to this end. They are also keen to see lorry traffic for freight much reduced by banning night driving over a certain weight and at weekends. Restrictions on noise levels, speed and weight limits should all encourage more use of the railways for freight.

The Green Party is only one of a growing number of environmentally concerned organisations throughout Germany which are having an often significant influence on German and European environmental policies. Many of them operate internationally, others only at a purely local level. The examples given here are only a fraction of the many such active bodies, but they demonstrate the enormous range of active concern for the environment and environmental protection to be found within Germany.

Greenpeace

Greenpeace is an international organisation which campaigns particularly to save the whale and other threatened species and fights against the pollution of the world's oceans and seas, and against the pollution and exploitation of the Antarctic, helping also to alert the world to the imminent dangers of global warming and the destruction of tropical rain forests. Its other concerns include transport, nuclear power (Germany has a large number of nuclear power stations), the export of dangerous waste materials and investigation into renewable energy resources. Its team of scientists, often at considerable risk to themselves, take vital soundings and measurements as early warnings of potential environmental hazards or draw public attention to ecological matters which need an urgent, authoritative response.

The German-based arm of Greenpeace is keenly involved at the present time in the problem of acid rain and the dying forests in the Alps and other mountainous areas, where the trees form a vital protective barrier against potential avalanches. Although Greenpeace's Bergweltproject – the Alpine mountain landscape project – is at the moment based in Switzerland, there are plans to extend it into Germany in the near future. Greenpeace does not directly concern itself with green tourism as such, but in response to many enquiries about whether skiing is ecologically acceptable, has felt the need to produce its own hard-hitting document about the impact of skiing and ski tourism on vulnerable Alpine environments.

The World Wide Fund for Nature (Germany)

The World Wide Fund for Nature, internationally recognised with its distinctive black and white panda symbol and the world's largest conservation organisation, has had a German branch since 1963 with its main office in Frankfurt am Main. The WWF Deutschland chose the Insel Vilm, a tiny island close to Rügen off the Baltic coast, as the venue for its conference in 1990, as a symbol of its great interest in and concern for areas of outstanding natural beauty in former East Germany which urgently need protection. An office of WWF Deutschland has been opened in Potsdam and joins the other seven centres throughout Germany which work on both regional and cross-border projects, such as in Poland and Czechoslovakia. WWF Deutschland has a full-time staff of seventy, plus hundreds of volunteers, and works together with conservation organisations in Europe and throughout the world. It influences German environmental policies both nationally and in the various federal states. For example, the WWF has already offered its help and advice to the Vorpommerische Boddenlandschaft on the Baltic, the Jasmund Nationalpark on Rügen and the planned Polish-German national park along the banks of the river Oder which will be known as the Untere Oder Nationalpark.

Naturschutzbund Deutschland e.V.

The Naturschutzbund Deutschland – the German society for nature protection – is one of the leading bodies campaigning for national and regional policies leading to the establishment of protected areas of landscape and nature reserves throughout Germany. It was formerly the Deutscher Bund für Vogelschutz (the German society for the protection of birds) but has now widened its brief to include other habitat conservation. The society works through regional branches which are now also active in the new Bundesländer; as an educational body it organises seminars and classes for individuals and groups, and publishes an authoritative journal, *Naturschutz Heute.*

Bund für Umwelt und Naturschutz Deutschland e.V. (BUND)

This German society for environment and nature protection, with its green and black 'hands round the earth' symbol, was founded in 1975 and is the Friends of the Earth in Germany, having more than 190,000 members with specialist research working groups active in a number of key areas of concern – nature protection, agriculture, rubbish recycling, the ecology of towns, traffic and transport, forests, sea and coastlines, water energy and intermediate technology and international issues. The Bund lobbies at federal and state level, and internationally. Major recent campaigns have been to clean up polluted streams ('Rettet die Bäche'), against the destruction of natural habitats by pesticides and other causes, the waste of scarce materials in unnecessary packing, the problems of 'Waldsterben', and the many causes of the greenhouse effect including high levels of carbon dioxide production. There are local groups in all Länder including the former DDR, as well as youth groups that organise a variety of educational and practical environmental activities for young people including the Europäische Forstwelt Programm. A campaigning journal *Nature and the Environment* is issued regularly.

Die Naturfreunde
Literally the 'Friends of Nature', this is a long established outdoor, walking and nature protection organisation which now has over 110,000 members in Germany, and a chain of hostels throughout the country. The Naturfreunde are very much concerned with the development of ecologically sound and socially responsible tourism, and not only put such principles into practice in their own activities and hostels, but campaign for such attitudes nationally and internationally and carry out educational programmes particularly with their own youth groups. At the Naturfreunde Kanzelwandhaus hostel in the Allgäu, Bayern, a special Naturfreunde Alpenschutz-Zentrum has been established as an educational centre to look at Alpine problems and to develop the concept of 'Sanfter Tourismus'.

Der Deutsche Alpenverein (DAV)
DAV, the German Alpine club, has 440,000 members and is one of Europe's largest and most influential Alpine bodies. It has developed a strong eco-political awareness out of a traditional base as a provider of maps, guidebooks and Alpine huts, to become one of the leading bodies concerned with the many threats to the Alpine environment, including that of 'Waldsterben', producing hard-hitting pamphlets and lobbying at national and international level to research and check the causes of dying forests. Their slogan 'Wir brauchen den Wald zum Leben' – we need the forests to live – has a compelling reality.

Verkehrsclub der Bundesrepublik Deutschland (VCD)
The VCD is a campaigning organisation for environmentally responsible transport and tourism policies in Germany. Linked to similar organisations in other European countries, for example the Environmental Transport Association in Great Britain, on the VCD agenda are better facilities for public transport users, bus and rail, better facilities for cyclists and pedestrians, investment in integrated public transport, control of car pollution and the development of alternatives to the car, and active concern to achieve a reduction of the greenhouse effect. A bimonthly magazine is produced and the VCD also operates extremely effectively at a local level through its regional branches.

Pro-Bahn e.V.
Like the VCD, Pro-Bahn is a pressure group for better public transport, with special emphasis on rail travel. It has a widespread active membership working at both local and national level, and offers information, advice and a programme of rail-based events for members as well as the magazine *Pro-Bahn* which is published every two months.

Allgemeiner Deutscher Fahrrad Club e.V. (ADFC)
The ADFC represents the interests of cyclists and cycling throughout Germany, and is involved in wider cycling route network planning and safety issues in both town and countryside. There are active local groups in every state.

Tourismus mit Einsicht and *Deutscher Naturschutzring (DNR)*
Tourismus mit Einsicht (tourism with insight) is a 'working group' or network of various environmental organisations in Germany and mainly other German speaking countries concerned about the impact of tourism on the environment and on local communities, not only within Europe but throughout the world, particularly the Third World. Tourismus mit Einsicht is, however, not only concerned with preventing the expansion of mass or hard tourism, but also with promoting the notion of 'sanfter' or responsible tourism, giving examples of good practice, and organising workshops, exhibitions and seminars to achieve this aim.

Deutscher Naturschutzring like Tourismus mit Einsicht is a federation, of no less than ninety-eight nature protection organisations and agencies in Germany, who work together nationally and internationally to achieve common goals.

Studienkreis für Tourismus e.V.
This is a voluntary agency co-ordinating information about green tourism initiatives throughout Germany, in Europe and throughout the world.

Useful addresses

Die Grünen, Colmanstraße 36, D-5300 Bonn 1.
Naturschutzbund Deutschland e.V., Am Michaelshof 8-10, D-5300 Bonn 2.
Bund für Umwelt und Naturschutz Deutschland e.V., Im Rheingartern 7, D-5300 Bonn 3.
Umweltstiftung WWF-Deutschland, Hedderichstraße 110, D-6000 Frankfurt 70.
Greenpeace e.V., Vorsetzen 53, D-2000 Hamburg 11.
Der Deutsche Alpenverein e.V., Praterinsel 5, D-8000 München 22.
Verband Deutscher Gebirgs und Wandervereine e.V. (representing climbing and walking organisations throughout Germany), Reichstraße 4, D-6600 Saarbrücken.
Verkehrsclub der Bundesrepublik Deutschland, Kalkuhlstraße 24, D-5300 Bonn 3.
Pro-Bahn e.V., Schwanthalerstraße 74, D-8000 München 2.

Allgemeiner Deutscher Fahrrad Club e.V., Radlerhaus, Steinstraße 17, D-8000 München.
Die Naturfreunde, Verband für Touristik und Kultur, Bundesgruppe Deutschland e.V., Postfach 600 4411, D-7000 Stuttgart 60.
Arbeitgemeinschaft Tourismus mit Einsicht, Mendelssohnstraße 34, D-8000 München.
Der Deutscher Naturschutzring, Kalkuhlstraße 24, D-5300 Bonn 3.
Studienkreis für Tourismus e.V., Dampfschiffstraße 2, D-8130 Starnberg.

Nature and landscape protection in Germany

Only when we learn to value nature for her own sake, will nature allow us to continue our existence long-term.

RICHARD VON WEIZÄCKER

The protection of natural beauty and wildlife habitats have a high priority in Germany, reflecting an overall awareness of the need for vigorous environmental protection policies to balance at least some of the damaging effects of one of the world's most highly industrialised and mobile societies.

German governments at both federal and state (Land) level have done a great deal to use legislative and other powers to protect what is a particularly rich heritage of natural beauty. Especially important is the Bundesnaturschutzgesetz of 1976 which empowered individual Länder to set up various categories of protected areas. Over 25% of the land in Germany now enjoys specially protected designation, and the percentage is increasing all the time with new national parks and nature reserves, especially in the former East Germany.

As in most other countries of the world, the term 'national park' is used to describe the highest category of landscape protection. Nationalparke in Germany may be defined as relatively large areas of mainly state-owned countryside or coast with natural features and wildlife habitats of national and international importance. A guiding principle is that in national parks there should be minimal disturbance of the natural environment by human beings, especially if there are any large centres of population nearby. This means that varied plant and animal species can flourish within their typical habitats. National parks are not compatible with any commercial use, though as long as adequate protective measures are in force, public access is freely available for quiet leisure purposes and for ornithological, botanical and similar interests. Nature conservation therefore has a higher priority than, for example, in the much larger national parks of England and Wales. Though most land is publicly owned, local people may have rights within it.

The usual practice is to divide the parks into management zones, ranging from the stringently controlled to those with less strict protective measures. The central area or core zone is given the greatest protection, with an intermediate zone acting as further protection, and a third less protected zone is available for suitable quiet leisure pursuits and relaxation, though access on foot is allowed even in the first two zones. A regeneration zone may also be designated in which the physical renewal of damaged landscapes is taking place.

Biosphäre Reservate (biosphere reserves) are a relatively new category of landscape protection. This is, in fact, a concept by UNESCO for a series of worldwide reserves on a large scale which will form a scientific basis for the conservation of landscapes with special natural and also cultural features. The main difference between national parks and biosphere reserves is that the latter aim to conserve and even develop a 'Kulturlandschaft' or traditional heritage landscape in which people live and work. It will also include the encouragement of traditional forms of agriculture and local industries, with a greater emphasis on the cultural and historical aspects of individual landscapes and their communities. Land in such reserves will be both privately and publicly owned. In some ways biosphere reserves are therefore much closer to UK national parks with their populated villages and farms than the more purely nature conservation German parks.

Naturparke in Germany are a newer concept than national parks and include areas of beautiful and typical and protected landscape in which people live and work and which usually also contain a number of nature reserves. Nature parks are inevitably extremely attractive for tourism, and usually contain quite large communities, and accommodation provision including campsites. In theory at least, tourism development and traffic should not in any way damage these protected areas, and what tourism development does occur, should be at an appropriate, small-scale level. Like the biosphere reserves their setting in a largely privately owned and farmed (or forested) 'Kulturlandschaft' makes them inappropriate for mass tourism. In practice many German conservationists argue that standards of protection vary. Nature parks can be extremely well managed, but sometimes they remain little more than lines on a map, hyped up in tourist brochures but with relatively little active conservation work actually taking place. Outside official nature reserves various forms of tourist and other development can and do occur, especially new road building, which can create great pressure on vulnerable environments. Where nature parks cross national boundaries as between Germany and Belgium, Germany and Luxemburg and Germany and the Netherlands they are known as Europa Parke.

Naturschutzgebiete – nature reserves – are, as their name implies, smaller areas of more stringently protected countryside, wildlife habitats, sometimes quite limited in area, but sometimes covering several hundred hectares. In some cases there is a strict limitation on public access through the complete or partial suspension of the overall German right of access to forest and open countryside – the Betretungsrecht. In most cases, however, ample footpaths are created from which to enjoy protected areas, sometimes using boardwalks to prevent trampling of marsh or peatland, and often supporting any access restrictions by good quality interpretation of what the visitor can see. A green and white triangle with the outline of a bird in flight or a black owl on yellow ground is used to indicate a Schutzgebiet.

Also to be found are Landschaftschutzgebiete (landscape protection areas), which operate in planning terms as areas where development is strictly controlled, rather like Areas of Outstanding Natural Beauty in England and Wales, where the state planning authorities will forbid or restrict building or industrial development. However, it is also true to say that planning in Germany is much more a pro-active than a re-active process, and examples will be indicated in the Länder sections of this book where former industrial areas have been regenerated and transformed to often surprisingly fine green areas of rural or semi-rural countryside through active policies of restoration and planting.

Environmental protection at all these levels is a state (Land) rather than federal function. State by-laws provide legal protection and the relevant state department or national park administration provides the necessary management powers and funding.

Conflict between public access to the countryside on foot and conservation of the countryside is not seen as a major issue in Germany, where potential problems are typically resolved not by blanket restrictions, but by tolerant compromise which secures co-operation between most users and nature conservation interests as well as with farming and hunting or shooting interests. Whilst the 'Betretungsrecht' has the force of law, in practice most people visiting the countryside are happy to keep to marked paths in the sensitive areas if they understand the reason for such restriction. Only the most ecologically sensitive areas are totally closed to the public as a 'Sperrgebiet', significantly more frequently found in the former East rather than the former West Germany.

Unlike in the UK, there is no 'definitive map' of footpaths and bridleways as such, as the 'Betretungsrecht' covers much of this requirement. Unless you are told otherwise you can walk freely along most paths, tracks and farm roads in Germany, and in forests, along foreshores and on mountainsides, though not across cultivated land. Outside towns and cities, walking and outdoor clubs as well as local authorities often undertake the waymarking of routes and published maps provide detailed route information.

On wider ecological questions, no doubt in response to pressure both from the Greens and from voluntary environmental organisations, successive German governments have been among the leading administrations in Europe to take action to reduce environmental pollution, for example by bringing in tough new laws on the use of catalytic converters ahead of European legislation, and setting targets to cut greenhouse gas emissions way below those of other European nations. The federal government has also promoted measures to protect soils from pollution and erosion, whilst individual Länder have set high standards in such matters as garbage disposal and recycling of waste products.

For some time Germany has led the way in Europe over listing environmentally friendly products which carry a 'Blue Angel' as a symbol that they are biodegradable or do not harm the environment. Recycling is seen as the responsible concern of most householders, who are prepared to sort their rubbish into different bins such as for paper, glass, organic waste, and many local authorities offer special collections for more dangerous polluting waste such as old batteries, paint residues and old medicines.

Further information

Information about individual national and nature parks is given in the Länder sections of this book. However, for an overview of the European national park scene from a German perspective with regular features on German national parks, see the quarterly magazine *National Park*, published by Morsak Verlag, Wittelsbacher Straße 2-8, D-8352 Grafenau.

The German national parks section of the European Federation of Nature and National Parks (FöNAD) can be contacted at Krölstraße 5, D-8352 Grafenau. Verband Deutscher Naturparke e.V., Niederhaverbeck, D–3045 Bispingen, publishes a full list of nature parks in Germany.

Official information about nature and landscape protection in Germany can be obtained from the Federal Ministry of Food, Agriculture and Forestry – the Auswertungs und Informationsdienst (AID), Postfach 20 07 08, D-5300 Bonn 2.

General environmental information is handled by the Umweltbundesamt, Bismarckplatz 1, D-1000 Berlin 33.

Getting around Germany without a car

The Germans, perhaps more so than many other people in Europe, might sympathise with green ideas, but are also addicted to their cars, regarding them as a precious status symbol – the ownership of a new or even secondhand Mercedes, BMW, Porsche, Audi or VW is a goal of almost every young adult.

And in some ways you can see, just as in the USA, UK and other European countries, the horrific effects of the car-dependency culture. Huge motorways link all major centres of population, concrete expressways smash their way through the suburbs of cities, their grade-separated interchanges taking in hectares of land. Every small town has its by-pass, while drive-in supermarkets, warehouses and hypermarkets now appear around the outskirts of every town.

Only in the former East Germany will you see landscapes not yet defiled by motorways, though the other side of that equation are town centres, not yet with by-passes, gridlocked with spluttering Trabbis and Wartburgs.

Urban public transport

But the other side of the coin is that German governments since the last war have invested heavily in public transport for environmental reasons, particularly urban public transport networks. In a typical large German town or city you may have three or even four distinct but closely integrated transport systems – an electrified fast suburban railway (S-Bahn), an underground or metro (U-Bahn), a modern street tramway (Straßenbahn, usually modernised into a modern light rapid transport system) which may in fact become the U-Bahn when it reaches the city centre, and conventional bus services, albeit using modern, low floor vehicles with huge standing space and space for pushchairs, wheelchairs and (at certain times of day) even cycles. Many of them are articulated, the familiar 'bendy' buses, whilst electric trolley buses are used in many smaller conurbations. In many larger cities very few buses actually enter the largely pedestrianised city centres, acting as feeders to the trams and S-Bahn lines at stations in the outer suburbs, rather than congesting urban roads served by parallel rail or light rapid transit services.

Ticketing systems encourage regular, low cost commuting, with cheap season tickets, multiple journey tickets (usually available at railway or underground stations, bus or tram stops from automatic machines) and integrated timetables making urban travel a real pleasure.

Significantly, investment in public transport is not seen in Germany as a political issue. On the contrary, good public transport is believed to help the road user by encouraging people to switch modes and make more space available for those who have to travel by car or are determined to do so. It has been said, with some justification, that public transport in Germany, along with Switzerland and the Netherlands, is amongst the best and most reliable in the world, which is another good reason for travelling in Germany without your car.

Not that the cities are without their traffic problems – but clean, efficient public transport using its own car-free reservations is considered an essential part of the infrastructure of any larger German city. Though car ownership is higher in Germany than in a country like Britain, actual usage of cars per head of the population is significantly lower, thus providing measurable benefits in terms of reduced congestion and pollution.

Traffic calming and pedestrianisation

Though an official speed limit on German motorways is only just in the process of implementation – a fact to deplore, in the suburbs 40kmh, 30kmh and even 20kmh are common in 'traffic calmed' areas, where streets are deliberately narrowed by chicanes consisting of tree tubs or extended pavements, and road humps or sleeping policemen help to slow down speeding cars. Most city and large town centres and even quite small towns and villages are now extensively pedestrianised, with medieval towns in particular now enjoying a festive 'Autofrei' atmosphere in their narrow streets and squares. Walking and cycling are positively encouraged, with cycleways along broad pavements (as a pedestrian you need to make sure you stand or walk in the correct pedestrian lane and not in the cycle lane where you might be hit by a fast moving cyclist!). The generally strictly obeyed street crossing lights also allow cyclists as well as pedestrians to cross at green. Often public transport enjoys priority over other traffic at traffic lights and is allowed, at suitable slow speeds, into otherwise pedestrianised town centres.

Getting to Germany

Air travel is, inevitably, a convenient way for anyone outside Germany to get there quickly and the only option for anyone coming across the Atlantic or from even further afield. There is a wide choice of flights from the UK, though with the opening of the Channel Tunnel the speed advantage of city centre to city centre air travel from the UK compared with Inter-City railways will decline. The majority of international flights are into Frankfurt Airport, from where linking domestic services extend to other centres of population – uniquely to Germany some of these 'flights', for example between Stuttgart and Frankfurt, being operated by train on specially chartered services by Lufthansa, Germany's national airline. There is also a choice of charter flights and bargain APEX fares, particularly on longer distance flights between London and the Far East that have a stop at Frankfurt or München. You can also travel to Germany by coach on a limited number of routes, including Europabus and Euroways, and on other privately operated routes. Many of these are designed to meet the needs of military personnel and their families travelling to and from NATO bases.

Easily the nicest – and greenest – way from the UK or elsewhere in Europe is, we believe, the 'classic' way of travelling by train and ship which has much to recommend it, if for no other reason than that the relative slowness of the ship gives the traveller time to psychologically adjust to a different culture. Whilst the short Channel crossings such as Dover-Oostende reduce time on the ship, the two main overnight crossings (both of which have excellent rail connections from the North of England and Scotland), Hull-Rotterdam and Harwich-Hook of Holland, have much to recommend them. They provide a comfortable overnight crossing and in the case of the Hook crossing, an early enough start the following morning in Holland to enable you to cross into Germany during the day, in time to reach such destinations as Freiburg in the Schwarzwald, Stuttgart, München, Hannover, Hamburg, Westerland, and even Berlin, before evening. After its opening the Channel Tunnel will, however, very much improve the attractiveness of through, overnight rail travel from the UK. Another very civilised way of reaching northern Germany is by direct DFDS ship – really a cruise ship – from Harwich to Hamburg. Most travel agents can provide details of these services.

Travelling by train within Germany

If you are travelling any significant distance within Germany, easily the best way of getting around is by rail. The Deutsche Bundesbahn (DB) – with which the former East German railway Deutsche Reichsbahn (DR) is currently being integrated – is in terms of moving people and goods around, one of Europe's most efficient railway undertakings.

It is still an extremely comprehensive network, with many cross-country and even rural branch lines surviving in a country where railways have always been seen to be of vital national and regional strategic importance, and social and economic value. Even when closures have occurred, replacement buses are generally efficient and meet trains. The former East German Reichsbahn has an even more comprehensive network of often delightful rural routes, a veritable spider's web of local railways, making travel over the network a rail enthusiast's delight.

Growing car competition has, however, left many of the rural branch lines vulnerable, and with DB now facing a substantial financial deficit, there are those who are arguing for a programme of rural rail closures, especially in the east where decline of industry and related unemployment is having an even more serious effect on travel patterns. Hopefully, more environmentally responsible arguments will counter the short term myopia of the cost accountants and most if not all the rural network will be allowed to remain and be modernised to provide a viable alternative to the private car.

In contrast to some quiet rural branch lines, DB's major trunk routes are, of course, all extremely busy with huge flows of both passenger and freight traffic. Financial support for railways for environmental reasons remains high, and massive amounts of freight still travel by rail (as well as by water) rather than on the overcrowded roads. Almost all of the principal routes in the former West Germany are electrified, with modern rolling stock. However, routes to and from the former East Germany were neglected, particularly in the east, for obvious political reasons, and are only now being modernised and electrified – for example the strategic trunk route between Hannover and Berlin. There is a backlog of work to repair, restore and above all modernise the DR network which will take years to complete.

Inter-city travel

On several prestige lines between major cities a new generation of high speed trains is now being introduced, InterCity Express (ICE), some of them operating over several stretches of purpose-build new lines – the Neubaustrecken – for example between Hannover and Würzburg, Mannheim and Stuttgart, Köln and Rhein. These and the more conventional fast express services, known as Euro-City and InterCity, and usually named after a prominent German poet, musician or historic figure or place, link all the principal cities in Germany and other mainland European capitals, including overnight services with couchettes or *wagon lits*. If you travel on these you must pay a supplementary fare (Zuschlag), at time of writing costing DM6.00 if purchased at the station before catching the train, or DM7.00 if paid to the conductor-guard on the train. However, your supplement also covers the cost for more than one InterCity train if you make a connection on a single through journey.

German InterCity trains are fast, efficient and an excellent way of covering huge distances. All have on board restaurants, cafeterias and usually a trolley service of coffee and light snacks to your seat. Our experience is that InterCity trains are extremely well used by German people for both business and pleasure and during the summer months at least, it is advisable to book your seats in advance. Thanks to computerised ticketing systems you can now do this up until the day before departure from any staffed station in Germany, as well as through international ticketing agencies outside Germany.

The next level of DB services are known as Schnellzüge (express) services, fairly fast trains usually prefixed by a D in the timetable. These provide an excellent choice of cross-country links, sometimes, especially in the former East Germany, covering huge distances. They are a very good way of seeing the countryside, often travelling through less well known and less heavily visited areas. They do not always carry even basic refreshments (look for the appropriate wine glass symbol in the timetable before you travel without at least some basic provisions). Sometimes they are called Fern-Express (FD in the timetable); these are less luxurious long distance trains and usually serve holiday areas from larger conurbations, for example between the Ruhr and Bayern, but they almost invariably have refreshment facilities. Look out in particular for the excellent new InterRegio trains (prefixed IR), which again operate as express services over a distinct network of longer cross-country routes, using new purpose-built rolling stock with comfortable, stylish compartments and a travelling bistro – all highly recommended.

Regional and local rail services

The next level consists of Eilzüge (E), or RegionalSchnellbahn (RSB), really a euphemistic term for semi-fast trains, that work their way across country at a more modest pace, albeit with an occasional burst of speed, but only missing out a few of the remoter halts. You can meet what are called Regionalzüge, operated, for example in Schleswig-Holstein, by comfortable little modern diesel railcars, not unlike the British Sprinter, at fairly high speeds. Finally there are the Personenzüge, or Züge des Nahverkehrs – local trains, more colloquially known as Bummelzüge, often operated with a locomotive and a couple of coaches or an elderly diesel railcar. These will meander along at a more gentle pace calling at every wayside halt and often pausing for quite a time at junctions to allow the express trains to connect or pass, a delightful way of travelling if you like trains and are not in a hurry. They often penetrate deep into the countryside along quietly neglected branch lines of great charm and antiquity. At time of writing some of these are still operated in the former East Germany along narrow gauge lines by steam, a preservationist's paradise.

There are also various private lines, some of them operated by private companies, for example a local bus company or municipal transport undertaking. In a land which has as many steam buffs as Britain, there are over a hundred preserved railways or Museumbahnen with a variety of narrow gauge and standard gauge, steam operated mainly over summer weekends and holiday times. Some but not all of these are shown in the DB timetable. Main line steam services are also operated from time to time with preserved locomotives. Full details can be found in a special timetable booklet mentioned on page 39.

Station facilities

It is also worth pointing out that most medium-sized towns in Germany have a station which, unlike in Britain, is still staffed, with a left luggage office or lockers where baggage or rucksacks can be left for an hour or two, leaving you free to explore an old town, perhaps hiring a bike at the station for the purpose. Even small country stations sometimes have a surprisingly good quality restaurant serving homemade food, coffee, cakes, soft drinks, wine and beer, all day from early morning into the evening. The former East German Mitropa restaurants are particularly good value and at time of writing survive in some amazingly small village branch line stations – though no doubt some accountant's calculator is already proving why such charming features of civilised travel are no longer economic and how, for the good of the community, unmanned and vandalised bus shelters on the platforms of demolished railway stations should replace them.

Cycles on trains

Deutsche Bundesbahn has an extremely positive attitude towards the carrying of cycles on trains. It is usually possible to take a bike in the luggage compartment of a train if such a compartment exists, which they still do on most trains, for a fee of DM7.80 – about £2.80, or DM4.40 for a journey of less than 100 kilometres. The existence of such a luggage compartment is often indicated in public timetables by a luggage or even a cycle symbol. In urban areas cycles are also carried on local S-Bahn services and even on trams at off-peak times where capacity exists; cyclists and their machines being directed to certain parts of the train where room is available by a symbol on the carriage door. You can even send your bike to a holiday destination in advance by paying the appropriate fee, using the same excellent service to have your luggage collected from your home and delivered to your hotel or guest house with guaranteed prompt delivery.

Where it isn't possible to take your own bike, or if you don't have a bike available, cycles with or without 3-speed gears can be hired for a modest daily fee from a choice of around 250 local stations in the former West Germany. The fee varies from DM6.00-DM8.00 for rail ticket holders, depending on whether the machine has gears, to DM10.00-DM12.00 for people not arriving by train, but who still want to hire a bike from local stations. You can even send your bike back on the train from a different station at the end of a cycle trip on payment of the appropriate and fairly modest carriage fee.

Timetables and information

Travellers outside Germany planning a rail-based trip can get at least an outline of major rail services through the excellent Thomas Cook European timetable, issued monthly. There is now also a special Thomas Cook German timetable, consisting of the German sections of the European timetable. However, the Cook timetables contain only a fraction of the rail services in Germany, for which you need the massive German railways complete timetable or Kursbuch, an enormous volume of telephone directory dimensions, costing around DM25.00 and covering all rail services in the united Germany. However, it does come in sections covering different regions, which can be bought separately and are a lot easier to handle in a rucksack or suitcase. An interesting point to note is that unlike British Rail, DB and most bus operators do not operate special, separate Sunday timetables. Sunday and holiday services operate to an identical timetable, with the exception of a certain number of weekday only workers' or commuter trains (marked with a crossed hammer symbol in the timetable), but augmented with recreational or tourist services indicated in both bus and rail timetables by a church cross symbol. It always pays to check such symbols carefully when making any journey by train or bus in Germany.

The Kursbuch doesn't just include rail service information, but also important regional bus routes, including buses that specifically link with trains or which have replaced rural branch lines that have been closed. You even see combined timetables where bus and train services intermingle rather than compete, and operate in the same timetable, the train operating at busy times, the bus at quiet times or serving different villages on the route.

All timetables in the Kursbuch fit into a logical numbering system, so that international rail services have a letter/number notation, national rail services a single or double digit, regional services a three digit, bus services a four digit number – used nationally – and boat services a five digit notation. Common numbering systems are used so that where possible local bus numbers relate to the local rail services, making planning and timetable cross-referencing a good deal easier.

Ticket prices are broadly similar to those in the UK and in some cases a little lower. There are, however, a number of excellent value-for-money tourist tickets available on DB. Two of these are the Inter-Rail Ticket and the German Rail Pass, only available for visitors from outside Germany, and therefore only purchasable outside Germany. Of outstanding value for overseas visitors, for older people as well as young, is the European Railways Inter-Rail ticket which now exists in two forms – for the under-26s and the over-26s. These are valuable in that they provide travel through Belgium and the Netherlands from Channel or North Sea ports to Germany as well as travel within Germany on all DB and DR rail services and some boat services. Equally excellent value is the DB German Rail Pass which is valid for any selected five, ten or fifteen days of travel within a month period, first or second class costing from around £100 to around £260, depending on number of days of travel and class type (first and second still prevail on DB). German Rail Passes are valid on all DB rail and also on DB bus services, as well as on the services of many regional bus companies (many of which are in fact DB-owned), on DTG long distance coach services including the 'Romantic Road' services, and on certain boat services along parts of the Rhine and Mosel. However, German Rail Passes have to be booked in advance outside Germany from DB or an approved DB travel agent.

Of special value to the traveller wanting to explore a specific region are the Netz- und Bezirkskarten (regional and local passes) which give ten days travel in a number of key regions on all local trains and some local DB-operated and other buses. These can be purchased within Germany or from the UK. Costs are discounted for travellers who also travel to Germany by rail and two people travelling together or families get a further discount. Another facility for young people is Eurotrain, which offers bargain fares for the under-26s to Germany. Combined with a German Rail Youth Pass (under 25) these can amount to an extremely cheap way of exploring Germany. Senior citizens in other EC countries can also get a pass giving them reduced price rail travel within Germany. A further possibility is a 'Fly & Rail' package with Air Europe between London, Gatwick and Düsseldorf at an all-in price for the air and rail pass. These facilities are summarised in an excellent DB Rail Travel Planner leaflet, in English, available from DB offices. Details of these and other appropriate addresses for further information to book tickets and passes (from the UK) are given below.

Bus and coach travel

There is nothing like the network of national coach services in Germany that exists in the UK or USA, but the most important national and international system is the EuropaBus network, owned by the European railways and operated between a number of major cities in Germany and elsewhere in Europe, including a service to and from London, and to popular tourist areas. These are supplemented by a number of privately operated Fernbuslinien (long distance bus routes). Again, details of some but not all such services are in the relevant section of the Kursbuch, together with timetables of ferry services to the various islands in the North Sea and the Baltic, as well as for Danube and Rhine cruise ships.

Bus services operate on a regional basis, as always in Germany complementing rather than competing with trains, operated both by regional transport companies (RVGs) and private companies, under the local control of regional transport agencies who co-ordinate timetables and provide bus stop information.

There is a good network of rural bus services in even quite remote parts of Germany, and local timetable information is easy to obtain once in the country, either from local tourist offices or bus information offices in the area. Most bus stops have timetable information boards. In the major conurbations such as the Ruhr, which has a totally integrated system of buses, LRT (light rapid transit) and trains, comprehensive timetable booklets are also readily available from bus enquiry offices. However, it is worth pointing out that in many rural areas evening bus services are often sparse or non-existent, and if you are making a longer journey by bus or with a bus element (say from a railhead) and don't have an up-do-date timetable, it will pay to plan your journeys to arrive at your railhead destination by late afternoon. Otherwise you might have to use taxis. These are usually readily available at most railway stations and even bus stations and the cost is generally reasonable – though it makes sense to agree a price with the driver before you start for more than a very local journey. In the Schwarzwald the regional transport authority actually puts recommended local taxi firm phone numbers on the bus stops for evening travel purposes.

An important point to note is that most rural bus services operate only from official bus stops – Haltestellen – marked with a green H on a yellow background. Stops are further apart – usually a kilometre or more – than is usual in the UK, nor will buses stop at any available point along a route by a hand signal. You must make your way to the official bus stop or watch the vehicle coast by.

Fares are reasonably low and in many areas you can also get discounted multi-journey tickets or weekly rover tickets at bargain prices to include unlimited travel over a whole local network of routes. Most buses have good luggage carrying facilities and there are even a few cycle carrying services.

Boat services

It is worth remembering that many of the major rivers in Germany, for example the Rhine, the Danube and the Elbe, and also some of their tributaries, have regular timetabled boat services, especially during the summer months. These provide real public transport as well as a delightful way to travel between riversides. Cycles are usually carried, but it is best to confirm this beforehand.

All the larger, inhabited off-shore islands in the North Sea and the Baltic have regular ferry services, usually linking with specific train or bus services.

Details of most but not all of these services are contained in the main and regional editions of the DB Kursbuch.

Cycling and walking

Cyclists and walkers are particularly well catered for in Germany.

Cycling is seen as a very cheap and practical form of local transport, as well as a mainstream recreational activity. Most cities and larger conurbations have extensive cycleways used by schoolchildren, shoppers and business people as a healthy and pollution-free way of getting to school, office or the shops. But extensive, waymarked routes have also been developed into the local countryside, using traffic free farm and forest tracks, quiet lanes and segregated cycleways. Many such routes are marketed by local tourist offices as among their top countryside attractions for visitors, often linked up with packages of accommodation and with luggage-carrying facilities between local guesthouses and small hotels to allow cyclists to enjoy easy riding without the weight and bulk of a massive saddlebag and panniers.

Rambling – Wandern – is a German national activity. Everyone, from the federal president and government ministers to schoolchildren, walks in the countryside for pleasure, and walking and outdoor organisations have a huge active membership, as have nature protection organisations. Rambling is often a group activity with walking and other clubs disappearing into the countryside, but is equally enthusiastically tackled alone, in couples or family groups. Love of the countryside, especially of the legendary forests and mountains, is a part of being German. The right to roam – Betretungsrecht – over wild and uncultivated places, over heath, mountain, forest and seashore, is built into German federal law. Almost every small town has its network of beautifully waymarked paths and trails from convenient forest car parks and bus stops, promoted by high quality literature. Often the waymarking takes the form of an attractive and distinctive symbol or may be colour coded.

Long distance walkers have a choice of routes and superb, waymarked long distance walks, some of which will be dealt with in the regional sections of this book. There are also a number of significant European long distance routes which cross Germany between the North Sea and the Mediterranean, the Baltic and the Black Sea. Many long and medium distance routes can be undertaken with the help of a luggage-carrying service to avoid the problem of overnight backpacking.

Maps for walkers and cyclists are no problem, there being a huge choice of walkers' maps mainly at 1:50,000 or 1:40,000 scale, but larger scale, more localised maps perhaps at 1:25,000 or even less are available for the more popular walking areas. We have found the popular 1:50,000 or 1:40,000 Kompass Wanderkarte (scales vary depending on area) to be particularly reliable, providing national coverage of the former West Germany. They include details of local footpaths and traffic free tracks and lanes, of waymarked long and medium distance routes, as well as cycle routes, and such valuable information as refreshment facilities, nature reserves, bus stops. They also have a wealth of good quality material concerning local geology, archaeology, natural and local history and tourist attractions printed on the reverse, as well as recommended routes, but for this you need to be able to read German. These maps can be purchased in the UK, or any small or medium German town will have one or more well stocked bookshops with a choice of maps and guides.

The former East Germany is a little more problematical, with some very good if old fashioned maps of popular walking areas published by the VEB Tourist Verlag which cost very little, if you can still find them, and these are full of excellent information – even though as former East Germans will warily tell you, certain items were omitted by the old DDR regime if felt to be of state or military importance. These are now being replaced by an avalanche of excellent new material, much, but not all, written and published in West Germany.

Useful contacts and addresses ⎯⎯⎯⎯⎯⎯⎯⎯⎯⎯⎯⎯⎯

Basic information about German rail services, rail passes and copies of the Kursbuch and regional timetables can be obtained from any staffed rail station in Germany, or (in the UK) from **German Rail,** Suite 118, Hudson's Place, Victoria Station, London SW1V 1JL.

Tickets and reservations from the UK to Germany and within the country are also available from **BR International,** Victoria Station, London SW1V 1JL (071-834 2345).

DB's own travel agency, **DER Travel Service** of 18 Conduit Street, London W1R 9TD offers a range of travel tickets and rail-based package holidays in Germany.

A number of independent international rail appointed travel agencies in the UK also handle DB tickets. **Ultima Travel** of 424 Chester Road, Little Sutton, South Wirral L66 3RB (051347-1717), has a particular interest in and specialist knowledge of the German rail system and has offered to provide a comprehensive and bespoke booking and reservation service for readers of *The Green Guide to Germany*, including Inter-Rail, German rail passes, regional rail rovers and Eurotrain tickets, and insurance services designed to meet the needs of rail travellers. When contacting Ultima, please mention this book.

Russell Hafter Holidays of 26 The Square, Ashfield, Dunblane, Scotland FK15 0JN (0786-824515) is the only UK travel firm specialising exclusively in walking holidays in Germany, as well as offering a number of attractive walking self-guided and guided packages, most with luggage-carrying facilities. Russell Hafter, like Ultima, is able to put together purpose-made specialist packages of travel and accommodation for green travellers. Again mention this book when contacting the company.

For further information about **Deutsche Bundesbahn** and its overall environmental and transport policies, write to Deutsche Bundesbahn, Zentrale Presse und Öffentlichkeitsarbeit, Friedrich-Ebert-Anlage 43-45, D-6000 Frankfurt am Main.

Cook's European Timetable is published monthly and is available from any branch of Thomas Cook plus certain bookshops, or in case of difficulty from Thomas Cook Publishing, PO Box 227, Peterborough PE3 6SB.

The *Kursbuch der Deutschen Museums-Eisenbahnen* (annual) can be obtained from Verlag Uhle & Kleimann, Postfach 1543, D-4990 Lübbecke 1, currently costing DM5.00 plus DM2.00 for postage.

A wide variety of walking maps of Germany, including the Kompass series and the Black Forest Society maps, as well as various larger scale Alpine Club maps, are available in the UK from **Stanfords,** 27a Floral Street, London WC2 9LP.

Food and accommodation

Green travelling is about enjoying the characteristic food and drink of a country, and in Germany, even if your budget is modest, you can eat typical German food and eat extremely well. For a variety of reasons, mainly we believe linked to Francophile snobbery, German food is dismissed by the ill-informed as being 'heavy' or 'stodgy', a kind of sauerkraut-and-sausage stereotype. You can, of course see plenty of sausages around in every possible shape, size and variety, and just occasionally you can find sauerkraut, a popular winter dish. Country food, in Germany as elsewhere, is often plain and plentiful. But traditional German food well cooked and presented can stand comparison with any in the world for quality and variety. As in all sophisticated European countries you can of course dine out in any German town at a variety of European, Indian and Asian restaurants – Italian, Yugoslav, Greek, Indian and Chinese are particularly popular. But it seems pointless to travel to Germany to eat Italian or Chinese food when there is a very good national cuisine.

Indeed one of the great delights of travelling in Germany is the variety and quality of locally produced food and drink, whether you are dining out in some luxurious restaurant or some unpretentious Gasthof or enjoying a quick snack in a local cafeteria or Konditorei. The sign 'gute bürgliche Küche' outside a Gasthof or restaurant is usually an indication that the proprietor will provide traditional German fare cooked with pride. The other very positive factor is that though you can eat splendidly, the cost of about £10 a head for a good quality meal, including house wine or beer, in a typical German restaurant is far less than you'd pay in the majority of English restaurants of a comparable standard. And you can often eat well – especially in the former East Germany – for much less than that. Regional specialities in food and drink abound, and are usually good value for money – but these will be mentioned in the context of the various regions themselves.

Frühstück (breakfast), in all but the smallest hotels and Gasthöfe and perhaps in some of the eastern regions, is often served buffet style so that you can help yourself from a range of fruit juice, fresh fruit or fruit compôte, a selection of crisp rolls, and dark rye bread, which is highly recommended as is the coarse-grained dark Pumpernickel and Korn bread, both excellent forms of roughage. Jams and preserves are frequently homemade and honey too can be local and of excellent quality. A variety of cheeses and cold meats – hams and salami – plus boiled eggs complete the usual fare. Tea or coffee are equally popular, so if you prefer tea to the excellent coffee, do remember that continental blends are weaker than English blends and taste better with lemon or 'schwarz', without milk or lemon, though you can of course take milk if you wish.

Germans eat well and enjoy their food. There is an emphasis on quality of produce and purity which you don't always find in other countries. Hot and cold snacks are usually available at almost any hour of the day at Gasthöfe (the nearest thing to a country pub). If you are in a small German town mid-morning or afternoon and feel a little peckish, indulge in one of the really excellent homemade cakes and fresh coffee available in most Konditorei or confectioners.

Most places which offer refreshment when you are travelling, including station buffets, offer surprisingly good homemade food rather than the kind of pre-packaged heated up hamburgers and pizzas so prevalent in England, though if you're into this kind of insipid instant food you'll find the world over, Pizza Huts and McDonalds abound. These are by no means the cheapest places to eat. And the ubiquitous Coca-Cola is everywhere to be found.

Savoury snacks available at street stalls and stand-up eateries traditionally include a couple of hot-dog style sausages (sometimes called Bockwurst or 'Wiener') with some bread or a roll and mustard. Regional specialities improve the range from the Thüringer Bratwurst (a meaty grilled sausage) which is freshly cooked, to various ham and cheese rolls, and fish snacks; for example rolls filled with fresh herring or shrimps are to be found closer to the northern coast.

Mittagessen (lunch) still tends to be the main meal for many Germans and you will usually find the Tageskarte or table d'hôte in a restaurant, café or hotel at two or three courses for a fixed price very good value. This could be soup – the usual are varieties of clear soup or broth, goulash (a spicy soup) or perhaps a thicker pea or vegetable soup – followed by a meat or fish dish with boiled, fried or chipped potatoes or salad or vegetables and maybe a sweet course such as fruit or ice cream, or a variety of cheese or apple cake. Pasta is popular, particularly in the south. Pancakes, savoury or sweet, are another German speciality.

Evening meals will be similar, though inevitably with a much greater choice.

Vegetarians are to some extent catered for, and in larger towns you can increasingly find specialist vegetarian restaurants, but it will not always be easy to find one in any given small town. If you do not want to risk too many omelettes or the rather flavourless 'Gemüseplatte' (plate of vegetables) sometimes offered to vegetarians, we recommend that you get an up to date copy of *Der Vegetarische Restaurantführer* or look up the vegetarian restaurants section in the excellent *Das Alternative Branchenbuch* which lists over 200 such restaurants in Germany. The *Branchenbuch* is also an encyclopedic collection of information about organic produce, organic farms (several hundred of which are listed, state by state, together with addresses and details of what produce is grown) and ecologically sustainable items and services – food, cosmetics, medicine, and technology, listing addresses of suppliers and of environmental organisations throughout Germany as well as containing excellent articles on current environmental issues.

However, it has to be said that away from the more alternative lifestyles, Germany is very much a meat eating country, with pork often dominant on menus in various forms including schnitzels, cutlets, and in casseroles, though beef, lamb, venison, veal (in schnitzel form usually) and even hare can be found on menus, cooked in a wide variety of ways. Poultry is also popular, especially chicken but also turkey and on occasion duck. Fish is almost always available in abundance, with superb trout and lake fish dishes inland and a quite amazing range of sea fish in the northern seaboard towns. Ham is often of excellent quality, whilst the range of sausages and salami has to be seen to be believed. A good range of cheeses is produced in Bayern in particular.

Compared with Britain and France fresh vegetables and salad dishes, although usually available, tend to be less imaginative, and a 'Salat Teller' can often be little more than a plate of lettuce and peppery cucumber. Nor have the Germans really discovered the art of the wholemeal salad-based sandwich, despite there being so much excellent bread available.

It is quite acceptable to have only a snack lunch at any establishment and save your appetite for the evening, so you could, for example, have just a soup course, and perhaps a sweet, if you don't want to tackle a heavy midday meat dish.

One aspect of German restaurants which we find compares unfavourably with Britain is the amount of meal-time smoking which goes on, surprisingly in so health-conscious a nation. No-smoking areas are rare and lighting up after or even during a meal is considered socially acceptable in Germany.

Many German families, especially in the north, prefer a simple evening meal called Abendbrot, which is basically varieties of bread, cheese, cooked meats and something to drink. Occasionally the same word, instead of the more usual Abendessen, may mean a cooked meal.

If you are self-catering, however, you will find a wide range of often superb fresh vegetables in the shops and street markets whilst almost every town has one or more 'Reformhaus' shops. These are the equivalent of UK health food shops and sell herbs, lentils and dried vegetables, spices, dried fruit and nuts, and perhaps organic wines. Specialist food stalls are often also to be seen in street markets. A real delight, too, is the wonderful variety of different breads on sale in any baker's shop, as well as cakes and savoury confections.

Beer is almost synonymous with Germany. The old Reinheitsgebot, purity law, of 1516 laid down strict guidelines for its manufacture, and German beer is invariably of high quality. Most beer in cafés, restaurants and pubs (Kniepe or Lokale) is the light Pilsen beer, a type of brewing which originated in Czechoslovakia, and which has little in common with the mass produced ersatz 'lager' suffered in England, USA and Australia. Fine quality Pilsen beer has a foaming head (it can take several minutes to pour into the characteristic round glass, usually with the brewer's insignia, and its drip-catching paper stem serviette), a nutty flavour and rich aftertaste.

But there are many other excellent brews to sample, from the bitterer and darker Altbiers of the north to the refreshing Weizenbier, made from wheat and still fermenting in the glass, so popular in Bayern. Many are specialist brews, such as the strong Bockbiers brewed in the spring, the double fermented steam beers, the extraordinary Franconian stone beers whose fermentation is helped by the dropping of red hot rocks into the brewing vat.

Quality of beer is always good in a country where brewing is almost considered an art form, its produce often, in beer drinkers' terms, rising to the superb. As elsewhere in Europe, a few famous national and even international companies dominate the market, for example the big Dortmund breweries such as Dort-munder Union, Dortmunder Actien, König Pils, and such well known names from other regions as Becks, Holsten, Löwenbrau, Warstein. On the other hand, many hundreds of extremely small private, local breweries survive, each with its own particular following and its aficionados. Both Bayern and the Schwarzwald are especially rich in fine local breweries.

German wine is again justly famous, though wine snobs tend to ignore some of the truly great German vintages. Queen Victoria popularised the fashion for Rhine wines in England, no doubt with her German husband Albert's encour-agement, when she so enjoyed her bottles of Hochheimer that she believed them to have curative properties, declaring that a good hock was superior to the doctor.

To a degree the reputation of German wine has suffered in Britain because of the over-production of the cheap sweet Liebfraumilch from the Rhine valley at a time when tastes favour the French dries. It has been said, perhaps with a grain of truth, that the Germans keep their finest wines for home consumption. In fact top quality German white wine will rival the classic French vintages and compare with the best in the world, ranging from Kabinett through to Spätlese, Auslese, Beerenauslese and Trockenbeerauslese, with fine bouquets and flavour; the best vintages are eagerly sought after by collectors. The sum paid by a wine collector for a bottle of Vollrads Riesling in 1972 in New York was the equivalent of £1,200; at that time it was the second highest price ever paid.

The German wines enjoy a variable but good winegrowing climate, even though they do not get the constant sun of vines in the south of France and Italy. The quality of the white wine is in fact improved by this variable temperature, which helps to bring out greater delicacy and as the acidity level decreases, the wine becomes fruitier in flavour. Climate, soil and type of grape as well as the vintner's skill are all crucial for good wine. The three main grape types are the Müller-Thurgau, the Riesling and the Silvaner, all producing crisp dry and semi-dry whites. Around 27% of the vines under cultivation are Müller-Thurgau, 23% Riesling and 16% Silvaner. The Riesling grape was probably a sport from an indigenous wild vine and is perhaps Germany's best known variety. It is planted particularly in the Rheingau, Mosel, Saar and Ruwer. In most of the great wine producing countries the main production is red wine, whereas in Germany the contrary is true with 80% of their viniculture producing white wine. There are, however, a few notable light reds, such as the Trollinger, the Blauer Spät-burgunder, and the newer Dornfelder from Rheinland-Pfalz. The Weisse-Herbst grape makes a very acceptable rosé. Sekt is a sparkling wine, the German equivalent of champagne (and very much cheaper – at least in the shops), and makes a good festive drink.

Most German wines come from the great Rhine vineyards of Rheinland-Pfalz and Hessen or around the Mosel and from Baden-Württemberg and Franken-land in the south.

Tafelwein – usually a hock – is the very acceptable house or table wine you get in most restaurants, though a lot of cheap French wine is imported for this purpose. But if you pay a little more, a superior product is a Qualität, a Kabinett or especially the excellent Auslese and the sweeter Spätlese – which still retail at a reasonable price, though a really fine vintage can set you back quite a sum. Prices in restaurants are only a little lower than in the UK except in wine producing areas, where you can get a Viertel (a quarter of a litre) of excellent locally produced wine for less than the price of house wine in the north. You will find that you pay more in Germany for any drink you buy in a place of refreshment, as it is taxed more heavily. Sekt in particular is expensive because it attracts an even higher tax. On the other hand, even the smallest drink or snack entitles you to sit in very comfortable surroundings for almost as long as you like.

Typically German too is schnapps, strong liqueur usually drunk in a single gulp as an aperitif or after a meal or even (not really recommended) after beer. Again, schnapps appears in many regional varieties, in the north mostly based on wheat – the typical Korn, strong and dry, though a weaker version flavoured with apple, Applekorn, is popular in Westphalia. The fruit schnapps from the Schwarzwald region of Baden such as Kirschwasser (cherry) or Mirabelle (small golden plums) is famous, whilst Obstler (a general fruit schnapps) is common everywhere. In remoter areas such as the Schwarzwald or the Bayerische Wald, schnapps was often taken medicinally, perhaps even to dull the pain until the doctor arrived, or until nature took its course.

If you are shopping for your own food or drink, do remember that shops open early and close late (usually 8 or 8.30 am till 6 pm) but often close for an hour or more at lunchtime (often 12.30-2 pm). Saturday afternoons are especially problematic in German towns, where most shops close at 1 o'clock except usually for a single Saturday a month. This can cause problems if you leave your shopping for Sunday's lunch too late on Saturday! On the other hand, many towns have a late Thursday opening for their shopping centres and larger stores.

Banks have similar hours to shops, but with no facilities on Saturdays and earlier closing – usually 4 pm. Many main railways stations, however, have banks which are open for cashing cheques over a longer period. All banks readily change travellers cheques and Eurocheques and will give cash on Visa or Mastercard/ Eurocard (Access). Increasingly, there are cash machines which now accept Visa for Deutschmarks, but it will pay to enquire in your home bank to ascertain availability. It is also very simple to exchange sterling or dollars at the current rate less a modest commission at banks. Avoid changing cash at travel agents or hotels except in an emergency, as they usually ask a higher rate of commission. Visa, Access and Eurocheques can now be used for purchase of goods or meals in most larger shops and restaurants in Germany, though it may be more difficult in remoter rural parts of the former East Germany.

Accommodation in Germany for an overnight stay or longer period is never a problem with endless choice, whether you wish to pay more for luxury at the top end of the market – not strictly for green travellers – or are content with the extremely comfortable quarters, often with en suite facilities, that most medium and small hotels and Gasthöfs in the former West Germany offer their guests. Private accommodation or farm accommodation at a budget price can be highly recommended if you prefer the small-scale, and is a very good way of meeting ordinary German families and getting well off the overused tourist trails. There are also numerous facilities for camping either with tents or caravans at official camp sites or Camping Plätze. Normally it is necessary in Germany to use an official site and these are usually equipped with good facilities – toilets, showers, a shop. They are indicated in tourist brochures and on most larger scale walking and leisure maps.

The Youth Hostel movement began in Germany, and German hostels are of an extremely high standard. There are plenty of them, giving the young and the not-so-young a huge range of budget accommodation. But do remember that you need your International YHA card with you, to be purchased in your own country, and the International YHA Yearbook.

Also recommended for walkers, and an excellent way of meeting other German conservationists and outdoor enthusiasts, are the walkers' hostels (Wanderheime) run by such bodies as the Naturfreunde, the Schwarzwaldverein, the Schwäbische Albverein, or the German Alpine Club. Most are available to non-members, but if you are using such accommodation regularly, you usually get a better deal if you are a member, and indeed will be supporting their conservation work and efforts by so doing.

Another possibility available in almost every region of Germany is to stay on a farm, 'Urlaub auf dem Bauernhof'. Farm tourism really began in Austria and Southern Germany and is seen as a way of helping to integrate tourism into the local community, giving visitors a 'deep' rural experience in which they – particularly children – are encouraged to participate in farm activities whilst at the same time supporting rural incomes and landscape conservation. Bayern and Baden-Württemberg are leaders in this field with a highly developed network of participating farms, but most state tourist offices have information and material available about farm holidays – see the individual Länder sections of this book.

Generally it is not necessary to book in advance whatever type of accommodation you favour out of season unless you plan a specialist holiday as suggested above, but it obviously makes sense to do so in the high season, especially in popular areas, including some of the Baltic and North Sea islands. The larger your party, the less easy it is to arrive speculatively, particularly in school holidays. German school holidays are staggered from early July right through to September. In certain popular walking areas such as the Schwarzwald, June and especially September are peak months because of the slightly cooler weather, more pleasant for walking, compared with July and August which can be hot (over 25° centigrade) inland.

Be prepared to make use of private accommodation in the former East Germany at times, as the process of restructuring has caused some premises to close though many are being renovated, improved and expanded to cater for a new clientèle. Good value in former East Germany are the former Betriebsheime or holiday homes – centres which belonged to various factories and manufacturing units and the like where workers could take their holiday breaks at subsidised rates. Some of these have now become hotels and offer a good standard of comfort at reasonable cost.

All regions of Germany have reasonably efficient local tourist offices (Verkehrsamt) that supply up-to-date lists of registered addresses of all ranges of accommodation from campsites and private rooms to luxury hotels, usually with phone numbers. In each regional section we list the main tourist office which will send you, usually by return of post and often in English, the general brochure of the Land, which lists individual district or town tourist offices with actual lists of accommodation providers. To save time, you will also almost certainly be able to get brochures of individual Länder from the German tourist office in your own country. The UK office is listed at the end of this chapter. Most accommodation providers will accept bookings by phone, though some may require a deposit or will only reserve beds if you arrive by an agreed time – say 6 pm. Larger hotels will generally accept either Eurocard/Mastercard (Access) or Visa or Eurocheques, but small establishments prefer cash for obvious reasons. If you are not sure if plastic money is acceptable, do check when booking.

Useful guides

Der Vegetarische Restaurantführer für Deutschland, Schweiz, Österreich, published by Naturata, Tauberstraße 25, D-6970 Lauda.

Das Alternative Branchenbuch, published by Alltop GmbH, Gotzingerstraße 48, D-8000 München 70.

Other information

German Youth Hostels Association (Deutsches Jugendherbergswerk), Bismarckstraße 8, D-4930 Detmold 1.

Deutsche Zentrale für Tourismus e.V. (DZT), Beethovenstraße 69, D-6000 Frankfurt am Main.

German National Tourist Office (UK), Nightingale House, 65 Curzon Street, London W1Y 7PE.

See the regional sections of this book for specific regional tourist offices which can supply addresses of local tourist offices with lists of all categories of accommodation and specialist countryside packages – for example walking or cycling packages with luggage-carrying facilities. Many, but not all, have brochures in English, and all can handle requests for information in English without difficulty.

Schleswig-Holstein _____

Mudflats glinting like some extraordinary moonscape, silvery beaches complete with highly coloured canopied double-seated basket-chairs, storm-tossed trees leaning out at perilous angles, and strikingly dramatic towers and churches in elaborately patterned red brick are some of the unforgettable images to greet the visitor to Schleswig-Holstein.

In prehistoric times, at the end of the last Ice Age, the proximity of the British Isles to the north German coastline was even greater than it is today as there was no intervening sea, but merely a continuous land mass. As the glaciers melted, England became part of an island complex, but the North Sea is not nearly such a division between the two cultures as many people imagine. Indeed the Angles, from which the Anglo-Saxons and ultimately the English derived their names, came originally from the region of Angeln, east of Flensburg and northeast of Schleswig, along the Baltic coast.

Today Schleswig-Holstein is Germany's most northerly state, bordering Denmark at the base of the narrow Jutland peninsula and having a coastline along both the North and Baltic Seas. Off the west coast, which is particularly bleak and stormy in the winter, lies the 15-30km wide flat tidal zone known as the Wattenmeer. Here are also the popular Nordfriesische holiday islands of Sylt, Amrum and Föhr and a number of additional smaller islands, known collectively as the Halligens. Helgoland (Heligoland), further out to sea with its steep red cliffs, which was formerly British, is also part of the state of Schleswig-Holstein and was formerly of great strategic importance.

Between the west and east coasts of Schleswig-Holstein lies sandy, less fertile land known as the Geest, mainly pastoral landscape. There is a limited amount of industrial development round such towns as **Neumünster** and **Rendsburg** and round the major ports. The east or Baltic coast has a milder climate and an almost tideless sea with a chain of seaside resorts. **Kiel**, the state's capital, and centre of the shipbuilding industry, has a splendid natural harbour looking towards Scandinavia which presides over the 99 kilometre long Nord-Ostsee Kanal or Kiel canal – one of Europe's busiest waterways. To enjoy a spectacular bird's eye view of the canal, take the little train from Kiel which climbs a high, looping viaduct over the great Transporter Bridge to make a dramatic entry into the old town of Rendsburg. Kiel's international sailing regatta known as the Kieler Woche is a well-loved sporting event.

The old Hanseatic city and port of **Lübeck** with its famous two-turreted redbrick gateway (see the section on Bremen for an account of the Hanseatic League) was originally the leading Hansa town and the northern terminus of the ancient medieval trade route or Salzstraße. Lübeck also has strong associations with the famous novelist Thomas Mann, whose partly autobiographical novel *Buddenbrooks* is set in the city. Lübeck lost its free city status in 1937, as a result of displeasing Adolf Hitler who was apparently not too delighted with his less than rapturous reception there. Today Lübeck is noted for fine architecture, and its celebrated marzipan – available in a wide variety of sizes and shapes, usually covered with chocolate. A newer speciality of the region beginning to gain ground is 'Kustenebel', literally 'coastal fog', a splendidly opaque pale grey liqueur flavoured with caraway and aniseed, served chilled, and looking for all the world as if some local sea-fret had actually been imprisoned in a bottle.

The visitor to Schleswig-Holstein could do worse than to spend time exploring some of its old towns such as Schleswig itself, Rendsburg, Flensburg, Heide, Eutin, and Friedrichstadt – founded by Count Friedrich III in 1621. Many have the remnants of medieval walls, narrow streets, mostly pedestrianised to make attractive shopping centres, remnants of defensive ditches turned into park lakes, and distinctive architecture with steep, tiled roofs with tall, narrow, gabled façades. **Flensburg**, on the border, has not unnaturally a Danish flavour, with its long narrow main street, the cathedral with its famous Renaissance organ, and its attractive harbour. **Husum**, as well as having ferry links with the inner Nordfriesische Inseln, has a castle, a seventeenth century town hall and the Nordfriesisches Museum in the Nissenhaus, close to the market place.

Denmark, Sweden and Finland are all easily reached from Schleswig-Holstein's Baltic ports, whilst the North Sea makes links with aspects of Scandinavian and even English culture easy to understand. Old Viking settlements around the Dithmarschen district and Haithabu (where there is a major Viking museum) near Schleswig are rich in archaeological interest. The state's more recent history has resulted in a much more varied mixture of people. After the Second World War, a million refugees and displaced persons helped to swell Schleswig-Holstein's population. Yet the present total of over two and a half million inhabitants, with a surface area of 15,720 square kilometres, makes it still a comparatively sparsely populated state, with fewer large towns than elsewhere in Germany.

For centuries Schleswig-Holstein was a source of contention with nearby Denmark, the region being used as a pawn in games of international power-politics. The small island of Föhr for example was half Danish and half German for a considerable period of time. A referendum in 1920 returned North Schleswig, consisting mainly of Danish speakers, to Denmark, while Southern Schleswig voted to remain in Germany. A model reform was introduced in 1955 as a joint initiative between the German and Danish governments to allow a South Schleswig voters' association to send a Danish-speaking deputy to the Schleswig-Holstein state parliament; the 5% of the vote normally demanded under the German constitution for political parties was specially waived here. In addition, the German government pays half the cost for anyone who wishes to educate his children in Denmark, while a Danish newspaper is printed in the border town of Flensburg. Danish schools and kindergartens ensure additionally that the Danish minority has its rights protected. It seems sad that other areas of Europe with cultural minorities cannot achieve similar just and rational solutions. Dairy farming and horse breeding predominate on the more fertile marshlands, with some pig and sheep farming generally further inland. The rich agricultural soil at Friedrichskoog also produces for example substantial quantities of white cabbage, mainly for sauerkraut which forms an accompaniment to various meat dishes or the hearty Bauernschmaus which is served with Bockwurst. Other food specialities of the region include a wide variety of fish dishes, including rollmop herrings known as Matjes, herrings served in a variety of ways including with fried potatoes and bacon, and shrimps (Krabben) served as they are or in soup.

A particular feature of this region are Knicks, ancient hedges built to protect the low-lying land from the strong prevailing winds, and also as boundaries and a source of firewood. They are also important for breeding birds. They divide meadows, woods, cultivated farmland and meadowland, English-style, and have been protected by law since 1973.

Yellow fields of rape for the margarine industry contrast with flowers grown often under glass, with windmills providing a focal point inland and colourful lighthouse towers closer to the coastal areas.

Tourism plays an important part in the region's economy, especially round the coastal resorts on both the Baltic and the North Sea. Much of the area between Lübeck and Kiel to the Baltic forms the Holsteinische Schweiz (Holstein's Switzerland). Though this description may be slightly misleading, it is in fact a charmingly wooded and relatively undulating area dominated by lakes including the Große Plöner See. At Bungsberg near Schönwalde the hills rise to 164 metres above sea level – high in this region – with a television tower on top, making it the highest point in the whole of Schleswig-Holstein.

This is a favourite part of northern Germany and popular for cycling and walking, and is well served by trains on the Lübeck-Kiel railway to such stations as Malente-Gremsmühlen, Plön and Ascheberg.

The Schleswig-Holstein regional rail pass provides access to the excellent network of local train services in the area. Most towns of any size are rail-served. The state is also co-operating with Deutsche Bundesbahn to secure a variety of improvements to rail services to reduce car traffic congestion and pollution. There is an extremely good network of local bus services from railheads and to villages off the rail network.

To the west, along the coast and offshore mudflats and islands, lies the Schleswig-Holsteinisches Nationalpark – an internationally important area of nature protection.

There are also Naturparke around Wittensee and the Westensee, near Rendsburg, and around the western edge of the Nord-Ostsee Kanal and by the Elbe-Lübeck Kanal in the southeast.

Schleswig-Holstein shares with the western-facing coast of Niedersachsen and the free city-state of Hamburg, a particularly precious heritage in the North Sea **Wattenmeer**, which actually stretches from Den Helder in the Netherlands to Esbjerg in Denmark; the German share of the Wattenmeer being around 60%. This very special ecological area, with much of its own fauna and flora and with its rich fish stocks and wonderful bird life, is increasingly threatened by pollution as poisonous river-borne chemicals reach the North Sea and the Wattenmeer, and further pollution is caused by shipping and oil-drilling platforms. The Wattenmeer is in fact a staging-post between the mainland and the open sea, flooded twice daily at high tide and drying out twice daily at low tide.

In 1985/6 the Wattenmeer on the North German coast was declared a national park and therefore able to avail itself of some fairly stringent regulations and legislation. The Schleswig-Holsteinisches Wattenmeer Nationalpark is distinguished by having its boundary stretching 150 metres out to sea as well as protecting part of the low-lying inland coastal regions. An awesome 5% of the world's fish catch originates from the Wattenmeer and two-thirds of the annual 30,000 tons of mussels caught along the German Wattenmeer actually comes from within the Schleswig-Holstein part of it.

The Schleswig-Holsteinisches Nationalpark, with its headquarters in the port of Tönning, divides into three key zones. Zone 1 corresponds to the most valuable – and vulnerable – ecological areas and has appropriately stringent protective measures, zone 2 has lesser protection and with less definite boundaries and is seen as a buffer between zones 1 and 3, the latter in turn having some protective legislation, but with a slightly more relaxed attitude to recreational activities and use. It is important to realise that it includes not only the actual Wattenmeer itself, an area of sand, water and mudflats, but also the sanddunes and part of the marshland, each of these terrains having their own particular mix of fauna and flora.

What is the Wattenmeer exactly and what makes it so special? Originally, in prehistoric times, it formed part of the European landmass. About 20,000 years ago as the earth became warmer and the glaciers began to melt, an enormous mass of water caused the watertable to rise 80 to 100 metres. In time the landscape along the North Sea coast became transformed with numerous islands which were greatly affected by tides and currents, causing over the centuries whole stretches of land to disappear. At the same time, fertile marshland was deposited in other areas, attaching itself either to an existing landmass or laying the foundations for new island territory. The coastline continually fretted by the sea broke up into a collection of islands, but the never-ending process of flooding and erosion was to leave only Sylt, Amrum, Föhr and Helgoland as the principal inhabited islands and others were to disappear entirely. Even now the islands exist under a dynamic process of change, with severe erosion by wind and sea in some places, such as the northern tip of Sylt, and deposition of sandbanks.

By the eighth century, the Frisians had spread as far as the river Weser and then into the area of present North Friesland, and there began to cultivate large areas of land and protect its low-lying terrain with dykes. But even these dykes were not able to withstand the great storm floods of the Middle Ages and not only was much land lost, but even more tragically, there was loss of life with whole towns and districts engulfed by the floods. Not for nothing has the North Sea been called 'murderous' or 'Nordsee, Mordsee'.

The Wattenmeer, which at low tide looks like a level area of sand as it dries out, is made up of soft mudflats and numerous channels and has strong currents. The mudflats consist of the finest clay sediment which is river-borne to the sea and also contains the fragmentary remains of animals, plants and plankton. The sludgy colour of the mudflats near the coastline makes the water itself look murky. The flood tide helps to deposit further sediment in the lee of the islands so in time new land is formed from what has been gnawed away in other areas by coastal erosion. Without this constant land recovery plus the building of dams on the islands, there would be less Schlickwatt (mudflats) which actually produces the valuable living conditions for the numerous fauna. The occasional unmistakable smell of 'bad eggs' is a chemical reaction, the result of human pollution as the organic sediments in the Schlick are killed by oxygen-using bacteria and form hydrogen sulphide. Iron hydroxide, which is also found in the Wattenmeer, becomes iron sulphide and causes lower layers in the Sandwatt to have a blue-black colour.

Pollution has done enormous damage, resulting from the phosphates from washing powders and the nitrates from fertilisers which have encouraged the growth of algae. Their remains leave behind great quantities of foam, which though unsightly is harmless in itself, but depletes the oxygen content of the water with disastrous consequences for other marine life.

The 100,000 creatures that inhabit each square metre of the Wattenmeer vary in size from microscopic organisms to the tiny Watt snails and rather large crabs. Lugworms, mussels, shrimps, cockles, starfish, sea-anemones and a wide variety of fish species such as eels, flounders, turbots, sole, mackerel and plaice are just part of the teeming marine life. The Wattenmeer is also used by several fish species as a nursery area, before the fish make their way to other waters. So any pollution of the

North Sea and Wattenmeer actually has even more far-reaching effects on the chain of human nourishment.

Enormous quantities of poisonous chemicals which are the result of industrial effluent pollute the rivers Elbe, Weser, Ems and Rhine and are stored up in the fatty tissue of various sea creatures. Radioactive substances from France's La Hague and Britain's Sellafield reappear in the Wattenmeer, and oil from ships, tankers and oil-drilling platforms is responsible for the deaths of thousands of sea-birds. The North Sea, and through it the Wattenmeer, is in danger of becoming a giant North European toxic dustbin. Recent international conferences on the North Sea have shown that Britian in particular has not yet taken the necessary action to help restore the North Sea to health. Stringent international legislation and its enforcement is now urgently overdue.

It took the plight of the seal to draw dramatic attention to what was actually happening in the Wattenmeer and North Sea, as the smaller and less prominent forms of marine life while just as much under threat made less appeal on television. The seal was formerly hunted for its fur and for its fatty layers which could be rendered into oil for domestic use in pre-electricity days, and it was regarded as a pest as it fed exclusively on fish. Today a short hunting season from mid-September till the end of October is allowed to cull the sicklier specimens. The sandbanks of the Wattenmeer are the seals' breeding grounds and also their basking area. The young are born in June/July at low tide and the new pups must cope with the water immediately the tide turns. The 'orphan' seals or 'Heuler' as they are called in German are usually one of twins, the mother finding it impossible to cope with both leaves one to howl out its woe. Fortunately nowadays they are picked up by specialists who take them to one of three centres, where they are fed a concentrated diet of milk and fish till they reach a certain weight and then returned to the Wattenmeer.

In 1988 the seals of the North Sea started to die on a massive scale, infected by a pollution-borne virus. People on both sides of the North Sea joined in protests to national governments. The people of the island of Amrum made a particularly spectacular protest as hundreds of local people and conservationists formed themselves into gigantic letters on the beach spelling out: 'Unser Nordsee, lasst sie leben' – 'Our North Sea – let it live'.

Fortunately the seal plague abated and populations appear to have improved to some degree. Special excursion boats from a number of Nordfriesische resorts take visitors to see the seals, but they take care never to intrude too closely. On some trips a net is thrown overboard, then drawn up full of sea-creatures which are placed in a salt water observation tank on board. The different forms of marine life are explained to the visitors by an expert guide or marine biologist and later they are returned to the sea.

Up to fifty different species of birds can be found around the Wattenmeer, including oystercatchers, redshanks, eiderducks and many varieties of geese and gulls. Virtually every island in the area has its bird sanctuaries and some are totally given over to bird protection, with wardens looking after them in the breeding season and limited public access. The Wattenmeer also plays host to many bird species migrating southwards who feed on the rich pickings.

Common and rare sea-plants abound, and include marram grass, a tall coarse grass that tolerates salt, sea holly and a number of salt-loving plants which are the first to colonise any reclaimed land in the polders or koogs as they are known. Some plants have evolved special methods to deal with the superfluous salt which occasionally can be seen crystallising on the underside of their leaves.

A type of sundew and marsh gentians are among less usual specimens in the marshier terrain.

The earliest written regulations regarding dyke building, called the *Rüstringen Rechtssatzungen*, show how crucial this skill was. It required the Frisians to build and strengthen their coastal fortresses which encircled all Friesland 'like a golden ring'. As early as 1180 Saxo Grammaticus stated that the land was very fertile and full of cattle, but unfortunately liable to flooding. The Spadelandsrecht declares that he who is not prepared to dyke must pay the penalty and leave the area. In fact all inhabitants whose land abutted the dyke area had to undertake to maintain a stretch of dyke and strict regulations were in force plus penalties for those who wouldn't or couldn't undertake this, usually resulting in the individuals being deprived of their land. Theodore Storm's novel *Der Schimmelreiter* gives a wonderful atmospheric impression of this special world. It was only at the end of the nineteenth century that the state took on the responsibility of protecting the coast and this also included land reclamation. Until fifty years ago teams of workers with wheelbarrows, horse drawn waggons and spades, digging and repairing the dykes, were a common sight. Now giant mechanical diggers have taken over.

It is worth calling into the Naturzentrum Nordfriesland at **Bredstedt**, north of Husum, open early May to late September, where there are exhibitions, displays, films and slide shows on the area's natural history as well as a programme of guided walks. Although expertly guided walks are taken across the Wattenmeer at low tide, it must be emphasised that even these are taken at one's own risk, and should *never* be undertaken on one's own initiative, as there are numerous deep channels and strong currents while unexpected mist can quickly descend, obscuring all sense of direction and causing fatal miscalculation. There are horrifying accounts both in past and recent history of individuals, family groups and even part of a school party who lost their lives. There is a route between the islands of Amrum and Föhr known as the Wattenweg; if you would like to sample the experience, dates of the organised events are advertised locally.

Slightly less demanding is one of the numerous official Nationalpark led 'Wattwanderungen' to look at bird, animal and plant life in the company of a marine biologist. These short walks across the edge of the Wattenmeer when the tide is out are arranged from several of the larger resorts in the summer months. Details can be picked up from local tourist information centres or by writing to the Nationalpark office – see the end of this chapter.

Schleswig-Holstein's three best known holiday islands are also under considerable environmental pressure and protection. The most heavily visited is **Sylt**, which can be reached either by air or over the Hindenburg Damm across the Wattenmeer by train. Those who wish to arrive at the island by car or coach are accommodated on a special two-tier train transporter of an amazing length. Drivers and passengers stay in their vehicles, their roofracks often crowded with bicycles, luggage and even boats. There are also excellent InterCity and local passenger services for non-motorised travellers and cycle-carrying facilities. You will notice a linear windfarm along the dyke as you cross the dam.

Sylt's main resort of **Westerland** offers the visitor a bewildering contrast of mass tourism development and stringent nature conservation. Perhaps Germany's most famous seaside resort, with some hideous modern tower block hotel development, you'll find promenades, smart pedestrian precincts, glamorous boutiques and restaurants and innumerable types of accommodation from private houses and camping sites to the smartest hotels. There is an excellent choice of facilities but prices are high. Away from the crowds are splendid thatched villas owned by the rich and famous.

All along the 37 kilometre long west coast, bordering the North Sea, there are fine sandy beaches with white breakers, clusters of basketchairs, and the option of doing without part or all of your bathing costume if you wish – at least away from the central areas.

However, the east coast overlooking the Wattenmeer couldn't be more different. Here you'll find miles of protected sand dunes, low cliffs and coastal paths through heath covered with heather and lovely pink and white rugosa roses. Most is Naturschutzgebiet or part of the Schleswig-Holsteinisches Nationalpark, with access restricted to footpaths. Some of the dunes form impressive ranges rising up to 30 metres in height, and from the specially constructed viewpoint above the Rote Kliff at Kampen you can enjoy an impressive view along the northern tip of the island. The island is barely one kilometre wide for much of its length, and the excellent island bus service from Westerland to Hörnum and List (from where there is a ferry to the island of Rømø in Denmark) makes coastal walking through this protected landscape particularly attractive. Buses also run to Keitum, where there is an old Altfriesisches Haus and museum, and from where the coastal path continues to Kampen and List.

The former narrow gauge island railway has been superseded by a bus, but part of the old track route is still used as a cycleway and as a path for walkers. There are already 180 kilometres of cycle paths on the island and more are in preparation. **Föhr** and **Amrum** are quieter than Sylt and less subject to the pressures of mass tourism. They can both be reached by the branch railway from Niebüll on the main line, operated by the local bus company (the Nordfriesische Verkehrsbetriebe). The little diesel rail cars leave the branch, crossing the street in front of their own local station platform to join the main line and collect a couple of 'through' DB coaches left by the main line express. These are then drawn at a gentle pace down the village branch line to Dagebüll Mole harbour station, from where flat-bottomed modern car ferries take rail passengers as well as motorists and cyclists to the two islands.

Föhr, known as the 'green island', was in fact the first of the three larger Nordfriesische Inseln to become a fashionable resort. This 82 square kilometre island was divided in its national loyalties for a considerable period, with the east of the island belonging to Denmark and the west to Schleswig. **Wyk** is the main resort, a charming old town which became the summer residence of the Danish King Christian VIII between 1842-7, thus becoming an extremely fashionable resort. It was later also popular with the Prussian aristocracy.

Föhr's greenness comes from the intense amount of cultivated land and it has a far milder climate than Sylt. There are few trees however. It is an especially attractive island for both walking and cycling, with a good circular bus service around the island and a special cycle-carrying bus service in the form of a trailer to carry tired cyclists and their machines.

Amrum is crescent-shaped and an aerial view of the island suggests a sort of lunar landscape full of craters among the sand dunes. Dunes cover a third of the island and another third is flat sand and forms a splendid beach where costumes are optional. As on Föhr there are bird sanctuaries and there is a particularly splendid footpath route from Wittdun along the southwest coast which allows the walker to see an enormous variety of bird life in an exquisitely beautiful area of dune and pond while a raised path on duckboards helps to protect the fragile environment. It is also possible to visit the rather photogenic lighthouse at certain times and climb up the 300 steps. At Nebel, a village of typical reed-thatched houses, there is an equally photogenic windmill which is also a museum. Again, a useful and extremely regular local bus service links with the ferries (both the Föhr and Amrum bus services are run by the ferry company – the Wyker Dampfschiffs-Reederei) and provides access to the whole island.

Other Nordfriesische Inseln which can be visited include the Halligens – Nordstrand (linked to the mainland north of Husum by a road dam) and Pellworm which consists mainly of marshland; but Langeneß, Hooge and Gröde are considered to have greater scenic interest.

All the Nordfriesische Inseln have adopted a high profile on environmental issues, including the greenhouse effect which could prove a particular disaster for the islands. Wyk subscribed the equivalent of £4,000 to become a corporate member of Greenpeace. Shops and supermarkets in Sylt, Föhr, Amrum, Pellworm and Nordstrand refuse to stock washing powders that contain phosphates and some of the islands have totally banned plastic bags, while some larger stores on Sylt restrict themselves to a biodegradable variety. There has also been an effective campaign on the islands against canned drinks, bottles which are not reusable and aerosols which damage the ozone in the atmosphere. Unfortunately, unlike the Ostfriesische Inseln which either totally ban the motor car or only allow cars with catalytic converters, the larger Nordfriesische Inseln have not yet been able to match this standard of environmental protection. Yet leading islanders have said that for them the private car is 'the environment's most deadly foe', just as on the mainland.

Further information

The Schleswig-Holstein tourist office: Fremdenverkehrsverband Schleswig-Holstein e.V., Niemannsweg 31, D-2300 Kiel. Among special packages available from this office are walking, cycling and nature holidays in the Nationalpark and other areas of Schleswig-Holstein.
Schleswig-Holsteinisches Nationalpark, Am Hafen 40a, D-2253 Tönning.
Wyker Dampfschiffs-Reederei Föhre Amrum GmbH, D-2270 Wyk auf Föhr.

Hamburg

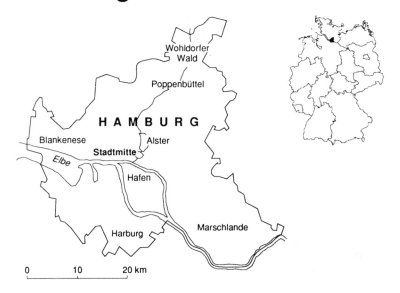

An old black raven made of wrought iron, a pair of spectacles poised on its beak, sits on top of a street sign reading 'Alte Rabenstraße'. This piece of street sculpture was erected in 1850 to commemorate an inn at the sign of the old raven, and is typical of the kind of quirky surprise that awaits Hamburg's visitors. The raven is part of the open air Skulpturpark on the left bank of the Alster.

But another and far greater surprise when you see the city for the first time is Hamburg's setting by its twin Alster lakes – the Innere and the Außere Alster – that dominate the heart of the city. More predictable perhaps but no less spectacular for that reason is the city's waterfront, the quayside area at St. Pauli-Landungsbrücken where the DFDS ferry from England arrives from along the Elbe, behind which soar the warehouses, offices, towers, domes and civic buildings of the city-state, with the green copper-domed tower of St. Michaelis, the sailors' church, reaching skywards, a key landmark.

The free Hanseatic city of Hamburg is Germany's largest port, with over 1½ million inhabitants, and covering some 750 square kilometres around the Elbe. It is also Germany's most densely populated area. The city was founded in the early ninth century and lies some 120 kilometres southeast of the mouth of the river Elbe and the North Sea. Like Bremen, Hamburg is proud of its former Hanseatic status with HH – Hansestadt Hamburg – on car number plates (see the Bremen chapter for background to the Hanseatic League). It is also proud of its ancient right of free trade and exemption from customs duties along the lower Elbe, which dates back to an edict of Friedrich Barbarossa in 1198. To this day unless goods actually leave the free port, duty is not charged on them. Hamburg's 'warehouse city' is a fascinating place and worth exploring, whilst her vast natural harbour on the Elbe accommodates large ocean going ships as well as coastal freighters. The port also lies at the head of and is a transshipment centre for a complex network of river and canal systems used for huge tonnages of freight movement. The Elbe Kanal provides a route for inland shipping to the industrial heartland of the Ruhr as well as to Germany's eastern regions, including Berlin, and even as far afield as Czechoslovakia. In recent years the Elbe was deepened to accommodate larger tankers, freighters and container ships. The port handles vast quantities of such goods as coal and iron ore, oil, chemicals, grain, cereals, animal feed, tropical fruit and vegetables. The domestic market throughout Germany also receives much of its fresh food supplies through the port. Boat tours of the port are arranged daily from the St. Pauli-Landungsbrücken.

In addition Hamburg is a leading centre for the electrotechnical industry, for oil refining, machine building, precision engineering, foodstuffs, aviation, aerospace and data processing, though shipbuilding has been largely superseded by repair work and orders for drilling platforms.

It is also a major commercial, administrative and shopping centre, a focal point for the whole of northwest Germany. Many people have suggested that Hamburg is also the most English of German cities, a fact reflecting centuries of close trade and commercial links. A local fishermen's and sailors' meat and fish dish (Labskaus) is identical to a dish found in East Anglian ports and even in Liverpool – a city with which Hamburg has much in common, though mercifully not sharing so much of the Merseyside city's economic decline. You'll also see many British goods in the shops and one of the city's leading restaurants is known in English as 'The Old Assembly Rooms'.

The city is a major cultural centre too, with a famed opera house and ballet of international reputation, with several major theatres, museums and art galleries such as the Hamburg Kunsthalle and the Museum für Kunst und Gewerbe with its fine collections of pottery, china and Jugendstil (or Art Nouveau). Much of Germany's publishing world is also concentrated in Hamburg. Despite the ravages of Allied bombing, which razed much of the city centre, there remains much fine architecture from the last century, including the magnificent neo-gothic town hall, recalling the wealthy merchants who were the architects of the city's prosperity.

What makes Hamburg particularly special for the visitor are the numerous parks, green spaces and nature reserves, so easily reached by an excellent integrated public transport system whether boat, S-Bahn, U-Bahn or bus.

The twin Alster lakes, covering 184 hectares in the heart of the city, were a tributary of the Elbe widened into an artificial lake just before its confluence into the main river. It dates from the time when the little river Alster was dammed in the thirteenth century to create a millpond near the Tröstbrücke, which was where the city was first founded.

The Alster with its fleet of elegant white boats – the Alsterschippen – is an integral part of the city transport system with a waterbus service from little jetties, complete with waiting shelters and timetables around the lakeside. Excursion boats operate round trips on the Alster taking about an hour, or you can take a trip through the network of canals which Venice-like penetrate the city centre. Such trips are a splendid way to see the city, its magnificent civic buildings in the centre, but also lakeside houses, gardens and green spaces further out. Regulations ensure that all buildings on the Inner Alster must be faced in light-coloured natural stone or light-coloured stucco and roofs must be in copper or grey to preserve the character of the area. In fine weather the Outer Alster is colourful with a variety of sailing or rowing boats on the lake (motor boats apart from the ferries are forbidden, to protect water quality) and people walking, sunbathing or just sitting along its banks.

Occasionally during a very severe and prolonged winter, the Alster becomes frozen and if the ice is declared safe, the entire population arrives to skate and enjoy themselves on the ice, drinking Glühwein (hot spiced wine) and eating hot thick pea soup and Wurst from small stalls that materialise like magic.

You can walk around both the Innere and Außere Alster along lakeside paths in three or four hours with ample places en route for any necessary refreshment. An alternative is to walk upstream from Fuhlbüttel Schleuse (lock) to Poppenbüttel, following the yellow triangle signs to Sasler Damm. The return could be by S-Bahn from Poppenbüttel and with a lunch stop this could take about three hours. A further possibility is to start from Poppenbüttel S-Bahn and walk upstream through Rodenbeker Quellental to Wohldorflock, returning on the 276 bus to Ohlstedt U-Bahn or Poppenbüttel S-Bahn. Again there is a chance for refreshment in the Wohldorf woods and the walk takes about two hours. Alternatively there are special canal tours on the Alster, a tour of Hamburg's numerous bridges or even an evening tour.

The celebrated Alsterpavilion on the Jungfernstieg waterfront is the right setting if you wish just to look out over the Alster and indulge in coffee (or perhaps something stronger) and superb cakes.

Cycling is actively encouraged by the city authorities and Hamburg's cycleways extend for 350 kilometres along a number of routes out from the city centre and through the suburbs and there are plans to increase this to 550 kilometres by means of further cycleways and quiet roads which are specially designated for cycle use and signposted.

Many of the suburbs are worth visiting in their own right. The old church township of Bergedorf in the southeast has old houses, churches, windmills, flower-rich meadows and marshes. Eppindorf has rows of houses each with their own riverside gardens and mooring places. You can walk along the banks of the Elbe by Altona, which was a Danish village till 1864, past Ovelgönne with its sea-captains' cottages and elegant merchants' mansions to the 600 year old village of Blankenese which clings to precipitous slopes with twisting steps along and between narrow streets. Artists' studios, boutiques and numerous restaurants offering fresh fish specialities crowd along the street fronts, the colour-washed cottages almost having a Mediterranean appearance. It is possible to reach this former shipping and fishing village by ferry in the summer or by S-Bahn S 1 or S 2 or by bus 36.

There is no shortage of restaurants in Hamburg offering such regional specialities as Labskaus (basically a sort of substantial potato hash with either fish or meat variations), an unexpectedly fruity yet delicious eelsoup, incredibly sized plaice of superb quality called Finkenwerder Schollen, or Matjes, marinated herrings. Rote Grutze is a traditional light dessert made from a mixture of red berries topped with whipped cream. Try also Pharisäer, coffee with a generous portion of rum topped with whipped cream which was apparently invented and secretly dispensed at a christening where the rather strait-laced parson had banned alcohol. The story goes that this drink had a highly convivial effect on the whole gathering, including the parson.

Hamburg is a city which is deeply concerned about the environment. In medieval times, Hamburg consisted of a huge woodland area which in time was considerably depleted by the growing city, especially during the industrial revolution, both for building materials and for wood burning. At the same time grazing animals helped to destroy the young saplings, and as natural fertilisers like leaf mould were used for the fields, the resulting impoverishment of the remaining soil caused heathlands to flourish.

The city-state authorities take environmental protection extremely seriously. They have banned the use of pesticides and herbicides in their parks and also the use of salt for de-icing roads and pavements in winter because of the damage caused to the environment. In 1988 the city commissioned a detailed study of its damaged trees and soils in parks and streets which seemed to show that road salt helped to leach nutrients out of the soil. Public involvement in environmental matters is actively encouraged. 'Environmental protection is seen as the concern of everyone, not just the state', as an official publication *Hamburg – Eine Stadt öffnet sich der Natur* (Hamburg, a city which opens itself up to nature) makes clear.

There are already no less than seventy-five groups taking part in the city's Bach-Patenschaften or 'Adopt a Stream Scheme', in which various organisations, school classes, youth groups or even individuals choose to look after a stream. This also includes its banks which are important habitats for numerous plants and animals. Help is given as well as advice, but the finance must be raised by the groups themselves for their 'renaturing', such as in some cases returning the course of a stream to its original channel, or planting the banks with suitable plants, cleaning and other protective measures.

Hamburg has an environmental protection advisory body which advises all official environmental authorities, and consists of independent experts from universities and colleges. Environmental groups also support the authorities with advice and look after protected areas. Six of these groups are especially recognised and empowered to take further action should they believe some erroneous environmental decision has been made.

Of Hamburg's twenty-one Naturschutzgebiete which have been established within the city-state boundaries, only a few examples can be given here to illustrate the city's extraordinary commitment to nature protection.

The internationally famous Heuckenlock area has a very special landscape. Its reedbeds lie in deep water channels of the Elbe and the mixture of sand and 'Schlick' on its marshy ground means that vegetation is particulary luxuriant here. Heuckenlock has over 700 species of plants which include fritillaries which were once so common that huge bouquets were sold in street markets. Other interesting plants include the marsh ragwort, water plantains, flowering rushes and beds of golden marsh marigold. Here the tidal flow and the unique sweet water of the Wattenmeer caused the evolution of a special habitat for plant and animal life. Poplar trees can reach a height of over 30 metres and the oldest elm is 400 years old and has a circumference of 4.40 metres.

The Fischbecker Heide Naturschutzgebiet was established in 1958 and uses an adapted Heideschnuckenstall (see the Lüneburger Heide section in Niedersachsen, page 67) for its headquarters. In order to keep the heath clear of encroaching tree cover, it is necessary to uproot tree seedlings, use the special breed of sheep who feed on the heather, Heideschnucken, to graze it, but also to mow the heath in order to encourage new growth and to reseed it where necessary. Remaining coniferous trees which obscure the light have to be pruned and paths have to be rationalised. There is also special protection for the sand lizard so that it has plenty of cover. No less than 2,500 species have their home in the heath, including reptiles, birds, small mammals and especially insects, with some of the rarer types of dragonfly and butterflies.

The Naturschutzgebiet Neuwerk Scharnhörn occupies two islands in the Wattenmeer area between the Elbe and the mouth of the Weser. It forms part of the Nationalpark Hamburgisches Wattenmeer, linked to the national parks of Schleswig-Holstein and Niedersachsen. Breeding areas on the islands must only be approached on marked paths or with written permission from the Hamburg environmental authorities. Neuwerk is a marshy island, which originally was formed out of old sand dunes and in time became increasingly covered by green vegetation, so that it became a summer grazing area for cattle; it was also used as a hideout by pirates. Scharnhörn is a floating island which is continually being changed by the winds and waves and like Neuwerk has extensive bird sanctuaries. It was formerly only known as a ship's graveyard with a dangerous reef till around 1900 when its remarkable bird life was recognised.

The two islands have between them one of the largest colonies of breeding terns on the North Sea coast. The various seabirds find rich pickings in quite different ways, the oystercatcher opens up mussels and sea-snails, the shelduck uncover worms and snails by treading on top of them, the brent geese which arrive in winter are plant eaters and the terns catch small fish, while other birds use their long beaks to poke the ground. A severe problem is the oil-polluted seawater, which not only covers the birds' feathers so they cannot fly, but also causes birds to die from swallowing oil. There is also harm caused to the breeding birds by eating fish which have been polluted. Zone 1 in the national park allows walking and riding on specially signposted paths, but the two island reserves of Scharnhörn and Nigehörn, a tiny island nearby, allow visits only by special permit. Dogs must be kept on leads. It is forbidden to leave boats beached outside special areas and bathing and fishing are not allowed.

Sea-bathing, walking and riding are allowed in zone 2, but there is still restricted access to the northern foreshore of Neuwerk. There is stringent protection for all plants and animals, which may not be collected, damaged or killed.

The Naturschutzgebiet Duvenstedter Brook in the extreme northeast of Hamburg has extensive groups of red deer and in season the stags fight for mastery of the herd with dreadful roarings before engaging in their ritual clashes. Occasionally wild boar can also be spotted. Bird species include birds of prey such as kestrels, common buzzards, sparrowhawks, goshawks and honey buzzards, while curlews, snipe, tree pipits, woodcock, warblers and golden oriole all seem to be at home in this particular habitat.

The Naturschutzgebiete Stellmoorer and Ahrenburger Tunneltal further to the east have varied terrain, from pools with rushes, reeds and various varieties of frog and toad and rich insect life, to the woodlands with their black poplars, birches, bird cherry, and varieties of original wild apple and wild pear trees. Equally important are the old field hedges called Knicks which would originally divide fields, but today are an ideal habitat for various old trees, herbs and ferns, and creatures like partridge, pheasant, hare and rabbit. Buzzards tend to use the Knicks as lookout posts before flying down on their prey. But the area is even better known for its archaeological remains from about 10,500 BC, from which era pottery and flint tools have been uncovered. There is an archaeological trail in the Ahrenburger area with interpretive boards.

Rodenbecker Quellental and Hainesch/Iland Naturschutzgebiete also in the north have a great variety of small fish in their pools and birds like the kingfisher, rarely seen elsewhere in this region and the dipper which can be seen ducking or even running under water in search of food. The area also has a Krattwald where trees were continually pollarded – cut down to their roots – ever since the Middle Ages so that the new shoots could be used as poles.

Finally the Raakmoor area in the northwest of Hamburg has made use of the principle of renaturing or Renaturierung, a process pioneered in Hamburg. Since the original character of the area had been disturbed by tree-felling, drainage and cultivation over the centuries, it was decided to fill in the drainage ditches and cut down some of the encroaching birch trees. As the water table rose, other remaining birches died and the rest of the original moorland vegetation started to flourish. Moss, heather and sundew were brought in from nearby moorland areas in order to accelerate the process and the area once more became a habitat for an interesting variety of fauna and flora which flourish in damper places.

All these sites can be easily reached by public transport. Hamburg Verkehrs Verbund – the Hamburg public transport authority – was a model on which passenger transport executives in the former metropolitan areas of the UK were based. HVV pursues a vigorous policy of promoting and developing integrated public transport over high quality bus and train networks. Facilities for visitors include the excellent Hamburg Karte costing about DM10.00, which gives unlimited travel on bus, trains and underground, free entry to a number of museums, and reduced prices on Alster boats, with an incredible value group ticket valid for up to four adults and three children at around DM20.00. The Hamburg Karte is available from tourist offices as well as HVV offices and some hotels and even theatre booking offices. There is also a choice of day, weekly and monthly tickets covering part or all of the network. Certain of these tickets are available at automatic ticket machines at S- and U-Bahn stations or even bus stops.

Further information

Hamburg tourist information: Fremdenverkehrszentrale, e. V., Bieberhaus, Hachmanplatz, D-2000 Hamburg 1.

Hamburg Umweltbehörde Naturschutzamt, Steindamm 22, D-2000 Hamburg 1.

Nationalpark Hamburgisches Wattenmeer: enquiries, tel. Hamburg (040) 2486-2227.

Niedersachsen

Niedersachsen (Lower Saxony), the second largest West German state, was part of the large area inhabited by the Saxons in early times, between Bohemia in the east and the Rhine in the west.

Niedersachsen has tremendous scenic variety – from the Wattenmeer with its immense seascapes and chain of islands forming the Niedersächsische Nationalpark, the bustling estuary ports of **Emden** with its vehicle assembly industry, **Wilhemshafen**, a major oil terminal and **Cuxhafen**, noted for its fish processing plant, to the rolling heathland of the Lüneburger Heide (Lüneburg Heath) and the wooded uplands of the Harz mountains.

Hannover, the state capital and focal point of a great industrial conurbation, is internationally renowned for its trade fairs. The city serves other major centres of industry such as nearby **Wolfsburg** which contains the main Volkswagen factory. Close by are such famous historic and architecturally rich towns as **Celle**, **Hameln**, **Braunschweig**, **Hildesheim** and **Wolfenbüttel**.

Hannover has its own share of fine architecture, such as the seventeenth century Schloß Herrenhausen. The palace stands mirrored in a lake; performances of music and drama in its baroque gardens take place in summer, while its 'Festivals of Light' feature authentic baroque firework displays. It is also renowned for its Schützenfest, the biggest marksman's fair in the world which takes place in early July.

Hameln on the Weser is the Hamelin of the folk tale. Most English children know Robert Browning's famous poem retelling the medieval legend of the Pied Piper, the colourful rat-catcher who rid the town of its plague of rats for an agreed sum of money, but took a terrible revenge when he was refused payment by enticing away the town's children. The drama is re-enacted every year with numbers of Hameln children enthusiastically taking part, but they do return home at the end!

Niedersachsen is also associated with the folk and fairytale collections of the Brothers Grimm, philologists and folklorists. Another folk hero was Till Eulenspiegel, a fourteenth century prankster and rogue whose character is portrayed in the Richard Strauss tone poem.

Niedersachsen, lying as it does on the North German plain and crossed by the shallow river valleys of the Elbe, the main tributaries of the Weser including the Aller and the Leine, and the Ems close to the Dutch border, is an extremely important agricultural area with its fertile soils producing cereal crops, sugar beet, maize and potatoes. Cattle, sheep and horse breeding are also significant to the economy, with fruit and vegetables being grown along the lower Elbe river and south of Emden. It is no surprise that the food processing industries are of major economic significance. Even today, cattle are often transported for fattening to the more fertile grazing grounds of the low-lying coastal marshlands and away from the poorer regions of the Geest area.

For forty years Niedersachsen shared a lengthy boundary with former East Germany, unable to communicate with neighbouring Mecklenburg or Sachsen-Anhalt. Access to much of the Harz mountains was denied to people on both sides of the Iron Curtain which sliced the Brocken, at 1142 metres above sea level North Germany's highest mountain. Even at the present time kilometres of tall, rust-proof fencing and a wide area of no-man's-land across the Harz and the summit of the Brocken remain.

The Harz mountains rise to a height of over 1,000 metres and are a range of Mittelgebirge (medium-height mountains) composed of slate and greywacke which has additional layers of granite and porphyry. In the west it is predominantly coniferous, contrasting with the abundance of beech woods and cultivated land in the east. Forestry and cattle rearing predominate in the western Oberharz and delightful villages and towns with well-kept half-timbered houses make this a favourite venue both for walkers and for winter skiers. The old town of **Goslar** on the edge of the Harz has an ancient imperial palace of the Holy Roman Emperors called the Kaiserpfalz and superb old half-timbered houses in the old town. Because most of the Harz lies in Sachsen-Anhalt, the Harz region as a whole is dealt with in that chapter.

The **Lüneburger Heide** originally was an area of wood and heathland which lay between the rivers Elbe and Aller, with the Wilseder Berg at 169 metres as its highest point. Beneath the morains, relics of the last Ice Age, mineral wealth resides in the Pleistocene loose sedimentary rock, and includes salt and oil-bearing rocks as well as limestone.

The Lüneburger Heide with its Naturparke and Naturschutzgebiete is visited by at least four million people annually, but the area was not always seen as having tourist potential. In the eighteenth century it was described as a desolate place, an empty landscape with neither house, stream, human being, animal nor even bird apart from hungry ravens to vary the monotony. As far as the eye could see was nothing but heather, sandy tracks, juniper bushes and perhaps pine trees on the horizon.

In fact the Lüneburger Heide is a man-made landscape, a result of the attempts of prehistoric man to make some grazing land for his animals which then effectively inhibited any tree growth. The landscape became increasingly park-like in the Middle Ages and any remaining trees were then cut down and used by the early salt industry for drying out the salt brine and turning it into salt blocks. Further tree felling and cultivation of the land was in due course to shrink the acreage of the heath within a century from 2,000 to 100 square kilometres. Since those days, the heath itself has become a Kulturlandschaft or heritage landscape with its own traditions and historic associations. There are numerous deer, wild boar, hares, pheasants, partridges, foxes, badgers and otters. Rarer species among the birds are the stork, black stork, crane and black grouse.

The Lüneburger Heide's famous Heideschnucken are a special type of small long-haired sheep, related to Corsican and Sardinian mountain sheep and also to the moufflon, which can be either grey in colour and horned or white without horns. Oddly enough they cannot cope with strong sun or much rain, as their wool is not very thick and oily like that of merino sheep, so that it easily becomes soaked through and gives them little protection against the sun. So at the first hint of either contingency, the Heideschnucken are led under cover by their shepherd. They graze the heather and their constant nibbling ensures that the heath renews itself. The crisp munching sound they make as they chew the hard heather sounds as if they are biting crisp biscuits. Areas of heather which the sheep cannot cope with are burnt in early spring.

The rich compost from the Heide was used in earlier days as a fertiliser, and the rootballs were strewn in the animal stalls. This type of fertilisation was exceedingly hard work, so much so that 'plaggen' as it was called became proverbial for work which took a great deal of effort – 'eine Plage'. In order to fertilise one hectare in this way, the farmer had to dig up four. The rather hard sheep wool is now hardly economical as it costs more to shear the animal than the wool is worth for the carpet industry, but the skins and meat bring in higher rates. 'Schnuckenbraten' is reputed to be delicious, as there is very little fat content and the flavour is perhaps nearer game than lamb. From the middle to the end of August is the best time to see the heather flowering and a number of centres like Amelinghausen and Schneverdingen start their festive processions with the crowning of a young girl as queen of the heath.

The rare black stork originally seen around the Wilseder Berg, now has increased substantially in numbers as part of the programme initiated by the Vogelschutzstation Lüneburg and the World Wide Fund for Nature. The future of the cranes in the area round the Elbe and Jeetzel in the eastern section of the heath was in doubt when it was proposed to build an atomic waste depot in the area. The cranes are seen by ornithologists as birds which act as 'indicators' of whether an area has been kept ecologically intact. Over fifty rare species of birds on the endangered list in fact breed here.

In the old style of agricultural management of the heath, farmer, shepherd and beekeeper were interdependent. The bees produced wax for candles and honey as a sweetener and the herds of sheep were useful in getting rid of the spiders' webs which they destroyed when grazing, which otherwise might well trap the bees. As artificial fertilisers took over, wool began to be imported from Australia and sugar beet superseded honey, the great sheep flocks shrank to only 12,000.

Then shortly before World War I, when much of the Heide had already been 'improved' either to woodland or cultivated land, the remaining areas began to be discovered as desirable and speculators moved in to build restaurants, Gasthöfe, summer residences and the like.

Wilhelm Bode, the pastor in the village of Egestorf in the north of the Heide, formed a 'Verein Naturschutzpark' – an association for a nature protection park – to protect the area. The association bought the Wilseder Berg which was about to be developed for weekend cottages and was able to influence many prominent politicians to support environmental protection. Even the Kaiser, Wilhelm II, supported a lottery which was for the benefit of the new park. But it was 1921 before the government declared the Lüneburger Heide round the Wilseder Berg, an area of 200 square kilometres, a Naturschutzpark.

After the Second World War the heath unfortunately became a centre for military manoeuvres for British and NATO forces and the huge array of tanks churned it into a sandy desert. Some of the area was finally returned by the British authorities after numerous protests by the German people, though it remains to be seen whether remaining sections will now be returned in the light of the reunification of Germany and the easing of tension with eastern Europe. The Verein bought up not only woodland and heathland, but also moorland and marshy areas, rebuilt and restored old farmhouses and churches and also built up a splendid system of paths and parking spots for the numerous visitors. In 1967 the Council of Europe presented the European Nature Reserve Diploma to the Naturschutzpark Lüneburger Heide, the first German nature reserve, which has become a model for many similar protected areas throughout Europe.

There is excellent access to the Lüneburger Heide by both train and bus, and superb opportunities for both walking and cycling across the Heide either by planning one's own route along waymarked trails or by taking advantage of several luggage-carrying walking and accommodation packages offered by local tourist agencies.

Horse riding enthusiasts are particularly well catered for by the Naturpark Elbufer-Drawehn in the Wendland towards the east of the Heide and special riding holidays are offered by a number of organisations. Walking and cycling holidays are also available in the Weserbergland along the upper Weser valley in the wooded hills above Hameln, and in the area round the Naturpark Soling-Vogler east of Holzminden, while there is a splendid 157 kilometre long distance cycling route from Braunschweig to Lüneburg which takes in many historic features of the Lüneburger Heide and its towns and villages.

The town of **Lüneburg** itself formed an important part of the Hansa story (see Bremen); it was the salt which was so attractive to the Hansa merchants. With its 500 salt workers, Lüneburg was the largest industrial centre in the region during the Middle Ages. In 956 AD King Otto I bequeathed the dues from salt manufacture in Lüneburg to the Benedictine monks of St. Michael by the Kalkberg. Salt was an early means of preserving fish and meat and Lüneburg had the monopoly both of its manufacture and trade for some time. Day and night enormous vats made of lead and filled with saline solution were heated by wood originally felled from the heath till the evaporated brine became salt – 'white gold'. Pictures of the town in earlier centuries show the huge palls of smoke to the west of the city which arose from those large vats. The salt was transported on the river Ilmenau and then made additional voyages along the Elbe, Stecknitz and Trave rivers towards the Baltic. Carts were also used on overland routes known as the Salzstraße, a name for the trade route which went on to Stettin, to Poland and then to Reval and Novgorod in Russia. Lüneburg won a special position for itself in the Hanseatic League because of the value of salt as a preservative and its merchants were able to manipulate and win concessions to the town's trade advantage. In all but name it became a free city, but the ravages of the Thirty Years War and the later development of sea-salt production brought much of that prosperity to an end. Today the brine bath in the Kurpark is one of the few remaining signs of this once great industry.

The **Steinhuder Meer** to the south of Hannover is a paradise for watersports of all kinds and, covering 32 square kilometres, is North Germany's largest lake. A special regatta is held for peat barges in mid-February. But since it is surrounded by moorland, woods and meadows, it also offers plenty of opportunity for the walker and cyclist including a nature reserve on its eastern side, with an atmosphere of tranquillity away from bustling crowds. Over 200 varieties of birds come every spring to the Steinhuder Meer and among them are cormorants and the great crested grebe. Flowers flourish on the moorland and the pathways are well marked everywhere. Cycling round the lake or through the woods and heathland is also possible and bikes can be hired at Mardorf. Eels, pike, carp and perch are part of a possible catch should you wish to go fishing or simply part of the splendid range on the menu when it is time for substantial refreshment. The area was already occupied by the Romans in 16 AD. In the mid-eighteenth century Wilhelm Graf zu Schaumburg-Lippe had an artificial island built on the lake. It was on this island that the Count planned the world's first submarine or U-boat. The island also housed a cadet school and one of its most famous pupils was Gerhard von Scharnhorst, who was later to reform and rebuild the Prussian army, an essential step on the way to Prussia's immense power and might in the nineteenth century.

Der Deister, a nearby wooded area to the southwest, also has some excellent woodland walking and the **Burgdorfer Land**, an area to the southeast, has walking country taking in rolling pastureland, meadows and woodlands. This is an area which grows the most superb asparagus, which is served in a variety of ways when in season during the early summer months.

The town of **Wolfenbüttel** recently rediscovered one of its great treasures – an early gospel of the time of Heinrich der Löwe (Henry the Lion), dating from the twelfth century and of exquisite workmanship. This manuscript disappeared for some fifty years before re-appearing at Sothebys in London in 1983, where fortunately the German government was able to buy it back for the nation. Wolfenbüttel was the residence of the Welfen dynasty or Guelfs as they are called in English, for 300 years. The philosopher Leibniz worked here and the dramatist Gotthold Ephraim Lessing wrote his drama *Nathan der Weise* in the town. The area of Niedersachsen between the rivers Weser and Ems and north of **Oldenburg** forms a distinct region of its own, much of it known as Ostfriesland although strictly speaking this only covers the area to the west close to the Dutch border and the Ostfriesische Inseln. The Frisian tribe were great dyke builders as well as sometimes rebellious fisher and seafaring folk, who had their own language and occupied an area which extends over the border into the Netherlands. Many of the towns and villages have typically Dutch-style mellow brick houses with high-gabled façades, stylish houses with elegant doors and high, narrow warehouses. The town of **Leer** on the river Ems is a fine example of this, with narrow streets of old warehouses, some converted into dwelling houses, yet still with old lifting cranes on their top stories.

Jever, easily reached on the Esens branch railway from Sande, near Wilhelmshafen, is another typical Ostfriesland town, a medieval settlement where the former defensive ditches are now ornamental lakes around a baroque palace, familiar throughout Germany on the label of Jever 'Ost-Friesen' Pilsner beer. The palace now houses the town's museum, with elegant chambers, but also extensive material relating to old Frisian life, with restored rooms and workshop including a traditional blue-tiled kitchen, whilst the old town hall plays a carillon of bells each quarter hour.

Jever typifies much of what is so civilised about a small German town – attractive pedestrianised precincts cobbled in warm brick in the town centre, narrow traffic-free streets onto which pavement cafés and stalls spill, a lively market place filled with colourful stalls on market day, beautifully restored older buildings, a relaxed, friendly atmosphere. But even the modern brewery producing (excellent) Jever pils proves how contemporary German functional architecture can look remarkably stylish and appropriate. A number of tall cylinders of the brewery tiled in mirror glass reflect the colours of the sky in the town park lake.

Jever is also a good place to try local food. Smoked eel soup and a variety of fish dishes are just some of the superb traditional dishes available in a carefully restored eighteenth century brewery restaurant.

Sadly, the Frisian language, distinct from both German and Dutch, and closer related to English than to either of these, is now reduced to a few small pockets of older people in rural communities in some of the islands and smaller villages. Words and even phrases often sound amazingly familiar to English speakers.

Interestingly enough the Frisians share with the English an almost obsessive love of tea which is usually served, with suitable ceremony, from a delicately floral china teapot. The tea is large leaved and the authentic way is to put one or two lumps of the large crystal-style sugar called Kandiz into the cups first, pour the tea over them and finally the milk (or lemon) which should not be stirred. Three cups are considered the minimum that politeness requires and the teapot is often set over a little ceramic stove or candle holder to keep it warm. Rum is also a greatly favoured drink and can be added to either coffee or tea, an excellent consolation in inclement weather.

The Frisians were always great seafaring people, and the sea played and continues to play a great part in their life. There is, for example a sailing harbour museum at Carolinesiel on the coast and a Buddelschiff (ship-in-a-bottle) Museum at Neuharlingersiel. The coast and islands now form a major part of the Niedersachsisches Wattenmeer Nationalpark, a section of the immense area of protected coastline which now extends along the North Sea from the Netherlands to Denmark and also includes the Hamburgisches Wattenmeer Nationalpark and the Schleswig-Holsteinisches Nationalpark.

The complex patterns of shifting tides and sandbanks are a key factor in the way of life of the wildlife of this protected area, and are in many ways more important than actual seasonal changes. Tides cause changes in temperature, in the amount of salt content in the water, and affect the movement of the water on the sea-bed and its oxygen content as well as affecting the nourishment content at given times. The salt level of the water varies between 25% and 30% though heavy thundery rain can actually cause the salt content at the ebb tide in the smaller pools to sink as low as 10%. In spring the sun's rays can heat the surface of the Watt to 20°C while the actual water temperature is only 5°C. Floods can also cause dramatic temperature changes to the warmer Watt areas in a very short space of time. The area's topography constantly changes as the sea nibbles away at the coast and then deposits silt in another area. The fiercer the swell of the water and the stronger its current, the more it transports larger particles of clay and sand, with the finer particles, the Schlick, being deposited where the water's energy is less fierce. Creatures which live on the sea-bed in the Wattenmeer such as mussels are able to take in the oxygenated water with their nourishment and at the same time are able to expel the used and filtered water from their systems. Several of the worm species build homes through which they pump the water and by this means they detoxify the hydrogen sulphide which becomes sulphur oxide and non-poisonous. These lug-worms are characterised by the worm-like rings which surround their dwellings. The salt meadows differ radically from the meadows of the mainland, as the latter are very much a man-made phenomenon and would soon return to woodland without being grazed or mown. But on the coast the irregular flooding of the area with salt water causes the salt meadows to remain as they are, with salt tolerant species but without bushes or trees.

This fragile and vulnerable area is at the mercy of modern industrial civilisation. Polluted rivers with dangerous effluents and North Sea shipping that treats the area as a giant dustbin pose a serious threat to this delicate ecosystem. It is salutary to realise that any polluted water for example in the inner reaches of the Deutsche Bucht (German Bight) takes three full years before it is fully purified by the cleaner waters of the North Atlantic. The whole North Sea needs comprehensive protection. Already the four coastal federal states of Hamburg, Bremen, Niedersachsen and Schleswig-Holstein have agreed a common programme for the disposal of ships' waste in their ports and harbours. The Marpol treaty is another step in the right direction – an international agreement to protect the North Sea.

The Niedersächsisches Nationalpark has three distinct zones in order to guard the areas which are most at risk ecologically. The Ruhezone or quiet zone has the most stringent protection and takes up 54% of the park. It includes salt meadows, vulnerable dunes, and seal basking areas as well as special resting areas for birds. Access is not, however, totally restricted even in such areas; however, walkers are asked to keep to paths. Only marked paths can be used through these areas, green for walkers and red for horse riders. Land used for agricultural purposes must not change its use, hunting is forbidden, though some commercial fishing is allowed. In the Zwischenzone or intermediate zone, 45% of the park, there are special restrictions during the main breeding season and again access is generally restricted to marked paths. The Erholungszone or recreational area can be used for bathing purposes and for quiet recreation, including walking or sunbathing. Motorboats are forbidden and planning permission must be obtained from the national park before any building is constructed.

The National Park Authority, a branch of the state administration, authorises appropriate biotope management, research, the planning of path networks and all necessary environmental protective measures.

The Ostfriesische Inseln are a chain of seven large and a number of smaller islands, the seven larger ones being: **Borkum**, **Juist**, **Norderney**, **Baltrum**, **Langeoog**, **Spiekeroog** and **Wangerooge**. These islands together with the sandbanks build a sort of barrier system against storm floods, currents and the like and therefore help to protect the Wattenmeer, the salt meadows and the coast.

The inhabitants of the Ostfriesische Inseln, all living within the overall Nationalpark designated area (though some township areas are outside the park boundary as such), depend heavily on tourism for their livelihood, but they are also extremely aware of the ways that tourism can damage the fragile ecology. They are also well aware of how the greenhouse effect and rising sea levels could threaten their very existence.

Fourteen major environmental organisations joined together in 1988 to produce a brochure for responsible tourism in the area called 'Strandspaziergang – Sanfter Urlaub mit Köpfen', which through a number of simple slogans tried to educate the public in the best way to husband natural resources and assist in protecting the Niedersächsisches Wattenmeer and the North Sea. In addition the Ostfriesische Inseln had a policy already in the mid-70s of biologically re-active sewage farms, which today have the benefit of even more advanced technology in this direction. There was also a ban on increasing tourist accommodation, and encouragement for the development of environmentally friendly energy resources such as wind pumps and heat conservation measures. Traffic regulations make most of the islands virtually car free and special measures to deal with litter were introduced. Even leisure activities educate the visitor by means of guided tours, seminars, protective measures and rest zones for fauna and flora, into a more environmentally friendly habit of mind.

All the Ostfriesische Inseln can be reached by public transport. The largest, which has the most popular tourist resort, is Norderney. This has a direct ferry link from Norddeich harbour served by InterRegio and express trains from all over Germany. The other islands rely on bus-rail links, from Esens, Jever or Sande where a specially timetabled 'tide-bus' with a trailer for luggage will take you by shallow-bottomed boat along narrow channels across to Langeoog, Spiekeroog or Wangerooge. Other services run from Norden to Juist and from Nessmersiel to Baltrum (which has an island railway), whilst Borkum has a boat link from Emden. A coastal bus service (Weser-Ems Bus) from Norden links all the ferries and coastal resorts. With the exception of Spiekeroog, cycle hire is available on all the islands and cycles can usually be carried on ferries. As boats and their linking buses depend on the highly variable tides, you must check out the timetables carefully (in the DB Kursbuch).

All the islands offer a fascinating blend of seaside tourism with long sandy beaches, Strandkorbe (the large basket-style deckchairs) and all the usual mass tourism attractions, and often quite astonishingly stringent degrees of nature protection and active concern for the environment. Two examples will suffice – Spiekeroog and Wangerooge.

The island of Spiekeroog is mainly within the Nationalpark. Visitors, especially young people, but also local people, are asked to help by following the park's zoning system that operates on the island and helping to protect the vegetation of the vulnerable sand dunes which safeguards the coastline and also to collect litter in the area. Spiekeroog even has a virtual bicycle ban as the island is keen to reduce erosion by cycles and concentrate on pedestrian movement. Apart from the doctor's vehicle, no others are allowed on the island, though there is a horse-drawn narrow gauge railway in use during the summer. Rubbish is carefully sorted and people are requested both to reduce the quantity of rubbish and to recycle as much as possible. Drinking water is saved by economising on its use in toilets and showers. The various places of accommodation and the shops offer locally grown organic and wholefood and it is possible to obtain freshly caught fish direct from the harbour. Buildings have to be built in an environmentally friendly form and in typical regional style.

When your boat arrives at the little island port of Wangerooge it is met by a DB narrow gauge railway which is the only means of mechanised passenger travel on the island. Passengers and freight go at a steady 8-12 kilometres per hour in elderly coaches, crossing the quiet zone on a narrow single track over an area of marsh, salt meadow and dunes, leaving the wildlife totally undisturbed. The rich beauty of birdsong to be heard from carriage windows as the little train eases its way across the marshland has to be experienced to be believed. It is however also possible to fly from the mainland for emergencies and for those who demand speed of access.

Wangerooge offers a long beach of silvery sand with safe bathing and the ubiquitous Strandkorben, but it has also a car-free village street where the bicycle is king and where little low small-wheeled carts are available from local hotels or guest houses to pull your luggage or shopping – or a novel way of giving young children a ride. Thatched roofs, photogenic lighthouses, coastal walks and rides, make this a paradise for anyone seeking to enjoy superb coastal landscapes and wildlife. There are two substantial nature reserves on the island specially for sea birds and a Nationalpark Zentrum with exhibitions, lecture rooms and teaching areas. Programmes of guided walks and other events are arranged.

Of the most important Ost Friesische Naturschutzgebiete, Langeoog has the highest dunes and it has one of the largest herring gull breeding colonies in Germany. Other nesting species to be seen include shelduck, curlew, lapwing, oystercatcher, redshank and common gull. Most of the island is a bird sanctuary.

The Elisabeth-Aussengroden Reserve is a 13.8 kilometre strip of mainland bank south of Wangerooge with mudflats of saltmarsh grass-land. It is situated on a migration path and is visited by an enormous number of birds. A few avocets nest here and it is remarkable how well they are equipped to deal with the conditions as they search for food in the Wattenmeer with their curved beaks and make semi-circular movements with their heads in the low water just below the surface, trawling for food. It is also believed that the redshank population is at its highest level in Europe here.

The small island of Mellum plays host to an enormous number of redshanks in late summer as well as curlews, grey plovers, godwits and ducks. Large numbers of shelduck also rest here on their way to their moulting grounds and the brent geese use the island as their winter quarters.

The Wattenmeer can be crossed by horse and carriage from Cuxhafen at low tide and there are special guided walks across. Never attempt, however, to cross the Wattenmeer without a professional guide. There are dangerous and unexpectedly deep channels and quicksands, and with fast rising tides and uncertain weather conditions, lives have too often been lost.

Further information

Niedersachsen tourist office: **LFVV Niedersachsen**, Gildehaus, Markstraße 45, D-3380 Goslar 1.

Fremdenverkehrsverband Nordsee-Niedersachsen-Bremen e.V., Postfach 1820, D-2900 Oldenburg.

Lüneburg Heide tourist office: Fremdenverkehrsverband Lüneburg Heide e.V., Am Sande 5, D-2120 Lüneburg.

Nationalparkverwaltung, Niedersächsisches Wattenmeer, Virchowstraße 1, D-2940 Wilhelmshafen.

Die Gemeinschaft der Ostfriesischen Inseln, c/o Stadt Borkum, Neue Straße 1, D-2972 Borkum.

Grüne Ferieninsel Spiekeroog, Nordseebad, Spiekeroog GmbH, Noordenpad 25, D-2941 Spiekeroog.

Bremen

Lehe
Geestemünde
Wulsdorf
BREMERHAVEN
R Weser
BREMEN
Vegesack
Worpswede
Stadtmitte
0 10 20 km

The Free Hanseatic City of Bremen has the distinction of being Germany's smallest federal state, covering an area of just 404 square kilometres with a population of 677,000. It actually consists of two cities, Bremen and Bremerhafen, which are about 60 kilometres apart from each other along the river Weser, but mutually dependent.

Though extremely small compared to other Länder, Bremen can be seen as a fascinating illustration of the democratic nature of the German federal system, which gives an important voice in both regional and national affairs to a state of this size. Bremen is a city-state which guards its independence and its traditions with pride, but at the same time it is one of the most progressive and even radical of German cities.

Bremen's crucial position at the mouth of the Weser on the low-lying North German coast determined much of its history. The name Bremen comes from an early German word 'Brem' meaning 'along the river' and its site proved a crossroads for the early trading routes, connecting the southwest with the northeast and the interior with the coast. The earliest settlers lived by a ferry landing on a small island between the dunes and the river known as the Tiefer and later moved to the area which was to become the heart of the city. Parts of the city's long sea-going tradition are still being discovered, such as the fourteenth century cargo ship used by the Hanseatic League, known as the 'Hansekogge' or cog which, though broken into thousands of pieces, has been painstakingly restored, and has proved to be a vital missing link in the understanding of Hanseatic maritime history.

The city dates back to the eighth century when the Frankish Emperor Charlemagne, or Karl der Große as he is known in German, made Bremen a bishopric. From his concessions were then established the right that anyone who lived in Bremen for a year was a free man and beholden to no authority outside the city. In 888 AD market rights were granted and Bremen's merchants were mentioned in documents as early as 965 AD.

From Bremen's earliest days the dykes that defended the coast were so essential that an ancient edict laid down that: 'If you are not prepared to dig and repair the dykes, you are not welcome in the area'. The care of the dykes along the whole of the North German marshes can be seen as an early example of mutual co-operation against natural forces and helped to foster a strong sense of community.

Bremen's low-lying terrain was always subject to great storm devastation by the North Sea, so that a system of dykes and seawalls played an essential part in her survival. They were also used as defences against enemies and an early archbishop, Friedrich, had the foresight to invite Dutch experts to construct a chain of dykes on the city's eastern side.

In 1358 Bremen became a member of the Hanseatic League, which was originally a confederation of groups of merchants on the North German coast who had banded together to develop their trade and to protect the interests of their members abroad. Lübeck was its main seat and most of the Hansetage (Hansa parliaments) took place there, though two were held in Bremen. The Hansa had strong links with England and their own centre in London included the Guildhall in Thames Street. Salt and cloth were among the earliest and most prized of the trading products. As the power of the Hansa grew, the League engendered great feelings of solidarity with the minimum show of force, always setting economic rather than political goals. It soon became the leading influence in North European trade. As its power increased, it was able to win more and more useful concessions for its trading agreements, an influence which extended as far as Novrogod and Smolensk in Russia.

Lübeck had become Western Europe's gateway to Eastern Europe, its superb geographical position in a deep sheltered bay enabling it to become head of the Hansa, while Hamburg with excellent natural harbours, and Rostock and Stralsund on the Baltic coast were just a few of nearly 200 Hanseatic towns that came to prominence. By the fourteenth century the Hansa had spread out its trade-routes southwards to South Germany, Italy, France, Spain and Portugal. In the later decades of the fourteenth century, in order to counter competition from the Dutch and South Germans, the League's second stage of development came with the banding together of a number of towns – the Hansa cities – rather than just groups of merchants, under the Hansa banner, thus succeeding till the sixteenth century in fending off most competition. The rise of independent nation states in the sixteenth century eventually broke the power of the Hanseatic League. After nearly 200 years of Hanseatic rule, the Hansetag met for the last time. Hamburg and Danzig (now Gdansk), each with free city status, prospered even more after the Hansa heyday.

Bremen herself was twice expelled from the Hansa after attempting to trade on her own initiative, but obviously felt it crucial to return to the fold. Her status as a member of Hansa is still recalled with pride and to this day she uses HB even on her number plates to emphasise the special status of the Free Hanseatic City of Bremen.

Although sixty per cent of Bremen city was damaged during the Second World War, the old part of the town survived virtually unscathed and this is particularly fortunate as Bremen, unlike a number of other German cities which suffered a similar experience, does not seem to have a strong policy of rebuilding in the old style. A walk round the city should start at the market place with its striking historic buildings including the superb Rathaus (town hall) with its great Renaissance façade where Charlemagne and the Seven Electors stand between tall windows. Visit the splendid wine cellar open as a restaurant renowned for its high-quality German wines, its enormous beautifully decorated barrels and row of special small dining alcoves for small private parties. Tradition claims that the doors closing off the dining alcoves are never shut if there are only two people dining there. The original Rathaus proved too small for the number of councillors, so that a decision was taken to march the councillors to the nearby Bürgerweide (common) where they formed a square and measurements were taken round them to determine the size of the new building.

One of Bremen's special traditions comes from the Haus Seefahrt, a charitable seamen's organisation, which organises a traditional meal or Schaffermahlzeit annually with specially invited dignitaries, with its main course consisting of the typical Bremen speciality of Kohl und Pinkel – kale with a special kind of local sausage made with coarse-grained oats.

The fine gothic cathedral of St. Petri alongside the Rathaus was founded about 1200. The cathedral also has a famous cellar, the Bleikeller (lead cellar), where lead used to be stored, which has the curious property of mummifying bodies, though this had nothing to do with the lead, but was due to its actual construction and aircurrents.

Bremen's relationship with its cathedral was a chequered one. An early dislike of church authority resulted in the famous statue of Roland in the market square apparently facing the cathedral in defiance. Roland is actually a figure representing citizens' rights and is found in many North German towns. He owes his origin to the bravest of Charlemagne's knights and is seen as a symbol of the city's freedom. Tradition has it that he must be re-erected within twenty-four hours should he ever fall down or that freedom will be endangered. Another much-loved city centre statue close to the Rathaus is the much more recent one of Die Bremer Stadtmusikanten (from a story by the Brothers Grimm): four domestic animals, Donkey, Dog, Cat and Cock, who had come to the end of their working lives ran off to seek their fortune as musicians in Bremen, as the town did employ a number of musicians for state fanfares and the like. The animals in fact never reached Bremen, but scared off some robbers and occupied their well-equipped house and lived there happily ever after.

In the Schnoor Viertel, close to the Rathaus, there are old cottages which once belonged to fishermen, many of them now small art galleries and cafés.

The Focke Museum in Schwakhausen has a great deal of material on Bremen's maritime and civic history, including a small tobacco museum recalling Bremen's long links with the tobacco trade.

Bremen is extremely well served by public transport, having an InterCity station which is a focal point of local train networks. The city also has a typically well-planned and integrated network of trams and buses. Interesting trips to take include a tour round the harbour and industrial areas on the banks of the Weser between Hemelingen and Gröpelingen which can be made either by bike or tram. Alternatively you can take a boat trip, perhaps as far as Bremerhafen, to enjoy the waterfront and skyline. Bremen and Bremerhafen form Germany's second largest port after Hamburg, handling both oceangoing and river and canal traffic and around 10% of all Germany's foreign trade.

You can also explore the city by cycle. One especially interesting trip is to take in the left bank of the Weser using all of Bremen's four ferries. This trip starts at Osterdeich and finishes at Farge. Another recommended cycle ride is to the Blockland on the banks of the Lesum and Wümme, renowned for their plant life, watermeadows and wetlands.

There is no shortage of attractive green recreation areas within Bremen. Many of the city's original wall and fortification areas and old branches of the Weser have been transformed into landscaped parks. The Bürgerweide remains a fine open space. A notable landmark in the centre is the old windmill on the Wallanlage. The Rhododendronpark also contains the botanical gardens, which display a splendid collection of 2,000 rhododendrons and azaleas. But it is along the river Weser that much of this city-state's interest lies and there are many opportunities for excursions either by using the ferries or excursion boats or by walking and cycling to numerous points of interest. Trips can also be made by local bus and tram. The tram kiosk opposite the railway station and close to the tourist office provides maps, timetables and details of bargain tickets.

Bremen's continuous problems with the silting up of her harbours caused the world's first artificial harbour to be constructed at Vegesack, which is now an attractive preserved area of the city. Beer was (and still is) a major export product, and the import of coffee, wine, cotton, timber, tropical goods, tobacco and later still cars was to add to Bremen's prosperity. But the Vegesack harbour also proved insufficient to handle the growing trade, and Bremen was forced to look outside her own territory for a new harbour at what was to become **Bremerhafen**, then ruled from Hannover. The Hanoverians fortunately were open to negotiations, realising that they too could benefit from an extension of the port. Bremerhafen was also to become a great whaling port. The skeleton of a whale that was washed ashore in the seventeenth century can still be seen in the Deutches Schiffartsmuseum – the German national maritime museum – in Bremerhafen, which traces the growth of German merchant shipping from earliest times through the Hanseatic era to the present day. Pride of place is the Hansekogge, whilst six old sailing ships, forming part of the open air museum, are moored in the Old Port.

Bremerhafen was also the departure point for thousands of German emigrants to America. By 1844 20,000 Germans had emigrated via Bremerhafen and by 1857 the Norddeutsche Lloyd had introduced a steamboat named 'The Bremen' and emigrants now reached New York in only two weeks as opposed to the long voyage of eight to ten weeks on the old sailing vessels. Bremerhafen is now a great modern container terminal and has an enormous banana storage depot and a gigantic car terminal.

Bremerhafen is easily reached from Bremen by frequent trains. You can walk along the Deichpromenade and the Weserdeich along the breakwater at the south side of the mouth of the river Geeste to the old town of Lehe to see boats arriving and leaving Bremen and Bremerhafen, and the great liner and container terminals. This can be combined with a visit to the maritime museum and the remarkable Tiergrotten (zoological caves) with bears, monkeys and seals and a Nordsee-Aquarium which specialises in the fish of the North Sea.

The peat growing area on **Teufelsmoor** is well worth seeing and you could include a visit to the Torfschiffmuseum and to a peatworks. Dried peat was brought by special boats or barges to Bremen on the narrow waterways and used for heating and then for industrial purposes up till the end of the nineteenth century. The peat workers lived a hard life, cutting first the Weißtorf or white peat for ordinary heating and for strewing in the barns and byres. Underneath lay the relatively dry Bäckertorf which could be cut out in the form of sods. These were dried for a time and stacked. The last layer or Schwarzertorf, which was regarded as the most valuable, was normally fairly wet and soggy. This had to be dried out in the fields by the women and children who ran over it in special wooden shoes to assist the drying process. After levelling the peat and letting it dry again, it was cut into squares, dried again and stacked up in round heaps, and then brought down in barges to Bremen to be sold. So hard was the life on the peat moors during the second half of the eighteenth century when the landless farmers were encouraged to settle there that the saying went: 'The first one will meet his death, the second one will suffer hunger and only the third will earn his bread'. Nowadays there is concern about the fragile ecology of the peat moors and there is debate about trying to return them to their original state. On balance it is felt they should be left in their present state because of the area's highly distinctive plant life. Another factor is that they lie on the flight path for many bird species on their way to and from the south.

The village of **Worpswede**, some 24 kilometres from Bremen and originally in the centre of the peat bog, became an artists' colony at the end of the last century, a leading centre of Expressionism where such painters as Fritz Mackensen and Paula Modersohn-Becker worked. Many of its attractive houses are now studios and craft centres.

Two popular small resorts easily visited from Bremen are **Wremen** and **Dorum** in the Dorumertief, as is the town of **Bederkesa** about 20 kilometres to the east with its restored castle. Eight hours sail away is **Helgoland** and the excursion allows several hours on the island before returning. Helgoland was taken from the Danes by the English in 1807 and later exchanged with the Germans for the more exotic spice island of Zanzibar. While still in English ownership, the island was able to follow a lucrative smuggling trade when Napoleon banned trade with England in the early nineteenth century. For Germany it became a useful defensive outpost. Nowadays the island is visited for its dramatic sandstone and chalk cliffs, its birdlife and its severe beauty.

Further information

Carol Claxton, *Bremen – the Story of the Free Hanseatic City* (Appel Verlag, Bremen).
Verkehrsverein der Freien Hansestadt Bremen e.V., Postfach 10 07 47, Bahnhofsplatz 29, D-2800 Bremen.

Mecklenburg-Vorpommern ___

Mecklenburg-Vorpommern is the most northeasterly of the German Länder, stretching from Schleswig-Holstein to the Polish border formed by the river Oder, with Mecklenburg to the west and Vorpommern to the east. It is still relatively unknown even to West Germans, and yet it is an area immensely rich in natural beauty and unspoiled wildlife.

One reason for this is the fact that this was never a wealthy area, nor were there mineral or other resources to exploit. Poor communications across marshy countryside also meant that it didn't fully share the industrialisation and urbanisation of other regions. Lack of investment by the old DDR regime has also paradoxically helped. Nature has been allowed to flourish in areas of landscape and coastline which now have international importance for conservation.

Its character reflects its particular history. By the twelfth and thirteenth centuries German-speaking peoples had colonised the land east of the Elbe almost as far as the Gulf of Finland. They built their system of agriculture on the pattern of the 'Gut' or large estate, a pattern of settlement only partially altered in Mecklenburg-Vorpommern by nineteenth-century industrialisation. Rye and potatoes are the chief crops on the poorer soil and wheat and sugar beet predominate in the more fertile areas.

Schwerin, the state capital, was the first German town to be founded east of the Elbe, 830 years ago. It is surrounded by no fewer than ten lakes, one of which, the Burgsee, contains a splendid neo-Renaissance castle built on an island in the style of a French château. There are magnificent water gardens opposite. The Schwerinsee, the second largest lake in the state, contains the Kaninchenwerder Insel, a popular nature reserve and wildlife sanctuary served by boat from Schwerin and attracting 80,000 visitors a year.

Until recently there were no large deep-sea ports on the Mecklenburg coast as the Bodden or shallow inlets with their sandbanks made shipping on a large scale difficult. However, the partitioning of Germany after World War II caused **Rostock**, one of the old Hansa towns, to become the chief port of the DDR with an emphasis on shipbuilding and fishing. It remains to be seen how reunification will affect its transport links with Sweden and the rest of Germany.

Stralsund, another of the old Hansa ports and the gateway to the island of Rügen via the Rügendamm, has splendid architecture and an almost Scandinavian atmosphere. The old town lies within a series of attractive lakes. About 15 kilometres to the southeast of the town at Niederhof on the Strelkasund straits is one of the most important cormorant colonies in Germany, where the birds have been formally protected since 1952.

Of the five new national parks created in the former East Germany, no fewer than three of them, the Vorpommersche Boddenlandschaft on the Baltic coast, Jasmund on Rügen further to the northeast and the Müritz-Nationalpark to the south are situated in Mecklenburg-Vorpommern. Additional specially protected areas are the Biosphäre Sudost Rügen including the outstanding Mönchgut area, and the Naturpark Schaalsee on the Schleswig-Holstein border. A substantial number of nature reserves by no means exhausts the list of protected areas. Ironically the old boundary areas between former West and East Germany and other areas designated for army manoeuvres and closed to the public, also allowed the protection of a great variety of bird and animal species and plant life. Such areas could now be under threat from developers unless special measures are taken to protect them.

The island of **Rügen**, more than anywhere else in Mecklenburg-Vorpommern, epitomises the beauty of the Baltic coastal landscape with its mixture of steep cliffs, level sandy shores, coves and shallow bays, varied with beech woods and rolling grass-covered hills or beautiful flower meadows dotted with cornflowers, poppies and marguerites. In the early nineteenth century poets and painters were already responding to the intense beauty of the land and seascapes. The German romantic painter Caspar David Friedrich (1774-1840), who was born at nearby **Greifswald** on the mainland, captured the mood of Rügen with his atmospheric paintings and drawings of the coast in sunlight and moonlight, twilight and mist. His celebrated painting of the Wissower Klinken in the Jasmund Nationalpark evokes more magically than any photograph the drama of the great chalk cliffs with their range of colour from an almost luminous greenish white to yellowish ochre against a background of ever-changing sea and sky.

When the German Federal President Richard von Weizäcker visited the island of Rügen in June 1991, he was reported as being so impressed with the outstanding quality of the landscape, that he declared that nowhere else in Germany could compare with it. He warned that any tourism initiatives would need not only very careful planning, but also the co-operation of the various interested bodies such as the tourism industry, local authorities, and conservationists. Hans Dieter Knapp, the director of the newly founded Naturschutzakademie (institute for nature protection) on **Insel Vilm**, voiced similar fears that suitably strong measures for protection of the environment and countryside were needed or there would be no guarantee that the countryside would be in existence for future generations. He compared the crisis in our countryside to the crisis in our society. In other words, our lack of a responsible attitude to our heritage runs parallel to our lack of concern for society as a whole.

Jasmund Nationalpark may be only 30 square kilometres and Germany's smallest national park, but it is certainly one of the most beautiful – and a landscape of European importance. Its eight kilometre long chalk coastal cliffs, crowned with beechwoods, which extend from Lohme in the north virtually to the old town of Saßnitz, rise to a height of 120 metres above the Baltic coast and are relics of the Ice Age. They date from the Pleistocene period and are formed from a mixture of compressed fossil remains, sand and marl. A huge forest area forms the inland part of the national park with beeches as the dominant tree though other varieties are equally at home. On the peaty, treeless heaths, cotton grass, mosses and sundew are in evidence, while in the damper and shadier areas near lakes and rivers, elms, sycamores and ash flourish. Such varying terrain plays host to whole legions of flowers, insects, birds and other animals, including many rare specimens. Interestingly some plant species found on Rügen are also to be found on the Russian steppes.

The woodlands of the Stubnitz section of the park, with its changing carpet of wild flowers in spring and summer, is also one of North Germany's finest areas for wild orchids, including the rare lady's slipper.

A network of footpaths crosses the park, none finer than the coastal clifftop paths from Lohme and Königstuhle (Stubbenkamme), both of which can be reached by service bus from Saßnitz station on the electrified railway from Rostock. The celebrated chalk cliffs of the Königstuhl with its large coach and car parks, cafés and pavilion shops, provides an example of how hard tourism could totally destroy the park as queues of visitors pay the toll to stand for a few seconds on the wellworn clifftop and enjoy the famous view, before escaping back to car, café and toilets. Yet a couple of hundred metres along the coastal path is relative peace with evocative views through the trees to the cliffs and the water.

The Baltic around Rügen is virtually tideless and shallow, and contains the Bodden, lagoon-like shallow water, particularly the areas lying between Rügen and the mainland, and within the island itself. The Bodden are interspersed with shifting sand banks which take skill to negotiate by any sea-going craft, but are rich in marine and bird life.

Much of the southeastern part of Rügen, including its adjacent Bodden, forms the Südost Rügen Biosphäre Reservat.

Mönchgut, the island's southeasterly extremity, demonstrates the particular qualities of a biosphere reserve. It was Swedish territory after the Thirty Years War. By the beginning of the seventeenth century, Sweden had already developed a highly sophisticated system of land surveying and measurement and as the Swedish crown wanted a clearer picture of what her new territories contained for taxation purposes, exact measurements were obtained in the later decades of the century. These were recorded in a number of volumes which now provide a fascinating, detailed record of the various settlements and manufacturing areas of the period. The calculations used triangulation and are therefore extremely accurate, so that changing population densities and settlement patterns as well as the way the coastline has changed, can all be reconstructed.

The landscape on Mönchgut is varied, with woods, bushes, grassy areas, cliffs, reed beds, beaches, salt meadows, cultivated fields and flower meadows. It is therefore the ideal environment for a suitably varied native bird life including, in autumn, birds fleeing the colder winters of the even more northerly regions. Among species to be seen are crane, wild geese, tern, osprey.

In previous centuries Mönchgut life was dominated by the traditional occupations of sailing, piloting and fishing. Herrings were in season early in the year, to be followed by flounders, pikes and eels, while in the autumn another variety of herring was the staple diet. The sea and land also provided an amazing amount of additional bounty for an adaptable community. Driftwood could be gathered both for building material and for firewood, reeds could be cut and dried for thatched roofs (it is still possible to see the grouped piles of drying reeds like small hayricks in various areas). A type of seagrass was collected for stuffing pillows, and rushes for straw plaiting and for nets. Seaweed was a useful fertiliser and birds were caught to supplement the household food stocks. The coast was also scanned for pieces of amber for jewelry. Though fishing through the centuries was the staple industry, it was of course only in the later decades of the nineteenth century that machine-made fishing nets were available and till then a wide variety of material such as flax, hemp, rushes, split or narrow pieces of wood, stones and even pieces of iron were all used to catch fish; in fact whatever raw material was to hand.

The little **Insel Vilm** off the south Rügen coast is 2.7 kilometres long and about 1 kilometre wide. Two to three thousand years ago high tides and currents helped to sunder the island from Rügen and some small islands nearby eventually totally disappeared. Vilm is of particular interest as a nature reserve as its island status has allowed it to remain relatively undisturbed, so that in quite a small area variations of the southern Baltic coastal region can be studied.

The name Vilm is derived from the Slav word for elm, though nowadays it is the beech and oak trees which predominate. Wood has not been felled commercially on the island since 1538 and some of the oaks are at least 500 years old. The woods on Vilm were also used as summer grazing areas for cattle which were even brought over specially up till the eighteenth century for this purpose. Archaeological finds have included neolithic flint tools and knives and early stone graves. In the eighteenth century tenant dairy farmers rented out rooms to visitors in the summer and provided food for tourists who enjoyed a 'romantic' island excursion.

Its popularity increased after the branch railway was built down from the main line from Rostock at Bergen to Lauterbach, but in recent years it became a private holiday retreat for DDR political leaders. It is now the state's Naturschutzakademie and as such access is strictly limited to a maximum of thirty students and guests a day, to keep the human impact on this remarkable ecosystem to an absolute minimum.

Visitors originally came to Insel Vilm largely as a result of the bathing establishment at Putbus-Lauterbach, conceived by Fürst (Prince) zu Putbus. It was he who founded the delightful little town of **Putbus** in the first decade of the nineteenth century, planned to be a rather grand spa town with some splendid buildings in a central area known as the Circus. His own palace no longer exists, but there is a charmingly renovated theatre still in use and the splendid English-style landscaped parkland is now the town's slightly overgrown and atmospheric park, while the former Spa Kursaal has become a stylish church next to a deer enclosure.

Putbus lies on a branch railway off the main electrified Baltic coast line from Rostock to Saßnitz at Bergen, and at the junction for the narrow gauge railway line to Göhren. It has great charm, a choice of inexpensive accommodation (mostly in private houses) and because of good transport links – bus and rail – it is a useful centre for visiting the whole of Rügen including Mönchgut.

The little Rügen beach resorts of Binz, Sellin and Göhren can be reached by that historic narrow gauge railway known as the Rasender Roland ('Flying Roland') from Putbus which also brought tourists earlier in the century when meals were served on the train. Up till 1917 there was a theatre train which took guests from the resorts to the beautiful little theatre in Putbus built by Fürst Malte zu Putbus and took them home after the performance – a very civilised way of enjoying a theatrical evening.

Attempts to close the railway in 1964 were foiled by public outcry and perhaps produced one of the first railway rescues in Germany. Since the roads on Rügen were in such a bad state, it was perhaps necessity rather than nostalgia which galvanised local opinion. Nowadays the metre-gauge railway with its delightful vintage steam locomotives and carriages is under state heritage protection, and is a tourist attraction as well as a valuable means of transport into Mönchgut. The journey at a sedate pace past beech and fir woods, flower-rich meadows, marshland and lakes, is a green traveller's delight and you are likely to see hares, roe deer and even the odd nesting stork from the carriage window.

Göhren in particular is an excellent centre for walks around the whole of the Mönchgut peninsula with a network of buses as far as Thiessow and Gager to enable a return to be made from the coastal path. Pathways follow the clifftop and beach and in summer the wild flowers form natural gardens of colour.

There were already grassroot initiatives at the end of 1989 to protect the **Bodden** by means of a national park. The Vorpommersche Bodden stretches from Hiddensee and the western side of Rügen to the isthmus of Darß and the Fischland and the Boddenkette. The formation of the Bodden started about 12,000 years ago as the great meltwaters of the Ice Age remained trapped above the moraines. Then as the water level rose about 7,000 years ago, the sea flooded most of the land masses, leaving only the highest points to become islands. Some 3,000 years on, as the silt eroded from these islands was deposited on their flanks, sand spits and dunes were created, thus making the Bodden area. Over the centuries, as the dunescape increased further silt was deposited, so that the original island area became covered by sea and sand dunes. Today great stretches of the outer coast of Fischland, Darß and Zingst for example, are being eroded and the Bodden area is silting up even more. Various protective measures are in force to stop the sea flooding in. Today Darß/Zingst, Hiddensee and Rügen are gradually coming nearer to each other.

Boats from Stralsund harbour, Schaprode on Rügen (linked by bus from Bergen station) and during the summer months Darß/Zingst, all call at the beautiful island of **Hiddensee** off Rügen's west coast. The island is 18 kilometres in length, but less than 1 kilometre wide in places, and it is an island of contrasts. It is mostly flat with sandy beaches, its long southern tip the Gelen an extended sandbank and nature reserve, but the ancient morains on the Dornbush side have relatively high grassy hills, thickets, and some woodland, and a lighthouse on a grassy knoll is particularly photogenic. Birds, insects and plant life flourish here in abundance.

The island is also totally car free, cars being banned, with a single bus service between Neundorf and Kloster, but visitors and locals alike cope perfectly well on foot or by cycle. Cycles are carried from the mainland or Rügen by boat, and there is cycle hire available on the island. Freedom from the automobile creates an atmosphere of peace and tranquility which has to be experienced to be appreciated, a slowing down of the pace of life and freedom from stress and danger. Reed thatched roofs, as elsewhere in the region, are a particularly attractive feature.

Hiddensee and especially the little resort of **Kloster** became particularly fashionable as a centre for writers and artists in the first two decades of this century, attracted by the fame and personal charisma of the writer and Nobel Prize winner Gerhard Hauptman (1862-1946) who made his home there and whose former house is now a museum. Hiddensee is also known for the uniquely shaped gold jewelry in its strange cross formation, discovered there some time ago and dating from about 950-1000 AD. Accommodation on the island is limited and if you travel there in the summer months, advance booking is advisable.

Darß on the mainland, the southern perimeter of the Vorpommersche Boddenlandschaft Nationalpark, has one of the largest and most beautiful woodland areas on the Baltic, including ancient coastal pinewoods, beechwoods, marsh and peaty heath together with areas of dunes. The reclaimed areas of land and string of small seaside resorts along the coast such as Zingst, Prerow and Wustrow are protected by dykes from high water and the dyke walls are grassed over. It is possible to walk some distance or alternatively cycle along the dyke walls from Zingst to Müggenburg, with a choice of linking paths through the forest or by the edge of the Bodden. An hourly bus service from the branch line terminal station at Barth links the resorts with Ribnitz-Damgarten on the main line and provides a valuable return transport service for walkers in the area.

This coast is famous for its amber. At Ribnitz-Damgarten there is a museum solely devoted to numerous beautiful examples of amber jewelry from the palest yellow to a deep warm burnished brown. Amber was formed in prehistoric times and is the hardened resin of ancient pine trees which were finally washed into the sea through various river courses. It became a much valued precious stone, to such a degree that it was called 'the gold of the North'. Originally quantities were found on the North Sea coast, but over the centuries this has dwindled and the Baltic coast became the area for larger finds. The German word Bernstein (amber) derives from the old Low German word börnen, to burn, and means stone which burns. Amber burns easily, for example when a match is applied.

Fish to be found in the Bodden include flounders, herrings, salmon, sea-trout, pike and eels, while red deer, wild boar, fox, badger, pine marten, hare and rabbit are some of the common mammals which can be observed nearby. Birds include geese, swans, and waders.

Not for nothing is the central part of Mecklenburg known as the Mecklenburger Seenplatte – the Mecklenburger lake plateau. Many of these lakes now form nature reserves or important recreational areas, including the Müritzsee Nationalpark.

The Müritz Nationalpark lies mainly to the east of the **Müritzsee**, in the south of the state, and is easily reached from the town of Waren on the main Rostock-Berlin railway line. A further area lies to the east of **Neustrelitz** south of **Neubrandenburg**. The name Müritz is derived from the Slav word Morcze, meaning the small sea. The lake is 27 kilometres in length with a surface area of 117 square kilometres and is Germany's second largest lake. It is also noted for a rather severe climate with its thunderstorms and bouts of fog and in winter such is the extreme cold, it becomes ice bound. A fifth of the surface of the Müritz Nationalpark is actually water, with the rest made up of marsh, moorland, large reedbeds and grazing land. The final section is ancient deciduous woodland with willows, birches, oaks, beeches and pine trees predominating. There is also a special area set aside for orchids, gentians and several varieties of sundew. Over 800 types of butterfly, innumerable kinds of insects, 700 plant species and 240 varieties of birds including several endangered species all make their home here. A special chained off area protects the banks for up to 12 kilometres along the shoreline, so that eagles, cranes and wild geese who frequent the area in late summer are not disturbed. As in other German national parks, a careful zoning system ensures that the central areas receive maximum protection, with visitors encouraged to leave their cars in fringe car parks and take footpaths and cycleways leading to observation points in the central park, whilst less active visitors can take an environmentally friendly horse-drawn coach along certain routes.

Less stringent controls apply to the Mecklenburgische Schweiz Naturpark around Malchin, Teterow and Demmin southeast of Rostock, which might bear little resemblance to Switzerland, but is an attractive area of mainly beech woodland, lakes and meadowland, popular for rural holidays and well supplied with waymarked footpath routes. A particular feature are the Ivenacher Oaks, reputed to be over a thousand years old, the largest with a trunk covering 16 square metres in area. Ivenack Tiergarten, where the oaks grow in a protected forest and deerpark, is only a short walk from Reuterstadt-Stavenhagen station on the Neubrandenburg-Güstrow railway line.

Usedom is a Baltic island shaped like an open V, with sandy beaches, which forms the easternmost section of the state; 85% of Usedom is under some form of environmental protection, with a chain of small resorts on its outer coast. Its steep cliffs give a splendid view far along the coast and out to sea and on a clear day, it is possible to see the southeast point of Rügen and even the ships sailing into the Pommerische Bucht. The flat stretches of sandy shore offer a sharp contrast to the small streets with their low-roofed traditional style houses and the area is also rich in remains of Viking, Slav and old Germanic culture. From Ahlbeck it is easy to cross over the border into Poland and stroll around Swinemünde or alternatively visit the nearby island of Wollin. It is fascinating also to note how many of the places and castle remains have Slav names, as endings such as 'ow', 'itz' and 'in' tend to indicate. All the little resorts strung out along the island coast are served by rail, and a coastal footpath between stations makes it an easy area to explore without a car. To reach Usedom, passengers must take the ferry from Wolgast across to Wolgast Fähre station, from where you can travel on to such resorts as Zinnowitz, Pennemünde, Bonsin, Heringsdorf and Ahlbeck.

Food in the region to particularly look out for includes excellent hams and cheeses, fruit, the delicious Rügen sausages, and a real old Pomeranian speciality – roast duck served with prunes, a variety of fish dishes, and Kummel, a strong schnapps flavoured with caraway seeds.

Further information _____

Naturschutzbund Deutschland (Mecklenburg-Vorpommern), August-Bebel-Straße 2, 0-2500 Rostock.
Mecklenburg-Vorpommern Fremdenverkehrsamt, c/o Fremdenverkehrsverband Rügen e.V., Hotel Nordperd, 0-2345 Göhren.
Nationalpark Jasmund, PF 22, 0-2355 Saßnitz.
Internationale Naturschutzakademie Insel Vilm, 0-2331 Lauterbach auf Rügen.

Sachsen-Anhalt _____

Stendal

MAGDEBURG

Schönebeck

Halberstadt

Wernigerode O

Bernburg

Dessau O

Quedlinburg

Halle

Eisleben

Nordhausen

0   50   100km

Sachsen-Anhalt in central East Germany reveals, in environmental terms, some of the best and worst features of the former DDR. There is wonderful, unspoiled countryside, a magnificent landscape heritage and some superb small towns and villages, but also despoiled areas close to huge old industrial plants, mines and power stations, many of them fired by lignite, which spew out poisonous fumes into the surrounding countryside and cover buildings with a darkening pall.

It is true to say that some of Sachsen-Anhalt's towns have actually suffered more damage since the Second World War than during it, as a result of being starved of essential funds for restoration and maintenance and through ugly postwar urban development. A bitter slogan sums up this state of affairs: 'Ruinen schaffen ohne Waffen' – creating ruins without weapons.

Things were not always so. Today's federal state of Sachsen-Anhalt with three million inhabitants and the ancient archbishopric of **Magdeburg** as its capital, has a great cultural heritage. The town of **Eisleben,** west of **Halle,** achieved renown as the birthplace of Martin Luther who was, in 1517, to nail his 95 theses on the cathedral door of **Wittenberg,** disputing the right of the Roman Catholic Church to sell indulgences or pardons and thus helping to precipitate the Protestant revolution. Composer Georg Friedrich Händel was born in the old salt town of Halle in 1685, and later followed his patron, the Elector of Hannover, England's George I, to London. In more recent times the town of **Dessau** achieved fame as the centre of the internationally renowned Bauhaus style of architecture in the '20s and '30s, reflecting a unity of art and technology, a movement which with its clean-cut modern lines still exerts an influence on both architectural styles and furniture.

In view of the industrial dereliction which may take years to be removed, protection of Sachsen-Anhalt's rural heritage is of paramount importance. Much of the finest landscape lies to the west, in the **Harz** mountains, a major part of which are in Sachsen-Anhalt.

Some of the villages of the Sachsen-Anhalt part of the Harz are of outstanding quality, largely untouched by the kind of modern tourist development and slick commercialisation which is sometimes all too evident in the West. Streets of old half-timbered houses in towns such as **Quedlinburg,** Harzgerode, Stolberg and Wernigerode have few equals in Germany. The danger is that after reunification, speculators and developers will transform this quality, ruthlessly destroying older town centres in order to construct modern hotels, fast-food chains, holiday villages, weekend retreats, department stores and high rise apartments of surpassing ugliness. In the western part of the Harz for example, every seventh house is a listed building; in Sachsen-Anhalt, with its superb architectural heritage, only one in a hundred is listed. A further concern lies with the impact of the car, and resultant demand for new car parks, improved roads, by-passes and new trunk roads.

Given the economic problems of the region, and the need for new jobs, the risk is that mass tourism could destroy an architectural heritage paradoxically protected by an inefficient centralised economy. Low land prices, together with easy road access from the overcrowded West and political demands for jobs at almost any price, could allow speculators and ruthless entrepreneurs to exploit a so far unspoiled landscape.

The Harz is a special area. The range of largely flat-topped, forested Mittelgebirge – medium-height mountains – that give the region its name lies midway between the Weser and the Elbe valleys and extends over three federal states, from the eastern end of Niedersachsen into Sachsen-Anhalt with a small southern section round **Nordhausen** actually in Thüringen. It is essential, given the future tourist pressures, that policies for the Harz treat the area as a single geographical region. It is encouraging to note that tourist authorities in East and West Harz – Sachsen-Anhalt and Niedersachsen – have already combined to promote the area as a whole.

The steep northern and western slopes of the Harz are noted for their high annual rainfall, yet Halle to the east has the lowest rainfall in Germany. Ancient mineral bearing rocks once gave great wealth. Although some silver, zinc and lead are still mined in the Rammelsberg area near Goslar in Niedersachsen, and there are copper deposits at Mansfeld on the eastern edge of the Harz, mining is no longer a major industry.

The Kranichsberg Bergwerk Museum in Lautenthal in Niedersachsen explores over a thousand years of Harz mining history whilst at **St. Andreasberg** the old silver mine can be visited. There is also a Heimatmuseum and large mineral collection there. Today St. Andreasberg is still a famous canary breeding centre, a slightly surprising venture which was introduced in the Middle Ages as an additional means of income by mineworkers from the Erzgebirge and Austrian Tirol, no doubt linked with the traditional use of canaries in mines as an early warning of lethal underground gas.

Silver mining in the Harz has left its particular mark on history. In the tenth century Heinrich I, the first Sachsen king, made the region the centre of his rule and an important focal point in the political and cultural life of the early Middle Ages. He built various castles on the edge of the Harz and founded the lovely towns of Goslar and Quedlinburg. It was the silver mines of the Harz which literally helped to swell Heinrich's coffers and expand his power, as well as those of the later Holy Roman Emperors who also used the palace at Goslar as their occasional centre. Geographically the area was also a natural defensive bulwark against the Magyar tribes from the east.

The timber industry is still of considerable importance in this heavily forested area. The landscape consists mainly of deciduous woodland covering the lower hills, punctuated by settlements – villages and farms – but with mainly coniferous forests, pine and spruce, covering the higher slopes, craggy outcrops, ridges and summits, which rise in many places to over 1,000 metres above sea level.

Because of its upland nature, the region has long been famed for its bracing climate and many natural mineral springs, which were the foundation for such well-known spas as Bad Harzburg, Bad Lauterberg (Germany's oldest hydrotherapy establishment), Alexisbad and Hahenklee. Bad Lauterberg is Germany's leading Kneippheilbad, which means it offers special hydrotherapy regimes, various physiotherapeutic and massage treatments, medical dietary regimes, and holistic treatments.

The Harz area is also famed for its associations with witches and old folk tales of buried treasure, amazing happenings, and sudden appearance of knights, robbers, spooks, witches and devils. On April 30th, Walpurgisnacht, the evil spirits of the underworld were said to meet on the summit of the Brocken mountain and the legend is perpetuated to the present day with various festivities. Goethe used the legend when he wrote his celebrated Walpurgisnacht scene in *Faust* and he also left numerous accounts in his diaries of how much the Harz landscape inspired him during frequent visits. Another famous visitor was Heinrich Heine, who wrote of climbing the hills and mountains and 'wandering through the awesome forests where the pine trees seemed to be shaking themselves out of their sleep and the fresh morning wind seemed to be brushing their dangling green hair'. Hans Christian Andersen also took a journey through the Harz in 1831 and wrote enthusiastically of his experiences. Other visitors included the poet Eichendorff, Carl Maria von Weber, composer of the romantic opera *Der Freischütz*, and novelist Theodor Fontane.

It is the landscape and natural beauty rather than literary associations that draw today's visitors to the Harz. It has a richly varied flora. The Oberharz is covered with bilberries and has a more Alpine character in contrast to the moorland where among the dwarf birch trees cotton grass, heather and sundew can be found. The Harz is also particularly known for the number of medicinal plants which grow there, such as arnica and the foxglove. The pharmacist Johannes Bürger who lived in nearby Wernigerode made the first effective drug there out of foxgloves known by its Latin name of digitalis. There is also a great variety of reptiles and amphibians in the marshy ground. Birds include various owl species, though the snowy owl and barn owl prefer the tree cover of the Unterharz. The rare peregrine falcon can sometimes be spotted, as can the more common crossbill. The chaffinch is the most common breeding bird of the Harz. In the tenth century Heinrich I was reputedly hunting these birds when the news was brought that he had been elected king.

The **Nationalpark Hochharz** was designated in September 1990 and consists of 5,868 hectares – 59 square kilometres – of Oberharz landscape, most of it in Sachsen-Anhalt. It includes the high granite area round the Brocken running from Wernigerode in the north to Bekennstein in the south. However, an equally large section in Niedersachsen is a protected nature reserve. As in other German national parks, it is managed in zones – a Kern or Ruhezone, zone 1, where no forestry work is allowed so that the woods develop naturally and access is only permitted on specified paths. Zone 2 is further sub-divided into a development zone or Entwicklungszone, zone 2a, which it is hoped to integrate step by step into the Kernzone, at the same time controlling the growth of coniferous trees and encouraging such deciduous trees as beeches which are suffering in the higher regions. In the Sanierungszone, zone 2b, a compromise has to be found between environmental protection and commercial forest use.

The Harz contains spruce woods, different types of upland moorland, crags, cliffs, swiftly flowing streams and a sub-Alpine meadow vegetation which is fairly rare in central Europe. The area round the Brocken contains the largest natural area of spruce in central Germany. The Niedersachsen part of the Harz has the larger share of moorland areas, but there are also a number round the Brocken itself which are important. Among the sub-Alpine vegetation, the Brocken anemone is one of the endangered species. The cliff areas are also covered in spruce and there are numerous streams. Since the national park is fairly small, it can easily suffer from undue visitor pressure unless sufficient stringent protective measures are taken.

The summit of the **Brocken**, at 1,142 metres above sea level the highest point in northern Germany, has, with its Goethe connections, long been a potent symbol for Germans. In the last forty years it was forbidden territory for both East and West Germans, lying as it did on the Iron Curtain boundary, covered by an ugly rash of radio and radar antennae belonging to both NATO and Warsaw Pact forces. The old Brocken summit hotel, served by railway, suffered the ultimate indignity of becoming a Russian army barracks.

Not surprisingly, it is a mountain every German wants to climb. It can be reached by five different paths in a sort of star-formation which are of varying difficulty. The Goetheweg, from Torfhaus, south of Bad Harzburg, where there is a huge car park, is a route made popular by the poet, his name linked to a small summit shelter, which is sadly overwhelmed by the radio station. It is already an enormously popular route; estimates are that over 250,000 people a year are visiting the summit and this could be only the beginning.

It is on the Brocken, more shockingly than anywhere else in Germany, that we have observed the horrific effects of Waldsterben, trees at that height being more vulnerable to pollution and in some cases reduced to mere skeletons. The causes of Waldsterben are complex and not fully understood, but it is assumed that industrial pollution and acid rain from both East and West Europe, including the UK, is largely to blame, together with the ever increasing emissions caused by road traffic. Dying woodland is not only an ecological disaster for the trees and their dependent species. Ultimately it presages the doom of mankind itself. Solving the particular problems of the Brocken, including its huge number of visitors, which threaten to erode even the Brocken's robust tracks, will be one of the greatest challenges facing the new park authority.

If you prefer to have a more 'green' and less crowded experience with gentle mountain climbing (the Harz offers hill walking rather than mountaineering), then the heights of the nearby Renneckenberg or the Ilsetal are to be recommended.

Before the establishment of the national park, apart from a small area in the Oberharz Naturschutzgebiet, the Harz was a major area for commercial forestry, which meant maximising wood production. Now the woods will be allowed to return to a more natural state. The over-abundant red deer will also have to be culled. The Nationalparkbeirat (the national park's advisory council) was established in 1991 with the aim of working out appropriate policies for tourism on the Brocken and developing the necessary field centres to deal with problems on the ground. It is hoped to make better use of potential helpers such as community service volunteers (eg. national service objectors), as well as other volunteers and students. By 1992 a Brockenmuseum is planned to be opened and by 1994 an information centre to allow the public to understand the concept of a national park. Already regulations limiting access are in force to protect the especially vulnerable nature of the environment. People are asked not to stray from the marked paths, plants and animals must not be damaged in any way, it is forbidden to camp or light fires or even smoke in the area and all water courses must remain unpolluted. Photography and filming for non-commercial use are allowed, but climbing rocks and cliffs is only permitted if they are on the routes of marked pathways and have been made safe for the public.

A leading voluntary body in the Harz region is the Harzklub which has already assisted the Nationalparkbeirat in waymarking paths and putting up interpretive boards.

The Harz is one of the finest areas of Germany for hill walking and it is possible to enjoy superb rambling throughout the seasons, provided the visitor is adequately equipped at all times for possible rough weather and difficult conditions in the Oberharz. There is heavy rainfall in the Harz and there can be frequent storms or sudden thick fogs round the ridges. Accommodation is plentiful in both Sachsen-Anhalt and Niedersachsen, and there is a choice of good waymarked paths and excellent public transport links, for example direct trains from Köln, Berlin and Hannover.

The Bund für Umwelt und Naturschutz Deutschland e.V. and the Harzer Schmalspurbahn und Brockenbahn e.V. have joined together to evolve an important and radical Verkehrskonzept (integrated transport concept) for the Harz region – Harz 2000. This ought to be a model for recreational transport development not only elsewhere in Germany, but in protected areas throughout the world. The goal of Harz 2000 is to develop a good network of public transport within the Harz area and to improve quiet recreational facilities in the Hochharz National und Naturparke. But it is also intended to limit environmental damage and the squandering of energy resources by restricting the use of the private car. Related goals include tough restrictions on building development and ensuring that the three responsible federal states of Niedersachsen, Sachsen-Anhalt and Thüringen work closely together to improve this very special European landscape for future generations.

One of the most fascinating legacies in the Harz of the DDR days are the Harzquerbahn and the Selketalbahn, a superb network of metre-gauge railways between Nordhausen, Wernigerode, Hasselfelde, Harzgerode and Gernrode, linking with standard gauge DB/DR lines to the north and south. Amazingly, these lines are still steam operated with a fleet of surprisingly modern and powerful locomotives, supported by diesels. One branch actually goes as far as the summit of the Brocken, though controversy rages as to whether the section of track which goes along the Goetheweg by the old boundary fence should have been reopened with consequent increase in visitor pressure.

Harz 2000 proposes to use this narrow gauge rail network as a centrepiece of their project. It is hoped to direct long distance car traffic away from the Harz and to build up an attractive package of measures by means of a Harzringbahn or loop railway round the Harz, with the network of Harz narrow gauge railways as the backbone of freight and passenger traffic within the area, both as a tourist attraction and for local use, supported by linking buses to complete the system. It is agreed by the authors of Harz 2000 that the railway must not only be preserved but also expanded where necessary both in the Harz and the Harz foreland, and till that is possible rail-linked buses are vital.

Traffic management measures would include high charges in all tourist car parks within the Harz to show a substantial price differential in favour of using the Harzringbahn and the public transport network. The income generated would be used to support and improve public transport. The creation of cycleways and the encouragement of cyclists and walkers are another priority. A combined tourist/walkers' ticket for trains and bus in the Harz is proposed. A Swiss-style 'takt' system of hourly frequency of linked buses and trains from the edge of the Harz into the central mountains and back is suggested. Such services will also benefit local people.

Such vision is vital if the Harz is not to disappear and be destroyed under an avalanche of cars and traffic pollution, demands for more car parks and road widening. The network could help achieve a careful balance between protecting the environment, transport needs, tourist and economic activities and recreational facilities. Such measures could, if implemented, become an internationally important pilot scheme for reducing the destructive effects of car-based tourism in the countryside of Europe.

Many of the small towns in the Harz have the suffix 'rode', meaning a forest clearing. Typical is **Wernigerode**, founded in the thirteenth century and with streets of beautifully preserved Fachwerkhäuser (half-timbered houses) of different colours. A particular feature of half-timbering in this region is a coloured decoration running along the beams between each storey.

Wernigerode is also the northern terminus of the 'Quirl', as the Harzquerbahn is affectionately known, where it connects with the standard gauge line to **Halberstadt** for Magdeburg. Although the line only took three years (1896-99) to build including the branch to the summit of the Brocken, it had taken thirty years to get permission for its construction from the Prussian government, which failed to see the economic necessity of a railway in the region to carry freight such as wood and minerals as well as tourists. When it was realised that narrow gauge railways actually cost a lot less to build than standard gauge, the Gernrode-Harzegerode line, the Selketalbahn came into being in 1880 and is actually the Harz's oldest narrow gauge railway. It is a delightful experience to ride behind one of these vintage steam locomotives as they pant their way portentously through the forest, calling at various villages and halts, and to hear their penetrating whistle as they round a bend or cross a level crossing.

Thale, which lies on the northern edge of the Harz at the entrance of the Bode valley, is not far from Halle, the former salt town. Surrounded by beech woods, it was laid out as a resort at the beginning of the last century with a network of footpaths into the Bode valley and was a favourite place for the writer Theodor Fontane. The rocky plateau of the Hexentanzplatz, the area where the witches were said to dance, can be reached by cable railway with views of the town, the precipitous rock faces of the Bode valley and the wooded mountainside of the northern Harz. The Walpurgis Halle is today a museum, while another attractive feature is the open air theatre founded in 1903 in a matchless setting. But there is no need to use the cable railway as there are well-signposted paths from Thale and over to Treseburg from the Hexentanzplatz, or on to

Allrode, Friedrichsbrunn or through the Bode valley back to Thale. The 10 kilometre footpath from Thale to Treseburg follows the course of the river through the narrow valley, which is enclosed by tree-covered rocks, bare slopes and steep mountain chasms. Rare fauna and flora led to the whole valley basin being designated a Naturschutzgebiet. Among rare plant species are saxifrage, daphne, Turk's cap lily, the blue Alpine daisy and hart's tongue fern, while bird species include the water ouzel and grey wagtail. Opposite the Hexentanzplatz is a 403 metre granite cliff known as the Roßtrappe, where legend has it that the beautiful princess Brunhilde, chased through the countryside by the knight Bodo, escaped him by spurring her horse and leaping across the deep chasm. To this day her steed's hoofprint can be seen in the rock. Bodo, however, was not so fortunate and was drowned in the river, called Bode after him. He was then transformed into an ugly hound, and compelled as a punishment to guard the princess' crown which had fallen off as she leapt across. It might be preferable to take the chair lift up to the Roßtrappe!

Stolberg, another beautifully preserved town in the east Harz, was also a centre for the mining of iron, copper, silver, zinc and gold. Thomas Müntzer, the contemporary of Martin Luther, was born here. Müntzer played a major role in the Peasant Wars. The town hall at Stolberg is a fine example of half-timbering and curiously has no staircase to the upper stories, which must be reached by a large flight of stone steps up the hillside on the outside of the building.

In nearby **Sangerhausen** by a sheltered valley known as the Goldene Aue – literally 'Golden Place' – is a Rosarium created in 1903 with about 6,000 garden roses, wild roses and an arboretum consisting of numerous shrub rose species; it is open from May to September. In the Rübeland there are limestone show caves with stalactites and stalagmites, with a depth of 68 metres in the Baumannshöhle with its crystal clear lake. The Hermannshöhle extends for 1,200 metres and the area known as the Kristalkammer is particularly splendid.

The **Kohlenstraße** was an ancient transport route used for charcoal from the Harz forests to the furnaces of Mansfeld southwards from the Harz, where copper was extracted. The actual route goes back to Bronze Age times, about 1800-700 BC, when the mining industry was in its infancy there. The charcoal and mining industries were mutually dependent and reached their peak in the sixteenth and seventeenth centuries, but the charcoal industry was still viable till the end of the nineteenth century. Much of the woodland never recovered and wood had to be imported from neighbouring Thüringen. In time, as wood supplies became exhausted, some furnaces had to be closed. Charcoal was used to smelt metal and large quantities were required for its production. The Kohlenstraßen were used to transport not just charcoal, but also hay, and on the return journey salt or copper ores were carried. Although coke was actually produced at Eisleben from coal as early as 1584, it unfortunately could not compete with charcoal manufacture because of transport problems. Bulk manufacture of coke had to wait for more than three centuries until the 1870s when the railway network made it viable. Smoking charcoal kilns were still a landscape feature in the 1950s. The whole job of firing, carbonising at a low temperature, adding water, cooling and taking out the finished charcoal needed great skill. The Kohlenstraße goes mainly through mixed woodland and makes an ideal walking, cycle or even ski-route.

Further east lies **Halle**, an important commercial, transport and industrial centre. Halle's salt deposits caused the site on the river Saale to be settled from prehistoric times and the salt was a major reason for the town's development in the Middle Ages and her growing wealth. In the second half of the nineteenth century the city evolved into a great industrial centre, but its geographical position has also helped to make the city an important transport centre. Historic buildings include the four-towered church of St. Marien where Martin Luther preached more than once. A Händel festival is held each June. The city also has a number of landscape parks and nature reserves nearby.

A particularly recommended walk from Halle is from the Peißnitz-Insel along the banks of the Saale river to the castle Burg Giebichenstein, from where there are also opportunities for river trips. On the south bank of Halle there is pleasant walking on the Rabeninsel, while to the west is the Dölauer Heide, which is actually an extended forest area and also ideal for walking. Not far away is the Heidesee where bathing is possible and bike and boat hire are available.

The river Saale can be further explored at **Bernburg** with its castle on the rocks, partly medieval and part Renaissance. The Süßen See region between Halle and Eisleben is an important conservation area and there are camping facilities, a sailing harbour, bathing beach and boat hire facilities nearby. About 12 kilometres northwards of Halle town centre is the 250 metre high **Petersberg** hill surrounded by extensive woodland and recreational facilities. There are waymarked paths to Burg Saaleck castle and the Rudelsburg castle set above the river Saale on limestone cliffs. The wine town of **Freyburg** lies in the lower Unstruttal surrounded by vineyards, meadows and fertile fields. Wine has been made here for about a hundred years and it is hoped to extend the area under cultivation considerably. Freyburg, with Lösnitz near Meißen on the Elbe, is Europe's most northerly winegrowing region.

Over 90% of the old city of **Magdeburg**, the capital of Sachsen-Anhalt, and birthplace of the composer Georg Philip Telemann, was destroyed by Allied bombing towards the end of World War II. Much has been rebuilt and restored, including the town hall, impressive state theatre and the cathedral, and the city is an important cultural, commercial and industrial centre. You can take 'Weiße Flotte' boat trips along the Elbe or visit the Rotehorn Kulturpark along the banks of the river, which unusually combines the role of traditional city park and outdoor museum including historic river paddle steamers.

An area of 430 square kilometres along the river Elbe south of Magdeburg (close to the town of Aken and served by a branch railway from Köthen off the Halle-Magdeburg line), incorporating the Steckby-Lödderitzer Forst Naturschutzgebiet, has been designated as the Biosphärenreservat Mittlere Elbe – the central Elbe biosphere reserve. The area contains the largest stretch of ancient riverine (waterlogged) woodland in Germany and is important for its beaver population which was on the brink of extinction, but thanks to conservation measures populations have recovered. However top priority is to reduce river pollution, and effluents particularly from the Elbe itself and its tributaries, so that habitats can avoid further degradation at times of high water.

The beaver and otter have been mercilessly hunted through the centuries as fish stealers. In fact the beaver is a herbivore and eats a large variety of plants, an adult beaver needing about 7.5 cubic metres of wood and plants annually. A beaver can fell trees up to 30 centimetres in circumference in one night and can gnaw through a 60 centimetre branch of soft wood.

Wood felled by the beaver usually grows again from the roots, so the beaver is really helping to pollard the woods. In addition beaver canals, ponds, and tunnels help to regulate the flow of the water. It has only recently been appreciated how much beavers' activities can actually help to protect the landscape. For a time there were only six beavers left in the Elbe between Magdeburg and Torgau. In 1920 the beaver colony and bird sanctuary were established at Stöckny and they became a nature reserve in 1961. By 1973 there were 400 beavers on the Elbe and four years later 600. New colonies were established at Mecklenburg in the Peenegebiet in 1976. The UNESCO research programme 'Man and the Biosphere' supported the programme for the Elbe waterlogged woodlands and in 1984, there were 430 different beaver colonies with 1,800 animals. There are now even beavers in the Oberhavelkanal and the Malzkanal in Berlin.

Letlinger Heide to the north, covering some 30,000 hectares, is an old hunting forest once belonging to the Brandenburg princes. **Tangermünde**, also on the Elbe, is a particularly attractive walled medieval town, a once important trading centre, with fine churches, a castle and half-timbered houses.

Further information

Landesfremdenverkehrsverband Sachsen-Anhalt e.v., Trothaer Straße 9, Nordbad, O-4050 Halle an der Saale.

Fremdenverkehrsverband Harz e.V. Geschäftsrasstelle Stolberg, Markt 8, O-4713 Stolberg.

Harzer Verkehrsverband e.v., Gildehaus, Markstraße 45, Postfach 16 69, D-3380 Goslar.

Interessengemeinschaft Harzer Schmalspurbahn und Brockenbahn e.v., O-4301 Rieder/Harz.

Nationalpark Hochharz, Aufbauleitung, Lindenall 35, 0-3700 Wernigerode/ Harz.

Brandenburg

0   50   100km

Löwenberg

Rathenow

Brandenburg

POTSDAM

Frankfurt an der Oder

Jüterbog

Wittenberg

Lübben

Cottbus

Brandenburg surrounds the city-state of Berlin. With just over 2½ million inhabitants, less than Berlin itself, it has **Potsdam** as its capital, a city situated on the southwestern perimeter of the new German capital. Brandenburg was never a real geographical or ethnic entity. Nowadays the Oder-Neiße rivers, with the old city of **Frankfurt an der Oder**, form the state's boundary with Poland.

In the seventeenth and eighteenth centuries immigrants arrived in Brandenburg from France, the Netherlands, Bohemia and the Salzburg area, joining the native Saxon and Sorb populations, the latter a Slav group in some areas who spoke their own language (sometimes also called Wendisch), which was widespread until the nineteenth century, and which still survives in pockets in both Brandenburg and Sachsen, with street signs, place names and even timetables being bilingual.

Brandenburg or Mark Brandenburg as the area stretching south of Magdeburg to the Oder is known, occupies a region of low-lying sandy plains and wide marshy valleys where the water often had to be drained before the land could be cultivated. It is a landscape shaped by the Ice Age. As the glaciers thawed, leaving huge moraines and meandering rivers, marshy ground and chains of lakes, they also left huge stones, many of which are to be found in the North Mark. The largest lake is the Scharmützelsee, famed for its clear water.

One of the most fascinating parts of Mark Brandenburg is the **Spreewald** region – much of it now forming the Spreewald Biosphäre Reservat. As its name implies, this is an area of forest, marsh and low-lying farmland drained by the river Spree and its many tributaries. It is some 75 kilometres in length but only 15 kilometres at its widest point. Channels drain into the Elbe and Oder rivers as well as into the Spree and its two major tributaries, the Maixe and Berste, and numerous lesser rivulets.

The Spreewald is divided into the smaller Unterspreewald and the larger and better known Oberspreewald. Originally access to the Spreewald was extremely difficult, but this has improved in recent times when much of the woodland was cleared for market gardening to serve the requirements of nearby Berlin, particularly for fresh vegetables.

Pickled gherkins, horseradish, sauerkraut, onions and plant extracts are amongst the best known Spreewald products. Many drainage channels were deepened, widened and cleared to form a network of shallow canals crossed by high wooden bridges, along which people and goods could be transported on narrow flat-bottomed barges called Kahne, traditionally propelled by the use of long poles rather like punts, though outboard motors are increasingly used these days.

Much of the Spreewald landscape is unique. There are wide water meadows, many of them flooded in winter after heavy rain or when the snow melts, dense mixed woodlands with alder and ash predominating, a network of rivers and canals, and small farms and villages. There are wonderful effects of light in the early part of the year as the bare trees form silhouettes framing the small settlements of mainly wooden thatched houses, while the lush overhanging vegetation along the narrow channels in the summer months almost turns them into tunnels of greenery. Not surprisingly, the Spreewald is a favourite destination for excursions from nearby Berlin, with good train services from Berlin to both Lübben and Lübbenau and linking buses into the interior. From **Lübbenau** in particular, there are superb walks along waymarked paths along old canalside dykes, going deep into the forest. Close to Lübbenau in the village of Lehde – Spreewald's Little Venice – there is a fascinating open air museum with traditional decorated Sorb farmhouses and farm implements, which can be reached either on foot or, during the summer months, by Spreewald Kahne from wharfs in the centre of Lübbenau. The area is particularly rich in wildlife. The whole of the Spreewald has game such as wild boar, deer, partridges, pheasants, while black storks, white storks and herons are to be seen in abundance, perhaps among the masses of water lilies that decorate the lakes and waterways.

On the southern edge of the Oberspreewald near the industrial centre of **Cottbus**, industry was quick to utilise the large deposits of lignite (brown coal), and there was a danger that this very special area with its fauna and flora might disappear. Fortunately the Spreewald's protected status as a biosphere reserve should safeguard its future.

Over the years, construction of dykes and ditches, artificial fishponds, and agricultural improvement in the Spreewald region resulted in the loss of much valuable plant and animal life. Now special areas of marsh – marshy biotopes – have been recreated in the dyke forelands. Water evaporates easily in the Spreewald, so that in order to prevent water shortages, fifteen dams have been built between Cottbus and Leibsch to regulate the watertable so that the plants in the Spree water meadows may get enough water to survive. Herons, ospreys, red kites, white-tailed eagles, cranes and marsh harriers are just part of the bird life that can be observed from a Spreewald Kahn. White storks, which have a habit of perching on dangerous overhead electric cables, with often fatal results for the bird, are now safeguarded by protective caps on the cables with an additional safe perch for the birds to use placed above them.

'Don't ever kill a mosquito,' says an old Spreewald proverb, 'or about a hundred will come to her funeral.' If you intend to come to the Spreewald during the summer or autumn this is a timely warning, as there are twenty different varieties of midge and mosquito in the area which makes a reliable insect repellent valuable if you plan woodland walks.

The Oberspreewald lies between Lübbenau in the southwest, Burg in the east and Alt-Zauche in the north, with its most beautiful section the Hochwald area. The Unterspreewald, the area between Lübben, Schlepzig and Groß-Wasserburg, is a large woodland area with unique plant and animal species and also with large areas of meadowland with a rich and varied pondlife, which includes rare dragonflies, storks, cranes and kingfishers. Guided walks are arranged by local tourist authorities, whilst self-guided routes offer detailed information about natural history from wayside interpretative boards. There are also bathing areas along the wooded banks of the Spreewald and plenty of opportunities for boat trips in the Spreewald barges or you can hire your own small rowing boat. Alternatively you can take a drive in the horse-drawn carriages known as Kremser or walk or cycle along 400 kilometres of marked paths, including a number of medium distance routes. There are numerous official camp sites on the edge of the Spreewald, though camping is not allowed within the protected area itself. Serviced accommodation is available in small hotels which are reopening in the area or in private houses.

Lübben makes an excellent centre to explore the Spreewald, even though no less than 80% of this historic town was damaged in the last war. It has a splendid and unusual large circular wrought iron sundial surrounded by flowerbeds which tells the time with amazing accuracy. The Salzgasse is a reminder of where the old Salzhaus stood in the times when all the inhabitants of the area had to buy their salt there by order of their liege lord. The baroque-style Ständehaus has a remarkable history including a narrow escape from the Prussian King Friedrich II (also known as Frederick the Great) who, in 1761 during the Seven Years War, was certainly not above plundering what was then a Saxon town. He demanded 20,000 Taler from the townsfolk of Lübben, which was to be paid to him in three days or he would burn the beautiful Ständehaus to the ground. He actually gave the order to do so to a certain Major von Marschall. The people of Lübben, who were poor, were unable to pay. Major von Marschall was so moved by the townspeople's predicament when faced with such extortion, that he paid the money out of his own pocket and saved the Ständehaus. His action was immortalised, using the name of Von Tellheim, in Lessing's play *Minna von Barnhelm*. The Wappensaal in the old Schloß has had its frescoes restored and the betrothal room with its delightful painted ceiling is an inviting place to sign any marriage contract.

Burg in the Spreewald is also part of the biosphere reserve and the eastern gateway to the Oberspreewald. Yellow and white waterlilies, swamp lilies, liverwort and woodruff, the latter used to colour the Berlin Weißbier green, grow here while storks, buzzards, kites and herons are numerous. Eels, pike and plaice can be fished and prepared in a delicious Spreewald sauce made of butter and cream. Other special dishes of the region include carp cooked in many ways, such as with a sauce made out of Lebkuchen, decorated with almonds and raisins, Saure-Brod-Suppe, a type of bread soup, and smoked trout. There is a definite delight here in mixing sweet and sour tastes in one dish.

This area has been inhabited for at least 5,000 years, as various tools made of metal or stone, a bronze wagon-like object and various human and animal bones testify. In the eighteenth century flax was grown in the area and a number of linen weavers settled in Burg, but this proved only marginally profitable and the handweavers were in time forced out by the weaving machines. Friedrich II colonised the area from 1763 by allowing settlers low interest rates on the land and freedom from military service. The land was very difficult to work and at times the colonisers were up to their waists in marshy ground. All the citizens had to fight against engulfing floodwaters, but attempts to interest the authorities in building dykes and canals were to no avail. They were forced to work together without any state help to erect the first bridges and paths. As late as 1842, when King Friedrich Wilhelm IV arrived in state at Burg on a fleet of barges, local people were still refused help. It took a further century before a government-sponsored dam was erected at Bräsinchen.

About a century ago, with the flurry of weekend excursionists on the then new railways, the Spreewalders discovered tourism as a new means of livelihood and starting punting visitors along the narrow channels. Fontane called the boatmen the Spreewald gondoliers. From 1899 till 1970 a narrow gauge railway called the Bimmelguste brought the tourists to Burg. Harbours were built and new roads, paths and bridges were constructed.

The current debate, however, is to ensure that mass tourism doesn't destroy this unique area, and that tourism only develops in ways which will support the area's conservation and local infrastructure and culture. Sanfter Tourismus – responsible tourism – is seen as the only way forward.

The Spreewald up to this very day is the centre of many old traditions like the Fastnacht or Zapust, its carnival in February. At Easter there is the Osterfeuer or Easter bonfire, eggs are intricately painted (a Sorb tradition), while harvest and Heimat feasts take place in autumn and summer.

The Sorb traditions are especially shown in the richly embroidered costumes such as headdresses, aprons and shawls worn by girls and women, mostly on special occasions. The wooden houses have a charac-teristic gable top decoration which looks like two stylised horseheads and there is a strong sense of community engendered by the teaching of Sorbisch in schools and its use as part of the Catholic church liturgy in the area. In the north the language is nearer Polish and in the south closer to Czech. Brandenburg's Sorb community in the Niederlausitz is clustered round the Lübbenau area, but the southern section or Oberlausitz is actually over the border in Sachsen round Hoyerswerda.

Brandenburg-Prussia and Potsdam are particularly associated with two Prussian monarchs, Friedrich Wilhelm I, the soldier king who also shaped much of the state administration and Friedrich II, the 'en-lightened despot' and friend of the great French philosopher Voltaire. Friedrich Wilhelm I helped to create the Prussian national stereotype with his insistence on punctuality and respectful obedience, fierce physical punishment for any infringements and general glorification of all things military – a phenomenon brilliantly satirised in later years by Heinrich Mann in *Der Untertan*. By the end of Friedrich Wilhelm's reign, no less than 80% of the state revenues were being spent on the army – even in peacetime. He was notorious for his elite corps of grenadiers who were among the tallest men in Europe.

Potsdam, set on an island in the Havel, is in the process of celebrating its millennium, though its real fame came much later when Friedrich der Große chose it as his main residence in preference to Berlin. This charming baroque town became therefore both the seat of growing Prussian power and a major cultural centre. In winter Friedrich lived at the Potsdam Stadtschloß, and in the summer at Schloß Sanssouci, built to his instructions. After the Seven Years War he gave orders for the building of Das Neue Palais with its huge reception rooms, richly decorated, including the famous Grottensaal with its thousands of semi-precious stones making a fitting setting for a great and successful European monarch. There is a charming theatre in rococo style which is still the venue for opera, theatre and concert performance. It was in the baroque-style Chinese teahouse in the Sanssouci grounds that Friedrich gave performances of his own and other people's music, including flute concerts, and received philosophers, especially Voltaire who had made his home in Potsdam. Although Friedrich II ruled from Potsdam and rarely graced Berlin, his successors preferred to return to the capital for the most part. It was only in 1945, at the end of the Second World War, that Potsdam once more was in the spotlight when the four Allied powers met to sign the Treaty of Potsdam in Schloß Cecilienhof. The room where the historic event took place is preserved and can still be viewed. In a final coda, the remains of Friedrich II have quite recently returned to Potsdam from the Hohenzollern family seat at Hechingen, in Baden-Württemberg, with much pomp, so that he could be buried as he wished with his greyhounds.

The **Märkische Schweiz** is a 147 square kilometre nature park that lies some 50 kilometres to the east of Berlin, and includes the town of **Buckow** and the Schermützelsee. It was here in Buckow that the dramatist Bertolt Brecht and his wife the actress Helene Weigel had two houses, the smaller one used by Brecht for his writing, while the ground floor of the larger house was for receiving friends and visiting writers. In what was originally the garage, the original waggon used on stage for the first production of *Mutter Courage*, Brecht's epic play about ordinary people caught up in the events of the Thirty Years War, can still be seen. The Märkische Schweiz has many typical features of the Ice Age-created Mark Brandenburg landscape – with low hills, heath, lakes, woodland, and rivers. In the woods over 800 species of plants have been recorded, and the area is also noted for its tall lime trees, growing to over 35 metres in height. Buckow and the Märkische Schweiz are easily accessible by train from Berlin via Strausberg and Müncheberg.

The **Scharmützelsee** to the south of the Märkische Schweiz lies among the Sarower hills and forms part of a nature reserve. The lake with an area of 1,500 hectares is linked to Berlin's waterway network through the Storkower Gewässer, another nearby lake. The towns of Pieskow, Silberberg, and the village of Saarow were Sorb settlements till about the year 1200. It is now a popular recreational area, within easy rail access of Berlin. Passenger boats on the lake link various settlements or provide scenic round trips.

A large area some 100 kilometres east of Berlin, along each side of the river Oder which forms the Polish border, and totalling some 32,884 hectares, of which 22,384 are in Brandenburg and 10,500 in Poland, is currently under consideration for an international Polish-German national park – the **Unteres Odertal**. Already a major conservation area with large nature reserves, but with an important cultural heritage, an appropriate designation is being sought.

This is an area of an internationally important wildlife habitat, mainly floodplain, containing water meadows, extensive reed and rush beds, streams and fragments of old riverine forest, whilst the valley slopes contain ancient deciduous woodlands with steppe vegetation on the southern slopes. It is also an area of little human habitation, only crossed by three public roads. On the Polish side the most valuable areas include the Zwischenstromland – floodplain areas – between the east and west Oder, whilst the marshy reed beds are the largest in Central Europe. Part of the reason for the area's richness as a natural habitat is derived from the fact that the original dykes to contain flooding fell into disrepair after World War II, particularly on the Polish side, allowing marshy conditions to return. However, river pollution is a continuing threat, as is the growth of fishing and motor traffic to the area, whilst the area's traditional dairy farming needs careful management in order that it does not impact on the wildlife reserves.

Bird species which inhabit the area include gooseanders, lesser white fronted geese, and Bewick's swans, whilst winter guests include rough-legged buzzards, merlins and white tailed eagles. Every autumn and spring huge flocks of geese and ducks, including white fronted geese, bean geese, shoveler duck, garganey and teal are to be seen. Among the fifty fish species are turbot and catfish, whilst rare plants include the pheasant's eye from the steppes, here at its most northerly point in Germany. Woodland species include varieties of oak, alder and limes.

Frankfurt an der Oder, a former Hansa town, was already an important transshipment port for the Baltic by the Middle Ages. A university was founded in the early sixteenth century, which counted amongst its students the writer Heinrich von Kleist, author of *Die Marquise von O*. Its superb gothic Hallenkirche is being rebuilt and its splendid late gothic style town hall has been restored. Other celebrities connected with the town include Theodor Fontane and Friedrich Schinkel who were both born at Neuruppin, the former immortalising Brandenburg in his four volumes written over a ten year period called *Wanderungen durch die Mark Brandenburg* and in many novels, while the latter was an architect famed for his buildings on a grand scale and his detailed drawings and stylish furnishing designs.

Theodor Fontane described the area around the **Werbellinsee** and the **Grimnitzsee** north of Berlin as being 'unsurpassingly lovely'. The Werbellinsee, easily reached by train from Berlin via Eberswalde on the Fürstenberg line, is 10 kilometres long and about 1 kilometre wide and has an artificial channel to the Grimnitzsee with a number of well-marked paths through the Werbellinsee-Grimnitzsee Landschaftsschutzgebiet itself and into the Uderheide nearby. At Chorin, a converted Cistercian monastery, is a museum and concert hall. There is even a boat service from Eberswalde to the Werbellinsee along the Finowkanal.

Part of this area lies within the largest biosphere reserve in Germany, the Schorfheide-Choriner Endmoräne Reservat which seeks to protect no less than 125,800 hectares of unspoiled landscapes in Brandenburg, in areas which show so many classical features created by the late glacial period in North Germany with forests, small scattered lakes and streams providing an unspoiled habitat for thousands of otherwise threatened species including black storks and eagles. The area also demonstrates what are essentially medieval agricultural patterns. There are proposals to make part or whole of the area a national park.

The **Liepnitzsee** in the Bernau area just to the north of Berlin is one of the most attractive lakes in the whole region. It is divided by an island called Der Große Werder, with a camping place on the northern bank of Der Kleine Werder. There is a splendid walk along the lake shore of about 8 kilometres and even on the hottest summer day, the beech trees offer plenty of shade. Another possibility is to take the old trade route, a country road which leads from the S-Bahn Bernau to Wandlitz and then goes through the Bernauer Heide, a mixed woodland rich in berries and fungi.

About 60 kilometres west of Berlin is the old city of **Brandenburg** that gives its name to the state. Founded by the Sorbs in the tenth century, Brandenburg grew to prominence in the seventeenth century through the activities of Huguenot settlers, but lost political importance to Berlin, becoming a major industrial centre in the nineteenth and early twentieth century. Though it suffered heavy war damage, some fine buildings remain, including the cathedral and part of the city walls.

About 30 kilometres north of Brandenburg is **Rathenow** (trains from Brandenburg and Berlin), which lies in Havelland, an area noted for its wild animals and water fowl. Around an area known as the Bolchow, great reed warblers, marsh harriers and bitterns have their habitat and storks, herons and cranes can also be observed. In spring and autumn huge groups of migrating birds cross over the area flying south, and an incredible 80,000 to 90,000 geese have been seen in one day. Visitors are asked to keep to the marked paths in order to disturb the birds as little as possible. Friedrich Wilhelm I and Friedrich II drained this Rhin-Havel-Luchs area in order to develop an industrial base. Otto von Bismarck was born in nearby Schönborn. There are plenty of opportunities for walkers or cyclists to wander or ride through wide forests, or to bathe in the lakes or hire a boat on the Havel and perhaps fish in one of her tributaries. Rathenow was also famed for its production of spectacles ever since the theologian Auguste Duncker invented a way of grinding lenses in 1800. The town is still known for its quality optics production. Friedrich II promoted the manufacture of cloth by founding a spinning centre here. It is a particularly good town for cyclists with the Stadtforst (town forest) being especially popular, and reached along marked cycleways. There are also paths round the nearby Wolzensee and across the Königsheide for both walkers and cyclists and a popular walk is to the summit of the Dachsberg with a view of the old town of Millow. There are also facilities for horse riders.

The great bustard is to be found in the Buckow area, a great rarity in Europe and normally only seen in Spain and Hungary. Its habitat is carefully protected. One of the oldest post windmills in the Havel area and dating back from about 1569 is to be found at Bamme; it is the centre of a festival in August. Also in August the inhabitants of Stöll celebrate the feat of Otto Lilienthal, an early gliding pioneer, who around a hundred years ago achieved a continuous 350 metre flight through the air.

The Naturschutzgebiet **Rietzer See** southeast of Brandenburg has a lookout point from where much of the lake can be observed. It's a shallow lake in a low lying part of the Potsdammer Havelgebiet. There are sedges which grow underwater on the south bank and it is a paradise for the various species of warbler and numerous other water loving birds. Migrating white fronted geese and the bean goose gather here up to 15,000 strong and the greylag goose is becoming a more common sight. The large number of geese cause a pollution problem in the lake and special protective measures are being taken in 1993 to deal with this so that the great variety of fish in the waters is not affected.

Further information ─────────────────────────────────

Fremdenverkehrsverein Spreewaldkreis Lübben e.V., Informationsbüro, Lohnmühlengasse 12, O-7550 Lübben.

Berlin

Berlin, with its symbol a black bear, is an astonishing city.

It is impossible to forget how central Berlin has been not only to German but to recent European history. It has been described as the 'Brennpunkt' or 'flashpoint' of Europe.

The decision by the East German government in 1961 to partition the city with a high concrete wall protected by searchlights, wires and guns, crossing streets and even gardens and keeping apart families and friends, has left its scars. Suddenly, on November 9th 1989 it all became a memory. After the bulldozers came the touts, with chunks or small pieces of wall exchanged for cash. A great swathe of derelict land across the city survives, soon to be filled with new development as the city adjusts to its old status as Germany's capital.

As a microcosm of a once divided Germany, reunited Berlin still suffers problems. For one thing much was duplicated by the two rival city and state authorities – opera houses, concert and exhibition halls, art galleries, museums. Many of the older public buildings, with the exception of the Reichstag (parliament building) were in the Eastern sector, duplicated by modern versions in the West. Even more dramatic perhaps was the contrast between the West's glitz and brashness typified by the bright lights of the Kurfürstendamm, the premier shopping and entertainment street and the communist state rhetoric of the Alexanderplatz and Palast der Republik.

Berlin is a city famous for its theatres, its cabaret, its visual arts. It can, at the same time, be stylish and vulgar, vigorous and decadent. Pub and café culture flourishes, often with music, live or disco, where you can sit all day over a coffee or one of the distinctive Berlin 'Weißbier' – usually served either red (with raspberry) or green (with woodruff, a herb). You can still find old Bohemian and Slavic areas with leafy squares, old cafés, churches and vast tenements, many of them now filled with immigrants, particularly Turks. There are inevitable downtown areas and fairly rough slums where you should not go alone, especially at night. Yet there are also gentle, traditional old Berlin suburbs with gracious, decaying houses and apartments along long leafy avenues, many of them traffic calmed to reduce the flow of cars which clog the main arterial routes into the city centre.

You'll also find amazingly unspoiled semi-rural areas, even entire villages, on the outskirts, villages such as Alt-Mariendorf, Alt-Britz or Alt Buckow, all within easy reach of Berlin's excellent transport system with interweaving U-Bahn (underground), S-Bahn (suburban electric railways), trams (former East Berlin only), buses and even boats. One real joy of Berlin is the fleet of British-style doubledeck buses, from the top of which it is possible to enjoy superb views of the city. Boat services operate across the Havel lake and there is a waterbus service along the river Spree between Jannowitzbrücke and Köpenick and Müggelsee. A variety of bargain tickets that can be bought at machines or kiosks gives you a choice of reduced price travel on all Berlin transport – for example the multi-journey travel ticket (Sammelkarte), an unlimited travel dayticket (Tageskarte) or the tourist ticket (Touristen Karte) available for two or more days.

But you don't have to travel to the outskirts to find green activity in Berlin. In Central Berlin is to be found one of the most vigorous flourishing 'alternative' cultures in Europe, where people, often enjoying tolerance unknown in other parts of Germany, are actively encouraged to experiment with new lifestyles, including different social, economic and ecological models. The Netzwerk-Selbsthilfe e.V. (selfhelp network) actually exists as a funding organisation to help alternative groups, whilst at the Fabrik für Kultur, Sport und Handwerk in Viktoriastraße in the Kreuzberg area, there is a remarkable cultural centre and workshops for alternative artistic groups. In and around such inner city areas as **Kreuzberg, Schönberg** and **Wilmersdorf** are a variety of collectives and groups supporting conventional shops, workshops, co-operatives, studios, radical newspapers, magazines reflecting everything from alternative political systems to macrobiotics, crafts, peace studies, feminism, anti-racialism, vegetarianism and veganism.

Such things are beyond the scope of this guide to explore in detail, as are the wealth of art galleries, museums, theatres, cinemas, conference centres, shops, cafés and restaurants which attract most visitors.

Yet if you are visiting or staying in Berlin, you'll find it one of the physically 'green' capitals in Europe, not just in the sense of the large formal central parks such as the Tiergarten, the Botanischer Garten or the gardens of the Charlottenburg palace (there are over sixty parks in Berlin), but in terms of informal green areas and walkways, gardens, bits of informal countryside. You'll find leafy avenues and walkways along the banks of the river Spree for example, and trees in every square, and allotments (Schrebergärten) extending into the outer suburbs. Unlike British allotments, German Schrebergärten are rarely just used for vegetable growing, but often contain flower gardens, lawns, and even a small cabin or lodge where people can spend a few nights as a summer retreat. German city dwellers love their gardens as much as the English, though it is the windowboxes and the Schrebergärten that often have to compensate for the lack of a suburban garden.

Even more significant than the city parks, perhaps, are the vast areas of lakeland and woodland within the city-state's boundaries. About a third of the city is still forest, lake, park or meadowland.

Berlin is built along a shallow, serpentine valley of the river Spree across what was formerly low-lying marshland. Its rising population increasingly demanded land for cultivation and Dutch experts were invited to construct efficient drainage systems which dried out the terrain and changed to some extent the character of the landscape. As the level of the water table changed again over the years and woodland took over, there was a danger that all the swampland areas would be destroyed and much fauna and flora, especially amphibious animals, virtually disappeared.

It was then decided to 'renature' the **Spandauer Forst**, to try to return it to what it once was and to remove superfluous tree cover. The moor soaked up the water fed into it like a sponge and various moorland plants such as the cotton grass plant again appeared, as well as insects and birds; thus demonstrating the success of the project. Gravel pits such as in the Luchland area are also a useful refuge for endangered birds, reptiles, amphibians and insects. Nowadays lapwings, short eared owls, various birds of prey and geese can be observed. Great reed warblers, yellow hammers and barred warblers can also be spotted. The various species of woodpecker delight in the area to the south with its suggestion of 'Urwald' or natural forest. Many endangered species in the plant and animal world find their ideal habitat here. The mixture of sandy and limestone grassland and the variety of damp ground and water meadows attract numerous butterflies.

The city has many lakes. The largest of these, the **Havel**, includes the **Wannsee**, which has Europe's longest inland bathing beach, for which the sand has had to be specially imported from Schleswig-Holstein, which is crowded on any fine day.

One delightful feature of the Wannsee area is that it is so accessible by public transport, for example from the S-Bahn station where linking boats take you across the lake, stopping at various landing stages to give a choice of woodland walks around the edge of the lake. It is now possible to continue into Potsdam (see Brandenburg) by boat or on foot. The **Pfaueninsel** is a remarkable island nature reserve in the Havel, noted for its historic buildings and its wildlife, though it gets so busy in the summer months that little wildlife is to be seen.

Other popular lake areas with attractive lakeside walks into adjacent woodland include the Grunewaldsee, the Schlatensee, the Kummesee, the Tegeler See and the Müggelsee.

Berlin's woods are beautiful and justifiably famous. They are mostly mixed woods, but with some dominant areas of beech, pine or fir where you are likely to see a variety of woodland birds including black and spotted woodpeckers. That such areas were preserved at a time when West Berlin was a small, enclosed island within a hostile DDR owes much to the foresight of the city authorities, but also to the need, as in and around such areas as the Spandauer Forst, to ensure the city retained unpolluted water supplies.

A favourite area for recreation is **Grunewald** in the southwest of the city, accessible by S-Bahn, with some exceptionally fine forest walks. Grunewald was already a protected landscape after the Second World War and for a number of years the development of the area for quiet recreational purposes rather than commercial forestry has been the main objective. Deciduous trees, especially oaks, are planted to 'soften' the monoculture of the coniferous trees. Owls, woodpeckers and dippers are among its inhabitants. Once again as the trees threatened to take over the terrain, the moorland was flooded with water from the Teufelsee so that it could be soaked up. Wheatears and woodlarks, butterflies and frogs were able to breed freely. The problem is that the Teufelsee area is also a popular bathing spot for Berliners, who pour into the vulnerable swampy ground as well as into the sandy drier areas and even into the nature reserves themselves.

Close by, on the banks of the Teufelsee, is the Berlin Ökowerk Natur-Schutzgebiet which includes part of a former Berlin waterworks. The centre has exhibitions and lectures, seminars and guided walks take place led by experienced staff. A regular magazine of Berlin natural history, _Ökowerk_, is produced.

Gatower Felder is another particularly interesting area. From Bronze Age times this area was under cultivation with cereal crops. Drainage ditches were in time covered over and once again the original landscape had all but disappeared. Through careful management the land has been to some extent returned to its former state and nearby meadows included in new protected zones. The renaturing in 1980 seems to have succeeded as there are now 132 plant species in the Hüllepfuhl area. Apart from the fields under cultivation with rye, barley, wheat, potatoes, carrots, cabbage and lettuce and many kinds of culinary herbs, there are 430 wild flower varieties not only in ditches, hedges, on the field edges and in the meadows, but also in the fields. Fungi, insects, butterflies and birds were endangered in the recent past as pesticides and artificial fertilisers were used to get rid of undesirable weeds for the sake of greater profit. The felling of trees, bushes and copses particularly affected partridges and other locally breeding birds. Flower-rich meadows are now reappearing, so that once again poppies, cornflowers and other attractive species are available to the returning butterflies.

Over 400 varieties of flower, 296 different butterfly species, numerous insects, amphibians and at least 150 varieties of bird have been recorded in the Flughafensee Vogelschutzreservat in the **Jungfernheide**. This original huge forest area was gnawed away in time by the growth of the Berlin and Spandau suburbs. The world 'Heide' is here a misnomer for forest, though there are areas of heather which were encouraged when beekeeping was an important industry. In the seventeenth and eighteenth century it was a favourite hunting area of the Berlin court since it was so rich in wild game. Military installations, flats, factories and suburban sprawl encroached. Many of the reedbeds also disappeared under tarmac, including motorways and airport runways. But the Flughafensee is now an area which is environmentally protected. Conflicting claims of bathers and ecologists have had to be amicably settled, to such good effect that in one area of about ten hectares, no less than 226 flower species have been recorded.

Berlin even has an area of dunes, around **Heiligensee**. Tar manufacture in the seventeenth century was responsible for the loss of much woodland in the area, destruction added to in more recent times when it was used by French troops for manoeuvres. However it now hosts up to 325 plant species, of which 70 are regarded as rare in North Germany. In the drier grassy areas this includes species of lily. Rare swamp plants in the wetter areas, as well as 133 kinds of butterfly have been recorded.

No mean achievement within the boundaries of a densely populated city-state of over three million people!

Further information _____

An excellent guidebook *Natur um Berlin* by Erich Hobusch and Udo Schwarzer (Arani Press, 1990) details a number of public transport-based walking and cycling trips, mostly with a natural history interest, within the city and into its outskirts, including Brandenburg.

Berlin tourist office: Verkehrsamt Berlin, Europa Centre, D-1000 Berlin 30. **Informationszentrum Berlin** (Berlin information centre), Hardenbergstraße 200, D-1000 Berlin 12, helps to organise educational tours and trips to Berlin, mainly for groups.

Sachsen

The federal state of Sachsen (Saxony) with 4.9 million inhabitants is bordered by Czechoslovakia to the south and Poland to the east. The state is surrounded by four other German states – Brandenburg to the north, Sachsen-Anhalt and Thüringen to the west and a small section of Bayern to the southwest. Sachsen's eastern borders in particular reflect an important part of her heritage and perhaps help to explain her cultural richness. The cities of Leipzig and Dresden, Sachsen's capital, have both played a significant role in European history.

Leipzig is for most people linked with the name of Johann Sebastian Bach (1685-1750) who, though he was born in Eisenach in Thüringen, lived with his vast and talented family in Leipzig for much of his professional life. His statue stands outside the St. Thomaskirche where he was cantor – director of music – from 1723 until his death in 1750. But Bach's contribution to the musical life of Leipzig was by no means unique. The baroque composer Georg Friedrich Telemann (1682-1767) had twenty of his operas performed here at Leipzig's oldest opera house, the Brühl. The opera house and famous Gewandhaus concert hall (now rebuilt) have seen the first or early performances of many great works. Composers such as Robert Schumann, Richard Wagner (born in Leipzig in 1813), Franz Liszt, Richard Strauss, and writers such as Goethe and Lessing were drawn here, many of them frequenting the famous tavern the Kaffeebaum, which as its name suggests was serving coffee from as early as 1694.

Leipzig has also long been a noted centre for training aspiring musicians, with a famous boys' choir and a school of music. The celebrated Leipzig Gewandhaus orchestra under its current director (and noted supporter of the reform movement) Kurt Masur, reflects the strength of its living tradition.

But many of the artists and intellectuals who saw Leipzig as their spiritual home would weep to see the damage done to their once beautiful city not only by war, but by insensitive development since that time by city authorities who, regarding fine architectural styles as 'bourgeois', erected utilitarian concrete monstrosities in some of the city's finest squares. Not that such a failure of imagination was unique to communist regimes – capitalist Britain has countless such examples.

Nevertheless, some beautiful buildings and delightful parts of this ancient city, including old courts and squares, remain to be explored on foot. The city also has a good tram system so that you can get around without a car. The railway station, built in 1913 on a grandiose scale, claims to be Europe's largest railway terminal with twenty-six platforms, making it a splendid place to arrive at. The richly decorated Altes Rathaus (old town hall) is another splendid building, as is the Altern Börse in front of which stands a statue of Goethe. In the Mädler Passage is a basement pub, better known as Auerbach's Keller where in Goethe's *Faust* Mephistopheles made Faust ride out on a barrel of wine.

Not to be missed is the Nikolaikirche. Its grubby and battered exterior, still with the odd bullet hole, hides something special. Within is a beautiful baroque interior of white columns and carved wooden pews, green palm fronds at the apex of its slender columns and dusty pink decorated ceiling. In the 1980s this was the church that became the focal point of dissidents in Leipzig and the whole of East Germany against the Honecker-led communist dictatorship. It was here that Christians and intellectuals came, lighting candles as symbols of both faith and protest, and demonstrating each Monday to bring together the forces of New Forum, which were to develop into massive nationwide peaceful protest and defiance – leading to the ultimate downfall of the regime.

This all reflects Leipzig's long tradition of being at the centre of new ideas. It has the oldest trade fair in the world, which transforms the whole of the city centre and not just the exhibition site itself. Its university was founded as early as 1407 and the first book was printed here in 1481, while Johann Breitkopf began printing music here in 1754. Today this tradition is continued with the annual printing of 20 million books. The Allgemeine Deutsche Arbeiterverein, a forerunner of the SPD, was founded here in 1863.

Dresden, the great city on the river Elbe, was before World War II known as the Florence of the North. Much, however, of this beautiful baroque city was destroyed in February 1945 by British and American bombs in a horrific attack resulting in a terrible fire storm causing the deaths of 35,000 people, many of them refugees. The 83-year-old writer and Nobel Prize winner Gerhart Hauptmann, as he looked on the ruins, was moved to declare, 'Wer das Weinen verlernt hat, der lernt es wieder beim Untergang Dresdens' – 'Whoever has forgotten how to cry, will remember how when he sees Dresden's extinction'. Richard Strauss, seeing the devastated city and the ruins of his beloved Semperoper (the opera house), composed his great late masterpiece 'Metamorphosen' as an elegy for a destroyed civilisation.

As in Leipzig, the city authorities were faced with an impossible task to rebuild from the ruins, and whilst much has been restored, including the famous Zwinger and the Semperoper, much remains to be done. Some astonishingly ugly buildings have been allowed to blot out the skyline and broad, empty boulevards were created. Once a symbol of grandiose communist civic pride, such areas are now ironically taken over by those pioneers of the free market economy, carpet and cigarette sellers and cheap clothes stalls. The Frauenkirche in the city centre has been deliberately left as a stark reminder of the city's destruction.

The Zwinger, Dresden's most famous and beautiful baroque building, erected in 1710-1732 during the reign of Prince Augustus der Starke, is an example of baroque architecture at its most delicate. It now houses Dresden's major art collections. Dresden was the centre of German expressionist art and the home of the early twentieth century group of painters calling themselves 'Die Brücke'. It is Augustus der Starke to whom Dresden owed much of the city's finest architecture. He turned the famous Grünes Gewölbe (green vaults) in his Schloß into a museum as early as 1723. The magnificent Semperoper, whose conductors in the past included Carl Maria von Weber, Richard Wagner and Richard Strauss, is now once again achieving an international reputation.

You can eat extremely well in both Leipzig and Dresden. The whole of Sachsen is famous for its hearty soups and good cuisine. The potato salad is a mixture which can contain sausage, vegetables, fish, apples, gherkins and the like. Kartoffelpuffer are light puffy potato cakes made of grated potatoes mixed with flour and onions and fried and then served with sugar and apple purée. Quarkkeulen, a variation, are made from a mixture of boiled potatoes, curds, flour, sugar and raisins and then baked. Carp is braised and served with red cabbage and potatoes in the Vogtland, while at Christmas Dresdener Stollen, a log-shaped rich yeasty mixture containing fruit and nuts, and Pulsnitz Pfefferkuchen or gingerbread are important parts of the feast. Eierschecke is a delicious cake filled with sweet curd served at coffee time.

Dresden has many green areas and parks including the lovely Große Garten and areas of public woodland. It is also an excellent centre, with an extremely good local rail network, for exploring much of Sachsen's exceptionally fine countryside.

Moritzburg can be reached by a delightful narrow gauge steam railway (not a preserved tourist route but a regular train service) which leaves Radebeul Ost on the electrified Dresden-Meißen line and steams its way, bell ringing, through suburbs, gardens and forests to Moritzburg. It's about twenty minutes walk through the town to the Schloß, but an excellent day's walk can be enjoyed by returning from one of the intermediate stations on the line between Moritzburg and Radebeul or Radeberg, the line's terminus. Special trains, the even older 'Traditionszug' with its preserved steam engines and coaches, are sometimes operated. Alternatively, the area can be reached by taking one of several Dresden tram routes through the suburbs to their outward termini. There are a large number of marked paths in the Moritzburg area including the Moritzburg Ringweg and the Lößnitzerhohenweg.

The Schloß Moritzburg is surrounded by the Moritzburger Teichlandschaft, an area of woods, parkland, meadows and small ornamental lakes and pools where over 200 varieties of bird can be observed, as well as many rare plant species such as arnica. There is also a deer reserve. Schloß Moritzburg is a handsome eighteenth century baroque palace, a former hunting lodge, painted in ochre and white and topped with four round towers. It contains a museum which includes period examples of porcelain, furniture and ornaments.

The area around the Frauenteich was declared a protected landscape in 1954. Sedges, marsh violets, mosses, reeds, bullrushes and water lilies can be seen. The black headed gull, various types of duck, reed warblers, white storks, the bittern and the lapwing find this a favourable habitat.

Northwest of Dresden, in the sheltered Elbe valley, wine has been grown for a thousand years round the old town of **Meißen**. Dominated by its late gothic cathedral on a high bluff above the river, the town has some quite magnificent architecture, much of it dating from Renaissance times. Particularly splendid is the town hall, while the Frauenkirche had the first porcelain carillon or chime of bells in the world. There are many superb baroque houses and shop doorways. The narrow streets and steep alleyways of the old town are a delight to explore on foot, with views across the river over a mosaic of terracotta pantiles which gives the town an almost Tuscan look.

Meißen is renowned for its porcelain manufacture which was actually first established in Dresden, but moved to Meißen in the mid eighteenth century when it was felt that it would be easier to guard the secret of the composition of the fine porcelain there. Ever since then Meißen, with its trademark of two blue crossed swords, has been a byword for high-quality handpainted porcelain. The works still produce an enormous variety of articles and some of the original exquisite designs like the famous 'onion' design are just as popular as ever. Guided tours of part of the works including the showrooms are arranged on most workdays. Enquire locally for times.

Meißen can be reached by direct train from Dresden (with a long walk over the bridge over the Elbe into the old town spoiled by the fumes of snarling traffic) or, preferably, during the summer months, by Weisse Flotte boat services along the Elbe. There is also some surprisingly attractive countryside around the town with hills, old villages and at Grabe Gustav an old mine open to the public.

If you take the boat along the Elbe from Dresden downstream you soon reach an area of spectacular beauty, the **Sächsische Schweiz Nationalpark** – Saxon Switzerland.

The Sächsische Schweiz or the Elbsandsteingebirge is one of Germany's newest national parks, covering 93 square kilometres on both sides of the upper Elbe valley. It consists of a series of gigantic crags and cliffs of weather-worn sandstone, towering more than 100 metres above the river valley and penetrated by deep rocky chasms and romantic gorges. Much of its splendour comes from the contrast between these dramatic crags and the quietly flowing Elbe below, which gives a sense of space and grandeur almost without parallel in northern Europe.

The Sächsische Schweiz was formed by the Elbe and her tributaries in the Cretaceous period. Wooded plateaux frame the steeply etched Elbe valley, which is broken up in the south by various striking rock formations. A number of basalt formations in some areas indicate a volcanic origin and these have a more fertile type of vegetation, with deciduous mixed woods on the Große Winterberg. Only fir and pine trees grow in the sandier areas or the damper terrain of the valley gorges or chasms, where cold air and snow seem to remain for considerable periods and the plants therefore have a more Alpine character. The higher, drier and sandier sandstone summits have sporadic spruce cover. A particular speciality is the rare labrador tea plant, a strong-smelling, evergreen leathery plant with white flowers and rusty young shoots, known as the 'Sächsische Edelweiß'. Various mosses, lichens and fungi occupy the shadier sheltered hollows whilst ferns and goat's beard spirea prefer the sunnier areas. Trout, otter and dippers share the swift flowing streams with the occasional kingfisher. In the woods are black woodpeckers, stock doves, owls and bats, with black storks near the Czech border.

From the thirteenth century the hard sandstone from this region was used for building and it became famous throughout Europe. It was particularly popular in the eighteenth century when the many quarries along the Elbe provided high quality building stone, transported by river, for such famous buildings as the Dresden Zwinger and Berlin's Brandenburger Tor.

As more intensive use was made of the woodland in the sixteenth century, the most accessible deciduous woodland was superseded by the more profitable, fast-growing coniferous woodland. Modern commercial forestry made further inroads even in less accessible woodland areas. Deer and wild boar spread unchecked through the woods causing much damage. Reversal of this damage to the natural environment will be an early objective of the new national park.

The area was first popularised by two Swiss artists, Anton Graff and Adrian Zingg who named it the Sächsische Schweiz in memory of their homeland. The writer Heinrich von Kleist described it as 'a moving sea of rocks which are formed with as much beauty as if the angels had created them while playing in the sand'. The romantic painter Caspar Friedrich, obsessed with crags, mist and lonely peaks, found some of his greatest inspiration here.

The tourist industry began in embryo when towards the end of the eighteenth century numbers of guides and bearers started to carry aristocratic tourists over the rocks and through the gorges in special sedan-style chairs in order to view the 'romantic' scenery.

The wave of tourists to the Sächsische Schweiz increased considerably in the last century and now there are about two million annual visitors in a relatively small area. Although tourist walkways have been built among the rocks, they are unobtrusively integrated into the rocky landscape, preserving a balance between safety and allowing public access. The Bastei Brücke is a dramatic artificial bridge erected last century over a wide chasm and provides a superb panoramic viewpoint, with the Elbe below with its boats and barges, threading its way through a gigantic loop like a long, silver grey ribbon. Certain of the sheer rock walls can also be climbed by the serious climber, with special permission and normally a trained guide.

The Sächsische Schweiz is best reached either by boat or by one of the frequent electric trains from Dresden to Stadt Wehlen or Kurort Rathen, from where ferries cross the Elbe under the towering cliffs to the small resorts from where a superb network of waymarked footpaths through deep, narrow gorges and deciduous woodland leads up to the Bastei.

Other good centres are Königstein, which has a remarkable hillfort, Bad Schandau and Schönau on the Czech border.

There is every chance that this national park will soon become a cross-boundary national park with the Böhmische Schweiz in Czechoslovakia, creating a huge area of protected landscapes where such threatened species as the lynx can flourish. This is an exciting concept and similar to initiatives in eastern Bayern with the Böhmerwald and Bayerischewald.

South of Dresden, running along both the Czech and Bayern borders, lies the **Erzgebirge** – the ore mountains – an area of rich and fascinating countryside. The region received the name from the mining of minerals, especially silver, discovered here in the Middle Ages. Small towns and villages, some of them extending for some distance along narrow valleys, served the once intensively active mining industry.

The Osterzgebirge to the east, with a region of 440 square kilometres, is a large protected landscape area. It has contrasting woodland, both forests and scattered hilltop copses, cultivated and uncultivated land. The bedrock of red gneiss creates a reddish, fertile soil. Red deer are common, and the otter is still found. Notable too in the area are grass snakes, the rare blue lettuce plant and chickweed wintergreen.

The Osterzgebirge's closeness to Dresden makes it an easy day's excursion by train from the city. A path from **Heidenau** goes through the Müglitz valley, which is scattered with castles and ruined towers such as the Bohna Burg, the Schlösser Weesenstein, Bärenstein and Lauenstein. **Glashütte** was originally a silver mining town, but changed over to clock-making in the middle of the nineteenth century and became an important centre of that industry. Nowadays it specialises in precision engineering. There is an unforgettable ride on the standard gauge Müglitzbahn branch railway from Heidenau (on the main line from Dresden) through part of the Erzgebirge. The diesel train climbs steep gradients at a steady unhurried pace through delightful woodlands around a hairpin bend to the old hilltop mining town of **Altenberg**. Sadly the prosperity enjoyed by many of the old mining and textile towns of the Erzgebirge, with their old fashioned factories in the woods, is very much a thing of the past and there must be concern about a future which tourism alone cannot support. But because tourism is relatively underdeveloped, this is a superb area to explore on foot and by public transport with good bus and rail links, and with remarkably inexpensive accommodation.

It is an easy walk for example, from Altenberg, the terminus of the Müglitz railway, over Geising hill with its nature reserve and viewpoint tower (refreshments available) through the woods via Bärenburg, a small, quiet forest resort, to **Kurort Kipsdorf**, a resort with a superb little Jugendstil station served by yet another narrow gauge steam railway. This line goes through the Dippoldiswald down a beautiful valley and forest route through the Rabenauer Grund, where footpaths link stations along one of the loveliest and most romantic of all the little east German steam lines, meeting main line trains between Dresden and Chemnitz at Freital-Hainsberg.

Zinnwald (linked by bus) nearby is the most important crossing point into Czechoslovakia, but is also a good centre both for walking and winter skiing through attractive countryside.

The Central and Western Erzgebirge are accessible by train and bus from the industrial cities of Chemnitz, **Zwickau** (birthplace of Robert Schumann and home of the infamous Trabbi) and **Freiberg**. They are an area of medium-sized hills, partly forested, partly moorland, an old mining town with Renaissance town houses and a gothic cathedral. This is an area still important for its many mineral reserves – granites, serpentine, tin. The upper Westerzgebirge has large commercial forests. Parts of the Mittlerer Erzgebirge around the Mothauser Heide are particularly important for nature conservation interests, with moorland birch and mountain spruce. Protected animals include wild boar, pine marten and ermine stoat plus some significant wildfowl.

The main centre in the Mittlerer Erzgebirge for both walking and skiing is the resort of **Oberwiesenthal**, linked by a picturesque narrow gauge steam railway from Cranzahl, a station on the line from Chemnitz and Zschopau to Bärenstein. From Oberwiesenthal a cable railway climbs to the summit of the Fichtelberge some 1214 metres above sea level, the highest point in the Erzgebirge.

The Erzgebirge enjoys special Christmas festivities when towns and villages are filled with huge wooden rotating pyramids of light, lit by large candles and containing nativity figures, miners, angels and animals. The Erzgebirge toymaking industry was traditionally an additional means of livelihood for the miners who often went through hard times. The brightly coloured nutcracker dolls, huntsmen, kings and ordinary peasant figures continue to be exported worldwide, though there is now competition from the Far East. A famous novelty is the Räuchermänner, little wooden men who appear to smoke pipes; scented candles are put inside them. At **Seiffen** traditional wooden Noah's ark animals are still made on a lathe with immense skill from a circular shaped piece of wood. Miners' wives developed lacemaking as a source of extra income and some of the beautiful laces can be seen exhibited at the special museum at **Schwarzenberg**. The western end of the Erzgebirge south of the textile and lacemaking town of Plauen merges into the Vogtland, an area of volcanic rock, gentle green hills, rivers (including a source of the Elbe), reservoirs and small textile manufacturing towns. This is an area well served by railways, with the little resorts of **Bad Elster** and **Bad Brambrach**, spa towns on the Czech border, being good centres to explore the area. To the north of Plauen it is worth making the trip to cross the astonishing Grölschtal viaduct at **Mylau**, built in 1845-6, a huge three tier brick structure and one of the highest in Europe.

Chemnitz, like Dresden, is close to fine walking country. Not far from the city is Sternmühlental, an area with a dense network of waymarked paths, whilst Chemnitztal close by the town is both a landscape conservation area and a nature reserve. A popular walk is to the 508 metre high summit of the Adelsberg, described as Chemnitz's 'local mountain'. Nearby is Augustusburg, an eighteenth century hilltop hunting castle, now a museum, youth hostel and restaurant reached by cable railway from Erdmannsdorf station on the Chemnitz-Annaberg-Buchholz line.

Lausitz to the east of Dresden is another region of great beauty, its lakes set amid rolling hills and with extensive areas of woodland. It was settled in the sixth century by Slav tribes known as the Sorbs who to this day maintain their own language and traditions. There is a similar group of Sorbs round Cottbus in the Niederlausitz in Brandenburg. **Bautzen** on the river Spree in the Oberlausitz (easily reached by train on the Dresden-Görlitz line) is the home of the Sorben Museum and is a centre of Sorb life. The town is considered one of the most beautiful in Sachsen with many fine buildings. The old watertower and weapon store is now a protected monument. The cathedral of St. Peter with its three naves is shared by Catholics and Protestants.

The **Zittaugebirge** – the Zittau mountains – in Sachsen's extreme southeastern corner occupies a peninsula surrounded by Poland and Czechoslovakia. It is an area mainly of sandstone, but with fertile areas of loamy clay soil. On the basalt tops of the Eibau the ground is more waterlogged. Because of the varying heights of mountains and valley areas, there are great differences in temperature and quite a high rainfall. In spring and autumn the prevailing winds from northern Bohemia and the cold air on the craggy summits combine to cause mists to form which are eventually driven away by strong winds. Even when the sun shines in the valleys, the mountain tops are often swathed in cloud. A fifth of the area is still woodland, with firs, pines and larches predominating. The deciduous woods contain great varieties of plants such as mercury, Turk's cap lily, anemone, lily of the valley and corydalis. The crags of the Zittaugebirge are also very popular among serious climbers.

There are two particularly important areas of protected landscape in the Zittaugebirge around **Görlitz**. It is hoped that a Czech section over the border in the Lausitz mountains will in time form a cross-border conservation zone so that the unity of the landscape and local building styles in Sachsen and Bohemia can be preserved on each side of the border. There are already well-marked paths on both sides. The Zittaugebirge is the start for a long distance footpath or Hauptwanderweg linked to the Rennsteig over Sachsen's and Thüringen's Mittelgebirge to Eisenach, forming part of a European route, while the Oberlausitzer Ringweg of 300 kilometres follows the southern Lausitz area.

There is a nature reserve at **Jonsdorf**. A footpath through the reserve follows gorges through a sandstone terrain and then goes through marshier ground before ending at some summits with volcanic influences. An unusual feature are the hardened column-shaped sandstone pillars. Further paths go from the Gondelfahrt over Falkenstein around the reserve. Rock climbing is only allowed from September till mid-December and needs a special licence.

Naturschutzgebiet Lausche is named after the highest mountain in the area and indeed in Germany east of the Elbe. The mountain is a superb vantage point and can be reached from Waltersdorf and also from Czechoslovakia. There are many interesting varieties of flowers here and in the spring white pestwort and cowslips bloom in abundance.

Zittau itself was an old trading town on the long distance trade routes between northern and western Europe and Bohemia. After the ravages of the Thirty Years War, Zittau became prosperous through linen weaving, cloth making and brewing. The traditional industries of textiles, vehicle and heavy machinery also include coal mining and metallurgy. The Weinaulandschaftspark is the largest local recreational area.

Görlitz Niesky has a hilly landscape to the south and a reservoir within a wooded conservation area. There are 150 varieties of birds on an island bird sanctuary. Four bathing beaches and a camping site, Kollm-Nord, make this a popular tourist area.

There is great concern about Waldsterben (dying trees) in this region and also in the Erzgebirge, caused by emissions of sulphur and nitrogen oxides from both local and also Czech industry which have polluted not only the air, but also the soil and the ground water. This has been worsened in some areas by metallic and chemical wastes, and in others by excessive use of fertilisers and by the over-production of silage. The landscape has changed over the centuries as trees were felled, courses of streams were altered and paths blocked. In future years car-related modern mass tourism could add to these problems as the former DDR begins to achieve western standards of material prosperity. In Sachsen as elsewhere the need for positive planning policies and adequate funds for their implementation have never been greater.

Further information ————————————————————————

Dresden tourist information office: Verkehrsamt, Prager Straße, Dresden O-8010.

Leipzig-Information, Sachsenplatz 1, O-7010 Leipzig.

Thüringen

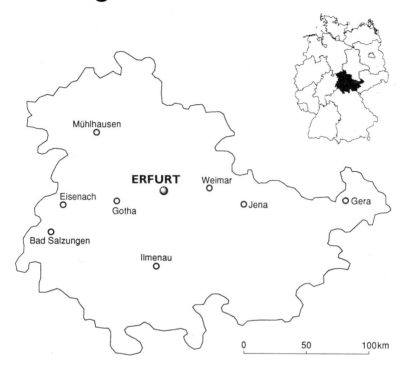

Mühlhausen
○

ERFURT   Weimar
◉   ○
Eisenach   ○
○   Gotha   ○Jena   ○Gera

○
Bad Salzungen

Ilmenau
○

0   50   100km

Thüringen describes itself with some justice as the 'green heart of Germany'. The high summits of the Thüringer Wald (Thuringian forest) form its southern border with Hessen and Frankenland (Bayern), whilst its northern border edges into the Harz mountains.

It is also one of Germany's most ancient states. Evidence from excavations in Weimar and elsewhere shows that Thüringen was already partly occupied in Neolithic times, whilst just after 400 AD Thüringen covered the whole of what is now central Germany, from the rivers Mulde and Elbe to beyond the Main. Feuds and battles and political change throughout the centuries have eventually reduced it to the size of today's state.

It is a region of forests, mountains, river valleys, churches, monasteries and half-timbered houses within the Thüringer Wald and the Thüringer Schiefergebirge and the lowlands of the Thüringer Kessel. In the west is the Eichsfeld area around Heiligenstadt where the writer Theodor Storm (see Schleswig-Holstein) worked at a district court from 1856 to 1864 whilst writing eleven of his novellas. The foothills of the

Rhön in the southwest continue with the Grabfeld in the south and the Gleichberge hills around Römhild. The rivers Werra, Unstrut, Saale, Weisse Elster, Schwarza, Ilm and Gera all flow through the state. But of special interest are the Thüringer Wald to the south, the beautiful old capital of Erfurt and above all the town of Weimar.

Much of Thüringen's prosperity arose in the later Middle Ages when several of the towns were on the important trade route eastwards from Frankfurt and also northwards, carrying copper and other produce to the city of Nürnberg.

Woad, a plant used extensively in medieval times for dying cloth blue, was grown around the five towns of Arnstadt, Gotha, Erfurt, Langensalza and Tennstadt. Other areas were noted for the manufacture of yarn and cloth, and the smelting of iron, copper and silver. Though these mineral deposits were already exhausted by the eighteenth and nineteenth centuries, the towns developed a good industrial base as a result of this initial impetus. Watches from Ruhla, machine tools from Erfurt, Gera cloth, tools from Schmalkalden and precision and optical tools from Jena manufactured by Carl Zeiss Jena remain among the region's main products. Zeiss, one of the world's top optical companies, was divided into separate western and eastern companies after World War II, and though there have been a number of problems for the Jena company entering the new world of free market competition, its future as a worldwide manufacturer of high technology optics looks bright once again. A museum at the factory in Jena is devoted to looking at the history of precious optical instruments from microscopes to telescopes.

In south Thüringen glass making continues, as does porcelain manufacturing dating back to 1760. Henneberg porcelain with its famous cobalt-blue glaze is still produced at Ilmenau on the edge of the Thüringer Wald.

The Thüringer Wald is a magnificent area of still largely unspoiled forest and hills, lying over mainly Carboniferous sandstone. Pine, spruce, yew, oak, birch and beech form superb sunlit mixed woods, in between which are areas of farmland and scattered villages. Wildflowers to be seen include gentians and columbines, with sundew in marshy places. The uplands are also the haunt of peregrine and eagle owls whilst kingfishers are common along riversides.

Three peaks, the Großer Beerberg (982 metres), the Schneekopf (978 metres) and the Großer Inselberg (916 metres) are the highest points of the Thüringer Wald. The forest is 20 kilometres wide at its widest point, but only 10 metres at its western end near Eisenach. The Großer Inselberg is perhaps the most popular summit of the three, with many waymarked paths leading along its crest, which is crossed by the Rennsteig, providing useful links to the Rennsteig from such centres as

Ruhla, Brotterode or Tabarz. The mountain appears to enjoy its own microclimate at times with bright sunshine on the tops when the valley is shrouded in haze, but at other times good weather down below with more threatening conditions above. On clear days the Brocken, the Harz's highest peak, is visible. A skilift on the Inselberg makes the area popular for downhill skiing during the winter months.

When walking on the 861 metre high Kickelhahn with its magnificent views above Ilmenau one September evening in 1780, and shortly after receiving a letter from his beloved Charlotte von Stein, Goethe was moved to write one of his most evocative poems, the Wanderers Nachtlied (Wanderer's Night Song), which was originally scribbled on the door of a wooden forest shelter near Gabelbach – 'Über allen Gipfeln ist Ruh' – 'There is peace on all the mountain tops . . .'. On another occasion, after walking in the forest, Goethe wrote to his employer Prince Karl August that he found the region 'beautiful, absolutely beautiful'.

There is now a Goethe footpath 'Auf Goethe's Spuren' between Ilmenau, Gabelbach and Stützerbach linking places with Goethe associations.

Königsee is a town in the Rinnetal with lovely half-timbered houses and an attractive path through the wood to Paulinzella. The ruins of an enormous church which once belonged to an eleventh century monastery can still be viewed. Steep cliffs, dense woods and narrow side valleys, quiet paths and fast-flowing streams make this a particularly attractive area.

You can walk the whole length of the Thüringer Wald to the ancient Schiefergebirge hills to the east along the **Rennsteig**, an ancient track which follows the summit of the long, wooded mountain ridges from Hürschel on the river Werra to its eastern end at Blankenstein on the river Saale, a distance of 168 kilometres. Most of the route lies between 600 and 900 metres above sea level. It is easily followed, with a distinctive white letter 'R' waymark. It forms part of a European Ramblers' Association long distance route EB and a former East European route rather pompously titled 'International Mountain Walk of Friendship' between Eisenach and Budapest in Hungary.

The Rennsteig dates from at least the tenth century, when it formed a messenger route and medieval trade route from Hessen into Bohemia. In earlier times the Rennsteig also formed the actual border between Thüringen and Frankenland, and later still between various other principalities. It is interesting to find some of the old boundary stones on the route, the oldest dating from 1572.

Access to the Rennsteig is fairly straightforward with linkpaths from Eisenach and several local railway lines crossing intermediate points along the route (there is even a station called the Rennsteig on the scenic route between Erfurt and Themar), bus links and a good choice of accommodation for walkers. Sadly, some parts of the ancient way have now been tarmacadamed for motor traffic and it will be necessary to create or work out new loops in the future to reduce the amount of heel-blistering roadwalking. Other sections, however, including its eastern end around the medieval Wildesau stone, provide superb yet relatively easy walking with magnificent views. Parts of the route are also suitable for mountain biking and riding.

The whole of the Thüringer Wald is a protected area because of its scenic beauty, with a number of actual Naturschutzgebiete. A Biosphäre Reservat covering 12,700 hectares has been created in the Vessertal at **Oberhof**, consisting of woodland, grassy mountainsides, and streams. Much of the grassland would soon be smothered by woodland, and many varieties of wild flower like the yellow arnica would vanish, but for careful grazing and meadowland management regimes. The essential qualities of a Kulturlandschaft – a traditionally farmed upland landscape – would also be lost. The area is only used for quiet forms of recreation.

At the eastern edge of the Rennsteig is the town of **Lauscha** (rail served) in a narrow valley squeezed between steep, thickly forested slopes. In 1597 Hans Greiner from Schwaben and Christoph Müller from Bohemia founded a glassworks there. Painted glass, glass figures, and especially Christmas decorations are still manufactured there today and glassmaking is also demonstrated at the glassworks. It was here that artificial eyes were first made in 1835.

Neuhaus, on the Rennsteig, is at 825 metres, the highest town in the east of Germany. It was formerly the centre of the glass industry. Not far away is **Sitzendorf**, where Thüringen porcelain manufacture had its infancy. In the town itself you will see enormous vases for sale, porcelain chandelier-style light fittings and mirrors framed in porcelain, not to mention great varieties of smaller objects.

Every May there is a race from Neuhaus on the Rennsteig to Schmied-feld 45 kilometres away to commemorate Christoph Gutsmuths, a pioneer of physical education for young people who tried to put his ideas into practice at the village of Schnepfenthal near Waltershausen. **Oberhof** on the Rennsteig is a major wintersports centre, but also a popular destination for walkers; its Rennsteig Gärten have thousands of Alpine plants.

The Obere Saale valley to the east, where the Rennsteig ends, contains the Schiefergebirge Naturpark. Further east, between the Saale and the Elster, lies a region known as the **Thüringer Holzland**, a relatively undiscovered area of medium-sized hills and fine half-timbered villages. A number of nature reserves and former country estates have enabled wildlife, including some fine forest fungi, to flourish. Centres include the resorts of Bad Kostritz, Bad Losterausnitz and the old town of Stadtroda.

The **Schwarzatal**, which runs through the northeast of the Thüringer Wald and the Schiefer hills, is named after the river whose dark colour comes from the ancient, hard slates that form its river bed and the dark shadows along its narrow banks caused by woods of pine and fir trees. The river Schwarza snakes its way for 35 kilometres until it reaches Rudolstadt on the Saale. The Schwarzatal is known for its damp and cool weather and long snow-bound winters. But north of Bad Blankenburg on the edge of the forest the climate is milder.

The old town of **Mellenbach-Glasbach** in the upper Schwarzatal is geologically a particularly interesting area, being on ancient Ordovician bedrocks. Guided geological tours are arranged. The **Limbach/Scheibe-Alsbach** area has its network of paths and a former glassworks and ore furnace. There is also a nature reserve containing the hardiest pine trees in Europe, the König and Güntertanne, and it is easily accessible from the Rennsteig. **Katzhütte** is another good walking area and **Lichtenhain an der Bergbahn**, served by the Oberweißbacher Bergbahn, is a resort known for both cool summers and winters, also for its bracing air.

The Oberweißbacher Bergbahn is one of many delightful railway lines to explore in Thüringen that cross the forest and link often otherwise remote village communities. The Bergbahn itself is an electric powered mountain cable railway between the spa resorts of Oberweißbach (on the scenic railway between Rudolstadt and Katzhütte), Lichtenhain and Cursdorf. The train is standard gauge and each unit can carry 150 passengers who enjoy superb views of the forest as they travel the 2.6 kilometre line which ascends 130 metres.

Gotha, to the north of the Thüringer Wald, is most probably best known outside Germany as the home of the Almanac da Gotha, an annual catalogue of German nobility published up to the outbreak of World War II, but it was also more importantly the home of the publisher of a wide selection of historical, physical and political maps and atlases. It has an early baroque palace at Friedrichstein and art collections in the Schloß museum, while the Ekhof Theater has examples of stage scenery dating back to as early as 1683. Sadly much of Gotha's architectural splendours are greatly in need of renovation.

The delightful Thüringer Waldbahn (in actuality Gotha tram route No 4) departs outside the main railway station at Gotha as an ordinary street tram. It then strikes across country at a good rate of knots via Waltershausen and Friedrichroda, the latter a popular health resort in a beautiful setting offering brine and pine-oil baths, past farmland villages and some spectacular crystal caves at Marienglashöhle and through deep forest to the small town of Tabarz. This must be one of the most romantic tram rides in the whole of Germany.

The Thüringer Wald teems with wildlife, fungi and wild berries, whilst rivers are full of trout. There are numerous waymarked paths for the walker which explore high ridges between intimate valleys. It is also an area of stately homes and castles such as the ruined Greifenstein, the Heidecksburg, the Dornburg, Schloß Großkochberg and many others. None is finer or more imposing than the **Wartburg Schloß** near **Eisenach.** The Wartburg contains, it has been said, much of the soul of Germany. Legend has it that when Landgrave Ludwig saw the towering rock above the forest when hunting in 1067, he declared it would be his castle and had soil carried from his own castle near Reinhardsbrunn at the dead of night. The following day twelve of his followers swore that the soil in which they put the tips of their swords belonged to Ludwig and according to ancient law, he therefore was able to claim the ground; the sword tips, it is said, defend the castle against it ever being conquered.

Less disputable is the fact that the Wartburg was the home of the Minnesingers in the thirteenth century, the first recognised German poets, such as Wolfram von Eschenbach and Walthar von der Vogelweide and many others who competed in song contests immortalised in Wagner's opera *Die Meistersinger.* Many of the Minnesingers, plus other legendary heroes and heroines such as Wartburg's Saint Elizabeth, are portrayed in the richly decorated art-nouveau style great hall.

Wartburg's most famous occupant was Martin Luther who translated the New Testament whilst in 'protective custody' there in 1521, outlawed and excommunicated by the Diet of Worms. The translation, from Greek, was completed in the short period of ten weeks, a literary masterpiece the power and authority of which was to help standardise and lay the foundations for the development of the modern German language. Luther's achievement gave enormous impetus to German literature, and also became a fountainhead of both humanist and Christian thought, with enormous influence throughout Europe. Goethe did not exaggerate when he declared that the German people became a nation through Martin Luther. It is a moving experience to stand in the small, bare room in the Wartburg complete with desk and primitive stool where he completed this great task.

The Wartburg was again at the centre of political ideas when students from eleven universities arrived there in 1817 to demand a united, democratic and free Germany. They ceremoniously burnt a long tail of hair and a cane as symbols of Prussian oppression. A monument in the Göpelskuppe hill survives to record the deed, as well as a flag in the banqueting hall and student gatherings which commemorate the Burschenschaften, as they were known.

Among superb walks into the Thüringer Wald from the Wartburg is the Drachenschlucht (dragon's ravine), a path through a narrow, winding chasm between huge sandstone crags above a stream. The path joins the Rennsteig at Sickelhan.

It is only a short walk to the Wartburg from the centre of Eisenach, though try and avoid summer weekends and go early in the day to avoid the inevitable crowds and queues.

Appropriately enough the Wartburg car was manufactured in Eisenach – until recently, a car with a good reputation, its factory now taken over by Fiat. Eisenach was the birthplace of Johann Sebastian Bach and Luther attended school there. There is a Bach birthplace museum in the town.

The town called **Sommergewinn** (summer's triumph) holds a delightful festival on the third Sunday before Easter which goes back to pagan times, when colourful processions pass the houses decorated with painted eggs and flowers. In the marketplace Frau Sunna (Madam Sun) decisively defeats Winter.

Three picturesque castles on hills between Gotha and Erfurt, known as the Drei Gleichen, dominate what was once a key medieval trade route. A popular footpath route links all three.

The town of **Arnstadt** has in its castle museum a remarkable collection of dolls known as 'Mon Plaisir', which were created by the Princess of Schwarzburg-Arnstadt, her ladies in waiting and a number of craftsmen between 1690 and 1750. It is really a miniature town, illustrating contemporary life at a German royal court and also the everyday life of its middle class citizens. There are 26 houses, 84 rooms and 400 dolls beautifully constructed with furnishings out of wood, fabric and wax.

Although most of the **Rhön** lies in Hessen and Franken, part of this Biophäre Reservat of volcanic hills is in the southwest corner of Thüringen, west of the resort of Meiningen. There are steep basalt columns, grassy meadows, craggy peaks, lakes and extensive forests as well as numerous historic buildings, churches and castles. Cattle breeding, weaving and woodcarving have been the main sources of income for a largely indigent mountain people, though there is now a certain amount of tourism. Yew trees, juniper bushes and flowers like spring snowflake, Solomon's seal, wood anemones and the carline thistle thrive here. It is also the home of Rhönpaulus, a legendary figure, rather like the English Robin Hood but dressed in a black coat with wide-brimmed hat, who robbed the rich to give to the poor. The Rhön is easily reached from Eisenach by rail via Bad Salzungen along the branch line to Dordorf, Dermbach and Kaltennordheim.

The city of **Erfurt**, capital of Thüringen, owes its foundation as a bishopric to the English monk and missionary Boniface in 742 AD. In

805 the Emperor Charlemagne established it as an important border trading post for trade with the Slavs, enhanced by its position on central Europe's most important trade route known as the Via Regia (king's way) which connected the west with the east of the continent.

Its earlier economic importance as a woad town declined after the import of far cheaper indigo as a textile dye and the development of Leipzig as a major industrial and commercial centre. But it was later to become a centre of flower growing, so that Goethe could write delightedly of the ring of brightly-coloured flower fields which surrounded the town on all sides. In 1802 the now Prussian Erfurt was under French rule for a time when Prussia was defeated at Jena and Napoleon held a congress of princes there in 1808 in order to demonstrate his power to Czar Alexander I. Nowadays Erfurt is a major industrial and administrative centre with a population of over 200,000, maintained by clothing and shoe industries and the manufacture of heavy machinery and micro-electronics.

The town itself has tremendous style and charm, with an ancient bridge in its centre called the Krämerbrücke on which is built a whole street of lovely half-timbered houses and shops. Close by is a remarkable, well-planned central area of green spaces and residential courts by the river. It has many other fine buildings, including some wonderfully renovated and very beautiful baroque houses in its centre at the marketplace, or Anger. These include the Haus zum Breiten Herd, the Haus zum Stochfisch with its very attractive stepped gable (now the town museum) and the Haus zum Roten Ochsen with its intricate doorway. The cathedral has among its treasures a romanesque carved figure 'Wolfram' dating from 1160, which is really a holder for two large candles. The town centre area around the cathedral enjoys UNESCO listing as a centre especially meriting preservation, and significantly enough, the state of Rheinland-Pfalz is offering considerable financial help with building restoration.

Erfurt's green lung is 700 hectares of deciduous woodland in the nearby Steigerwald, penetrated by more than 36 kilometres of footpaths.

Johann Wolfgang von Goethe (1749-1832) the 'universal genius' – poet, dramatist, scientist, statesman – lived in the little Thüringen town of **Weimar** for fifty-seven years and transformed it into a focal point of intellectual and cultural life. Earlier inhabitants of the town had included Lucas Cranach the elder who painted his great altar piece for the church, later finished by his son, and Johann Sebastian Bach who came to the town in 1708 as court organist and conductor, before going to Leipzig. But when the 26 year old Goethe arrived, Weimar was regarded as a backwater of 6,000 inhabitants. The poet became both administrator and writer-in-residence to the court of the young Duke Karl August.

When Friedrich Schiller (1759-1805) joined Goethe in Weimar the two became twin pivots of the Duchess Amalia's famous social and intellectual gatherings. A warm friendship developed between the two men in spite of a considerable difference in age, with Goethe writing and responding to his younger friend: 'You gave me a second youth and once more made me a poet', as Schiller had already written to Goethe, 'You set the whole mass of my ideas in motion'. Today the Goethe Haus has much of biographical and literary interest, as well as actual furnishings used by the writer. His Garten Haus, where he wrote various works, is also open to the public in a riverside park. Schiller's house is also a museum. Goethe was director of the playhouse in Weimar and together with Schiller transformed the German theatre, putting on the first performance of many of Schiller's major works, among them *Maria Stuart* and *Wilhelm Tell*.

Franz Liszt also came to Weimar and stayed seventeen years to teach and compose music and also initiate a music school. It was here that Liszt performed Wagner's *Lohengrin* in 1850. There is also a Liszt museum. Richard Strauss was a conductor here between 1889 and 1894 and gave the first performance of Humperdinck's *Hänsel und Gretel*. Heinrich van der Velde's Kunst und Gewerbeschule, established in 1902, was hugely influential, with many fine Jugendstil buildings surviving in Weimar itself. In 1919 Walter Gropius founded the Bauhaus school of architecture in Weimar, again forming a focal point of artistic life, until forced out by the rise of xenophobic nationalism in the 1920s when it transferred to Dessau.

Weimar became a political focal point when on 11 August 1919 the National Versammlung declared the establishment of the First German Republic – or the Weimarer Republik as the ill-fated regime came to be known.

To the north of Weimar and Erfurt lies an area of relatively flat countryside known as the Thüringer Bekken. To the northwest is the **Eichsfeld**, which forms the foothills of the Harz mountains, rolling countryside of wooded heights and old villages linked with textiles and tobacco growing. **Heiligenstadt**, now a spa, probably owes its name to the church of St. Martin, established in the eighth or ninth century. The poet Heinrich Heine (1797-1856), although Jewish, was baptised here to allow him to 'get access to European culture'.

Nordhausen, on the edge of the Eichsfeld and a gateway to the Harz mountains, was already the site of a royal settlement under the first Sachsen King Heinrich I. Its Renaissance town hall has a particularly impressive medieval statue of Roland, the symbol of civic liberty set up when a town received its municipal charter. The town became famous for the Nordhäuser Doppelkorn, a strong-tasting schnapps, and was also known for its chewing tobacco which was flavoured with a number of pleasant tasting herbs. Being the centre of V2 rocket manufacture in World War II, it suffered heavy war damage. It is now an important railway junction with through express services from Kassel, Köln, Erfurt and Dresden, whilst the narrow gauge Harzquerbahn starts from Nordhausen Nord station close by the main station.

To the south of Nordhausen lie **Kyffhäuser** and the Kyffhäusergebirge, a nature park of typical karst limestone scenery, covered with fine deciduous woods, wild flowers, crags, caves, underground waterfalls and dry valleys. The ruined castle of Flakenberg makes an impressive viewpoint across the valley of the Goldene Aue.

The little rail-served spa town of **Bad Frankenhausen** to the south of the Kyffhäusergebirge makes a good centre to explore this area. Five kilometres away above **Rottleben** (next station along the railway line) is the Barbarossahöhle – the Barbarossa caves. Layers of anhydrite make spectacular formations hanging down from the ceiling looking like animal skins in one cave, sparkling like a milky way on the ceiling of another or piled in layers like sides of black and white cured bacon in a third. An enormous natural rock formation like a throne is known as the Barbarossa chair and is shown to visitors.

Barbarossa himself sits sculptured on an immense and more lifelike red sandstone throne on the Kyffhäuser Denkmal on the summit of the Kulpenberg, about 10 kilometres to the north, as though awaiting a summons to Germany's assistance as numerous legends infer, rather like Britain's King Arthur. The statue forms part of a great monument and viewing tower built to commemorate the uniting of Germany under its first Kaiser – Wilhelm I – in 1871.

Mühlhausen in the Eichsfeld, reached by train from the main line via Leinefelde, has many medieval buildings and also reminders of the Peasant Wars. It was here that Thomas Müntzer, the great sixteenth century peasant leader and revolutionary, lived, preached, fought and was finally executed. Under the leadership of the charismatic and eloquent Thomas Müntzer, a theologian and contemporary of Martin Luther, a major revolt by peasant farmers took place against their feudal overlords.

On the Kyffhäusergebirge at Weißen Berg near **Bad Frankenhausen** (a short, hilly walk from the town centre, but bus services operate), close to the actual battlefield where thousands of peasants were massacred, a special circular building has been erected to house the world's biggest painting, undertaken by the East German scholar and artist Werner Tübke between 1974 and 1987. This vast panorama was inspired by and is a national memorial to the battle of 1525, when 6,000 peasants were slaughtered by advancing mercenaries. It is presented as a piece of theatre. After an initial talk visitors are taken into the darkened chamber, a kind of auditorium, where slowly the lights rise and the astonishing panorama surrounds them on all sides. The gigantic painting on linen is 14 metres high and 123 metres long and contains over 3,000 figures. It is undoubtedly a masterpiece of social-realism, yet at the same time is a highly symbolical and allegorical representation of currents of thought and ideas contemporary with Müntzer. It depicts feudalism, the rise of the bourgeoisie, the Catholic church and the Reformation, scientific discoveries and technological developments. Included within it are portraits of many famous figures from German culture including Müntzer himself, with his symbol of the rainbow, Albrecht Dürer, Martin Luther, Lucas Cranach and many others. It is an extraordinary work, powerful and visionary. Though created as a propaganda piece, perhaps as a piece of socialist art, it transcends such limitations to become a profound, ultimately optimistic statement about the human condition.

Further information ————————————————————

Erfurt-Information, Bahnhofstraße 32, O-5020 Erfurt (also handles information for the state of Thüringen on request).
Weimar-Information, Marktstraße 4, O-5300 Weimar.

Hessen

Hessen, in the very centre of the newly united Germany, has much that is very typically German in terms of landscape and townships, without being subjected to anything like the same kind of tourist pressures as the better known regions. Hessen is certainly a Land in which to experience what middle Germany is like.

Hessen lies between the uplands of the Odenwald and the Taunus in the Rhine-Main plain. Though it was briefly important as a dukedom in the sixteenth century, it only really came into being after World War II during the restructuring of West Germany, being welded together out of a number of fragmented regions. Yet it soon became one of Germany's most prosperous states, with the old Frankish city of Frankfurt am Main expanding rapidly as Germany's main financial centre, home of the Bundesbank (federal bank) that controls the destiny of the Deutschmark. Hessen is also reputed to have a higher percentage of forest – around 40% – covering its land surfaces than any other state in Germany, a large proportion of which is protected and made available for recreation in the form of no less than nine Naturparke. There is also a total of thirty-two official spa towns and health resorts from which to enjoy this countryside. Significantly enough, in recent times Hessen has been the first German state in which the Greens have had a modicum of power, sharing with the SDP a coalition or 'red-green alliance'.

Wiesbaden, created by the Romans as baths around hot thermal springs, lies in the Rhine valley, across the river from Mainz, and is the state capital. The Rheingau Gebirge and the Taunus mountains form a backcloth to this attractive city spa, still famous for its curative mineral springs, twenty-six in number and now mostly serving the spa hotels and the elegant Kaiser Friedrich's Bad. The hot springs bubble up from a depth of 2000 metres, and are reputedly good in rheumatic disorders. You can taste the mineral waters in the Kochbrunnentempel in the Krantzplatz in the Kurpark, where the Kochbrunnen with its water at 154° Fahrenheit bubbles to the surface.

Wiesbaden was the seat of the newly created Dukes of Nassau in 1816 and became a fashionable centre for European royalty and aristocracy up to the outbreak of the First World War. In the city centre by the gleaming white ducal palace of Nassau, there is a bustling market square and streets with elegant shops and arcades such as the Wilhelmstraße. The city is also an excellent cultural centre and convenient public transport node from which to explore a wide area of countryside; for example the Neroberg, crowned by a beautiful Greek Orthodox chapel with five golden domes, or the Sonnenberg with its superb, panoramic views. Close by the Rhine is the Rheingau region with its castles, cloisters and vineyards. Also within easy reach is the Limes, the Roman boundary wall originally guarded by towers and fortifications and the German equivalent of Hadrian's Wall.

Wiesbaden is also ideally positioned to reach the Rhein-Taunus Naturpark to the northwest, an area of hills which is almost two-thirds forested and which has 131 waymarked footpath routes (around 500 kilometres of paths) from which to explore the area. A delightful way of getting there from Wiesbaden is along the Aartalbahn, a preserved railway which runs from Dotzheim station (bus link from Wiesbaden centre), mainly on summer Sundays, to Bad Schwalbach. Alternatively, the Niedernhausen-Limburg line – cycles carried on most trains – goes through the northeastern section of the nature park. There is a frequent rail link to Niedernhausen from Wiesbaden, and ample bus services. It was the Romans who first planted vines on the Rheingau, on the more sheltered reaches of its southern slopes. Here the Riesling grape is king and there are ample opportunities to taste the vintage en route. The 65 kilometre Rheingauer **Riesling-Pfad** (Riesling path) stretches from Wicker to Lorchhausen; the best way to reach the start is by bus or train (Flörsheim on the line to Frankfurt Höchst). The walk is divided into six parts, all close to public transport links to enable you to walk the route in stages and return if required to Wiesbaden. On the other hand some of the inns along the route are keen to promote their wine by offering a Rheingauer Frühstück, a hearty breakfast accompanied by a dryish wine, so overnight stops have their attractions. Local Riesling wine is also used in a variety of delicious sauces, a Riesling sorbet or Handkäs mit Musik, cheese soaked for some hours in the wine and served with onions, oil and vinegar.

The Benedictine and Cistercian monks were the original wine-making pioneers in the Rheingau and they made some very important discoveries about winemaking, including types of grapes and the special qualities of Spätlese and Auslese, the Kabinet-Keller and techniques of bottling. There is a Weinbauschule in Eltville and a research centre in Geisenheim, forming Germany's premier wine academy. Winegrowing plays an increasingly important role in the Rheingau economy, and this is also a major recreation area for the Rhine-Main conurbation. In the thirteenth century the Rheingau farmers called themselves 'cives', the Latin word for citizens; they enjoyed considerable political freedom, although the rulers of Mainz tried repeatedly to undermine this, with only limited success. Up to this very day, the Rheingau vintners are noted as being among the most highly qualified winegrowers in the world. Virtually every independent vintner is fully qualified as either a vintner's assistant, master vintner or vintner engineer. In England Riesling wine became known as 'hock' from the name Hochheimer. There is also an excellent if less well known red wine, Blauer Spätburgunder, which matches the white Riesling for quality.

The **Naturpark Hochtaunus** is Hessen's second largest nature park and lies to the north between the conurbations of the Rhine-Main and **Gießen** and **Wetzlar**, making it easily reached from these large centres of population, particularly Frankfurt. The scenic railway line from Friedrichsdorf to Grävenwiesbach serves the north of the nature park, but sadly has no weekend or holiday services. Wetzlar and Braunfels on the Lahntahl Bahn (Koblenz-Gießen with connections from Frankfurt) both have good footpath links into the nature park. There are also bus links from both Frankfurt and Wiesbaden.

Heidetränkel in the Hochtaunus was an old Celtic settlement and the area was also on the route of the Roman Limes. Later a chain of medieval castles and fortresses guarded its trade routes. About two-thirds of the park is forested but the original deciduous woods have to compete with conifers. More than 140 waymarked circular routes are available for walkers and many paths are described in detail in the guide to the Naturpark Hochtaunus. The Lahn-Hohenweg, the Limesweg and the Taunushohenweg are particularly fine long distance routes, while the European Ramblers Long Distance Routes No 1 Nordsee-Mittelmeer and No 3 Atlantik-Böhmerwald also intersect the nature park. Interesting places to visit include Germany's oldest parsonage in **Rod am Weil** and the fortified towers and castles such as Braunfels, Runkel and Kronberg. There is plenty of opportunity for a keen walker to get away from the crowds on the popular Großen Feldberg by just going a short distance away from the summit, and by choosing routes away from the popular villages and car parks.

The city of **Frankfurt**, now the region's major financial, commercial and industrial centre, and inevitably ringed by such un-green things as motorways and airports, was as its name implies first settled by the Franks and was also once the seat of the Emperor Charlemagne. Its site on the river Main was already settled in Neolithic times and became an important Roman settlement. Relics of Roman Frankfurt are kept in Der Historische Garten in front of the cathedral's main entrance, where there are also the foundations of a Carolingian imperial palace. The city's greatest glory was her medieval old town, the largest in Germany until damaged by bombing in the last war. Fortunately the heart of Frankfurt, the Römerberg, with its splendid red sandstone and steeply stepped gables, has been rebuilt and renovated. The Römer, a collection of fifteenth century town houses, containing the city's old town hall and the Kaisersaal, was the site of the old imperial coronation banquets after the old German Emperors had been elected by the princes.

The Pauluskirche is famed as the site of the German National Versammlung which tried to transform Germany into a democratic national state in 1848-9. Despite war damage, the church has been rebuilt in more simplified form as a meeting place, exhibition centre and symbolic site of unity and freedom. The Saalhof, originally medieval and an exit point in the twelfth century when Frankfurt was still surrounded by a wall, is now part of the Historisches Museum. The Goethehaus, where Goethe was born in 1749, is preserved and stands adjacent to the Goethe Museum.

A brightly painted trolley-bus called the Ebbelwei-Express will take you on a city tour with a glass of apple wine and pretzels, making a round trip from the Ostbahnhof to the Zoo, Sachsenhausen, Römer/ Pauluskirche and Domstraße. Frankfurt is a major centre for opera, theatre, concerts, art galleries and museums. It has also numerous smart shops, large department stores and boutiques in such areas as the Hauptwache and the Zeil, the latter with modern pedestrian zones, and there is also the more exclusive Goethestraße. The Zoo, Palmengarten and Botanischergarten are all attractive spots while the Anlagering dates from the nineteenth century, when it was decided to raze the fortification wall round the city to the ground and transform the area into a public park; now a five kilometre ring of green encircles the city. The large Stadtwald has innumerable pleasant paths and trails while the old Goetheturm near Sachsenhausen gives a wonderful view of Frankfurt and the Taunus mountains.

Frankfurt specialities include apple wine which can be ordered by the glassful, a 'Schobbe', or by the jugful, a 'Bembel'. Grüne Soße, which is made with seven specific herbs, was Goethe's favourite dish, and has a light, delicate flavour.

The city is surrounded by hills and numerous pretty small towns and villages with the Taunus, Odenwald and Spessart hills being within easy reach as well as the valleys of the Wetterau, the Main and the Rhine. Excursions can be made by rail to the famous spa of **Bad Homburg** in the Taunus foothills or to the medieval castle of **Burg Kronberg** and the nearby partly ruined castle of **Königstein**. Take the Frankfurt-Königstein railway, operated by a private company (though regional travel tickets apply), from Frankfurt's Höchst station.

The winegrowing town of **Rüdesheim** on the Rhine is only an hour away by train, whilst the famous old university town of **Heidelberg** on the Neckar in nearby Baden-Württemberg can be reached in under an hour. The town of **Offenbach** houses Germany's leather museum, where exhibitions of handbags and leather containers give interesting insights into various periods and styles in different countries and the shoe museum contains artefacts from Coptic times to the nineteenth century.

The city of Frankfurt and its outlying regions are linked by a network (FVV) of city and commuter buses, trolley buses, U-Bahn and S-Bahn in a zoning system. There are also a number of attractive public boat trips which explore the rivers Main and Rhine.

The **Naturpark Bergstraße-Odenwald** lies in the south of Hessen, overlapping into the Bayerische Odenwald. It is not far from Darmstadt but is also easily accessible from Frankfurt along the Odenwaldbahn, running from Hanau to Wiebelsbach-Heubach and Eberbach, and also from the Darmstadt-Mannheim railway, well served by local stations, to the west. There is also a branch line to Fürth from Weinheim to the south.

The area was already settled in Neolithic, Bronze Age and Iron Age times and its Celtic inhabitants were later defeated by the Romans, who built fortifications along the Limes in order to defend their conquered territory. The stretch called Mümmling-Limes and Limes-Germanicus-Hadriani is particularly interesting and can be followed by footpath, while the Riesensäule on the Flesberg at Reichenbach are also Roman. The Romans were followed by the Alemanni, whose traces can still be found in place-names ending in 'ingen'; later, they in their turn were overrun by the Franks who left their mark in the form of place-names ending in 'heim'. In medieval times with the founding of various monasteries and abbeys, the economic importance of the area increased till the Oberrhein, the Bergstraße and the Odenwald became a key part of the old Germany.

The beauty of the blossom-laden flowering trees in spring makes this a popular area in late April or early May. The Odenwald area is composed of red sandstone with ridges and V-shaped valleys. The area northeast from Bensheim, the nature reserve round the Fellsenmeer, is rich in geological interest. More than half of the nature park is covered with forest, which is partly deciduous and contrasts with neighbouring cultivated fields and meadows. Deeper into the forest there are larger more impenetrable areas of woodland which are dark with spruce, firs, and pines. There are also a number of nearby spas such as Bad König (on the railway), Grasellenbach and Lindenfels which make useful centres to explore the region.

There is good walking on the excellent network of waymarked paths. A characteristic feature by the side of many paths are worn stones with letters, shields and symbols – these are in fact old boundary stones which recall the region's complex history. The Sensbacher Höhe is another favourite rambling destination between the Sensbachtal and the Gammelsbachtal. The Melibokus at 517 metres, easily accessible from Zwingenberg station, is one of the most popular summits of the Odenwald, with a view to the west of the Rhine plain, the Haardt and the Pfalzer Wald, while to the east there is a fine panorama over the rounded summits and the woodlands of the Odenwald. Numerous castles can be reached on foot such as the Burg-ruine Frankenstein, the Schloß Heiligenberg, the Fürstenlager at Auerbach and the Königshalle in the former monastery at Lorsch, the latter being the oldest building of the Carolingian era on German soil which is still in good condition. In the steeply sided Neckartal which forms Hessen's southern boundary with Baden-Württemberg, lie such attractive towns as Hirschhorn and Neckarsteinach.

Kassel dominates the northern part of Hessen. The city claims that no less than 63% of its surface area is green space available for recreational use. The present city has its origins in the decision of Landgrave Karl von Hessen (1670-1730) to invite French Huguenots to establish industry close to his ducal residence on the Fulda. In 1705 the exiled French inventor, Denis Papin, demonstrated the first experimental use of steam for power for his patron. Kassel's tradition of innovative research in engineering and technology continues to this day. The folklorists and philologists Wilhelm and Jakob Grimm (1786-1859, 1785-1863) were born in Kassel and collected much of their material from this region. There is a memorial to them in the city centre which is attractively pedestrianised; a model of a modern, civilised urban environment.

The Landgrave's magnificent eighteenth-century castle (where Jerôme Bonaparte, King of Westphalia, held court) and its superb park, Bergpark Wilhelmshöhe, have survived, with a spectacular series of cascades and fountains leading up to a great statue of Hercules at the park's apex. There is an interesting collection of paintings in the Schloß. The parkland and surrounding countryside and the riverside at Karlsaue have excellent networks of footpaths from which to enjoy the parkland. A special feature is an annual Lichtspielfest on the Wilhelmshöhe when thousands of people make their way up with lanterns; the climax is a splendid firework display.

Immediately to the west of Kassel, and bordering on the city, is the **Naturpark Habichtswald**, which includes the northern summits of the Hessische Bergland and borders on the Weserbergland to the north. To the west lies the Waldecker Land. The core of the park is the Habichtswald itself with the 615 metres high Hohen Gras and the Langenberg at 556 metres. The area was originally settled by tribes known as the Chatten 2,500 years ago, who were then called Hassi in medieval times which eventually became Hessen, thus giving their name to the federal state.

Neolithic and Bronze Age settlements have been discovered here and there are remains of the Altenburg, an extensive fortification at Niederstein, built by the Chatten. Numerous ruined medieval fortresses and towers in the area were built to protect the towns and trade routes. Limestone in the north and west and sandstone in the central region and the west, as well as faults and rift valleys west of the river Fulda, make this a dramatic landscape. There are also basalt formations here which indicate a volcanic origin.

Mountain beech dominates the forest areas, with luxuriant plant cover everywhere. On the warmer limestone slopes around Zierenberg there are unusual steppe-type plants. Spring flowers cover the scree-strewn slopes, with various ferns and mosses on the red sandstone areas. There are seven nature reserves within the park reflecting its special fauna and flora.

Typically for Hessen, walkers have an excellent choice of paths, including 130 circular routes from car parks but also some important linear routes. In the south of the nature park are houses and farms built in the Frankish style, and in the northwest in the Saxon style, explaining a great deal of the region's earlier history. There are also twenty-one towers and fortresses, with the oldest dating from the twelfth century; the medieval Weidelsburg at Ippinghausen and the Kugelsburg at Volkmarsen are in the best condition, while the old towns of Zierenberg, Naumburg and Niedenstein from the same period are worth seeing.

Access from Kassel is particularly convenient along the railway to Volkmarsen via Zierenberg, Altenhausen and Wolfhagen. The old scenic line to Naumberg is closed to ordinary traffic, but operates as a preserved line with steam power from Kassel Wilhemshöhe station via Hoof on a limited number of weekend days per year; at other times there are good bus links from Kassel.

Melsungen to the south of Kassel on the Fulda, and served by rail, is one of the finest half-timbered towns in Germany. It lies close to the **Meißner-Kaufinger Wald Naturpark** to the southeast of Kassel.

At least half this nature park is wooded, the rest being gentle farmland with cherry orchards whose spring blossom is famous. There is a huge choice of waymarked routes for a day's walk or even a week or more through the area as well as other routes. Old salt ways are to be found around Bad Sooden-Allendorf (rail served from Kassel via Bebra).

It was in this area that many of the stories of the Brothers Grimm had their origin. There is also a small museum which tells the story of local mining for lignite.

The old university and cathedral town of **Marburg am Lahn** was once a great pilgrimage centre, with thousands drawn to the relics of St. Elizabeth of Hungary, a child bride of Landgrave Ludwig von Thüringen who died of plague in 1227. The thirteenth century cathedral, which once contained Elizabeth's remains, is the first gothic cathedral in Germany. At the Reformation Marburg became a centre for Protestantism. The old town has a fine sixteenth century town hall and a market square of half-timbered houses and inns.

In the **Knüllgebirge**, a region of forest, limestone hills and farmed valleys between Marburg and Bad Hersfeld, a local society, the Knüllgebirgsverein, campaigns to protect this vulnerable area. On a 'red list' of endangered species of flowers are greater spearwort, water avens, yellow pimpernel, common wintergreen, pheasant's eye and bird's nest orchids. An interesting new footpath is known as the Ruhland Pfad after

Johannes Ruhland, the medieval creator of an eight kilometre watercourse from Sachsenhausen to Trysa which provided the village with water from an artesian well for almost 500 years. The new path follows the water course and returns by a circular route.

The **Naturpark Diemelsee** in the northwest of Hessen, north of Marburg and west of Korbach, actually has a third of its area in Nordrhein-Westfalen and is part of the Rothaargebirge which is better known as the Sauerland. Its highest points are the Langenberg and the Hegekopf, both 834 metres high. Two rivers, the Diemel and the Aar, flow through the area, which was already settled in prehistoric times as the ending 'lar' on placenames indicates. The Frankish kings preferred the valleys where they could make use of grazing land and cultivate the fields, retaining an outer fringe of woodland. The mixed deciduous woods and beech woods are threatened by coniferisation, though the higher moorland areas round Usseln and Willingen still have tundra-like flora which has made their protected status into a key feature in this area.

Devonian slate, quartz, marl and limestone form the bedrock of this district, with the Eisenberg 562 metres in height, virtually the only mountain which produced gold in Germany, though these veins had already been worked out by the time of the Thirty Years War in the seventeenth century. There are numerous paths and long distance routes which form a variety of attractive ways through woods, fields, mountains and valleys. Worth seeing is the high Diemeltalsperre, a dam built to prevent possible flooding by the river Weser and which includes a lake 166 hectares in area. By this lake lies **Heringhausen**, founded by Charlemagne, with a romanesque basilica. The churches of Rhugena and Welleringhausen date from the same period. The Oserkopf at 708 metres can be easily climbed from Usseln, as can the Diemelsquelle, the source of the Diemel. Jäger's Weinberg and the Bühler Höhe are of particular interest to geologists. The town of **Korbach** itself dates from at least 980 AD and has medieval buildings and old walls and towers. The railway line from Korbach to Brilon Wals, with stations at Usseln and Willingen, serves the south of the park.

The **Hessische Rhön** lies east of **Fulda** and along the boundary with Thüringen and Bayern, all three parts of the Rhön forming a major Biosphäre Reservat across the three states. The Hessische Rhön Naturpark includes part of the Rhön foreland, the Küppigen Rhön and the Hohen Rhön. The massif of the Hohen Rhön lies in the east on an enclosed high plateau of over 800 metres above sea level with few passes across it. There are treeless areas and wooded summits with Hessen's highest mountain – the 952 metres high Wasserkuppe. There had been some prehistoric settlement and Christianity arrived when the British missionaries St. Kilian and St. Boniface converted local people. The religious overlords of Fulda and **Würzburg** tended to encourage individual farmsteads and small hamlets instead of larger settlements, which today have a charming, almost Alpine character.

Geologically the Rhön dates from the Trias and the Tertiary periods and consists of limestone or red sandstone covered by marl and clay layers. Volcanic upheavals and movements of the earth's surface formed the basalt-topped summits of the Hohen Rhön. The area is only a third wooded after much tree cover was felled in the time of early settlements. Spruce pushed out the indigenous beechwoods which were the Rhön's original tree cover, though there are still plenty of mixed beech woods. Plants include arum, gentian, arnica, orchids, anemones, yellow foxglove, Turk's cap lily, sundew and the carline thistle.

There are 360 kilometres of waymarked paths through the nature park including a 10 kilometre geological path on the west slope of the Wasserkuppe and a prehistoric trail on the Milseburg. The Hochwildschutzpark is a high-level deer park at Ehrengrund near Gersfeld. Other fascinating areas include the Blockmeere at Schafstein and the Rote Moor, whilst the Gluckaikessel with the Guckaisee, Eube and Pferdekopf are very attractive scenically. Particularly fine is the Milseburg hill, 835 metres high with a nature reserve, a mountain chapel and extensive views. The chapel was formerly a place of pilgrimage. Schloß Bieberstein on the Kugelberg, and the Rhöner Museum at Tann, are also particularly interesting.

Access by train from Fulda is along the Röhnbahn to Gersfeld, but other former rail links have sadly vanished. There are however good replacement bus links and other local bus services.

The **Spessart Naturpark** in the southeast of Hessen is much better served by rail transport, lying to the south of the busy Fulda-Hanau-Frankfurt line, with useful local stations such as Gelnhausen and Schlüchturn and a little local 'Kleinbahn' between Wächtersbach and Bad Orb which at busier times is a train, but at quiet times of the day and week is operated, pragmatically perhaps, by buses. The nature park covers only the northern part of the Spessart, one of the largest forested areas in Germany, which again has a history of early settlement. It is composed of red sandstone with two basalt outcrops, the Beilstein and the Alsberger Olatte. It is particularly rich in red deer and wild boar and there are numerous orchid species, fritillaries, foxgloves, Turk's cap lily and sundew. In this 729 kilometre long nature park, with its four hundred kilometres of footpaths, there are opportunities to walk without carrying luggage ('Wandern ohne Gepäck') on two long distance paths which were ancient trade routes, the Eselweg (donkey path) from Schlüchtern to Miltenberg on the Main, and the Birkenhainerstraße from Neuwirtshausen to Gemünden. A very attractive medieval town is Gelnhausen with numerous churches and buildings of early date.

The **Hohe Vogelsberg** lies in the centre of Hessen, west of Fulda, and has a hilly landscape broken up by woodlands, an expanse of moorland known as the Breungeshainer Heide, and by areas of farmland. There are numerous plant species including globeflowers, thyme, and various mosses and lichens. The region is also known for its archaeological interest, including Bronze Age remains. Half-timbered houses are quite a feature here, as in Schotten's town hall and the Teufelmühle in Grebenhain-Ilbeshausen. Some interesting four, five and six day circular walking packages in the region are offered by the Vogelsberger Höhenclub and the Vogelsberg and Wetterau tourist office.

The Hessen Fremdenverkehrsamt is especially well organised to cater for green travellers. An excellent range of publications detail a variety of walking and cycling routes in different regions of the state, as well as combined accommodation and activity packages of walking, cycling, farmhouse holidays, some with 'ohne Gepäck' luggage transfer facilities. There are no less than eleven state sponsored long distance footpaths or Wanderwege through the state, all individually waymarked and with corresponding 1:50,000 scale maps produced by the Hessische Landesvermessungsamt.

But a particularly fascinating 'sanfter Tourismus' or responsible tourism initiative in Hessen involves a co-operative of twelve accommodation centres which have a particular character of their own. All in fact are traditional buildings, for example an old mill, a blacksmith's shop, a forestry house, traditional farmhouse and a wine pressing centre. Each of the centres offers food and accommodation with a wide and varied programme of special 'green' facilities and courses such as canoeing, pottery, horseriding, cycling, gardening, using energy from the sun, theatre, music and meditation. There are excursions to find edible wild plants, a 'four elements' cycle tour, a cycle tour for gourmets, musical experiences in four different towns, a canoe journey which instructs on the ecology of the waters and streams, and a delightful Märchen Tour (fairytale ride) for children through the country of the Brothers Grimm.

Green for this group means that they are conscious that Hessen is a region through which so many visitors travel from all directions to reach their particular destination, but where relatively few actually stay. The Arbeitsgemeinschaft Hessischer Tagungshäuser or AGHT works to make a stay in Hessen a positive environmental experience. Environmental concern is the keynote with the four medieval elements – earth, air, fire (energy) and water seen as symbolic of the four elements of the modern world which need safeguarding from over-exploitation by industrial civilisation. But it is important, too, that there is social and cultural integration with nearby village communities and small towns, all of which are well away from the major, over-used recreational areas. The group is keen too, to encourage visitors throughout the year, and not just in the main holiday season.

The AGHT exists not only to help develop the right kind of tourism initiatives within the state of Hessen, but well beyond Hessen's boundaries. A key concept is that encouragement be given to the visitors to choose and direct their own activities, experiences and adventures, rather than absorbing a package of ready-made experiences. Yet it is equally important for the visitor to be aware of local conditions and help to support the local economy. Finally the holiday should be a positive experience for the participants which should influence and enrich daily lives when they return home.

Further information _____

Hessischer Fremdenverkehrsverband e.V., Abraham-Lincoln-Straße 38-42, D-6200 Wiesbaden.

Hessischen Landesvermessungsamt, Schapenstraße 9, D-6200 Wiesbaden, for maps of waymarked routes.

AG Hessischer Tagungshäuser & Bildungstätten in Selbstverwaltung e.V. (AGHT), Am Steinbruch 12, D-3553 Cölbe.

Rheinland-Pfalz _____

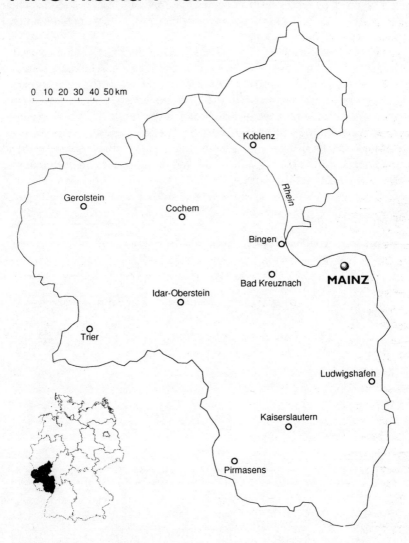

0 10 20 30 40 50 km

Koblenz

Rhein

Gerolstein

Cochem

Bingen

Bad Kreuznach

MAINZ

Idar-Oberstein

Trier

Ludwigshafen

Kaiserslautern

Pirmasens

It was English travellers, writers and painters above all, who, in the late eighteenth and early nineteenth centuries, first discovered the romantic beauty of the Rhine. A Rhine journey soon became an essential part of a fashionable tour of the Continent for an educated young aristocrat on his first trip across the North Sea.

The most influential of such visitors was no less a figure than Lord Byron, who in 1816 came to the Rhine to use part of the landscape where 'the river nobly foams and flows' as a backcloth to his immensely popular and influential narrative poem of romantic love and heroism *Childe Harold*:

> The rolling stream, the precipice's gloom,
> The forest's growth, and Gothic walls between,
> The wild rocks shaped as they had turrets been . . .

Not surprisingly a copy of *Childe Harold* became an essential part of the luggage of any young or not so young seeker of melancholy beauty in continental Europe. Byron's tall friend Shelley was suitably impressed by the scenery, but he also complained about the shortness of the beds in his Rhineland accommodation which caused his feet to hang over the edge.

But it was the landscape painters, working in both watercolours and oil, who added most to the perceptions of romantic Rhineland scenery. J.M.W. Turner, one of England's greatest painters, filled a whole sketch book with his Rhine drawings and painted over fifty watercolours from his very first Rhine journey. Many other painters and aesthetes were to follow. The impressionable John Ruskin was first taken to the Rhine as a boy of fourteen.

Significantly, 1816, the year of Byron's 'Childe Harold visit', was also the year that the first passenger steamboat appeared on the Rhine. It had been built in England especially for Rhine traffic. Within a generation, and with the coming of the railways, the tourist trickle was to become a flood as tens of thousands of visitors from all over Europe came to take a Rhine cruise or enjoy the river scenery from the railway lines along both banks. By the middle of the nineteenth century there were already over a hundred travel books published describing the glories of the Rhine scenery.

There were soon complaints about the exorbitant amounts that inn-keepers, riverboat captains and even the customs men on the Rhine demanded of foreign visitors. Thackeray declined to describe the Rhine scenery in his writings, because he declared that everybody from high to low had already been there, and the poet Thomas Hood who lived in Koblenz for two years, stated in 1840 that the flood of visitors meant the customs men who guarded the passes had no time even to refresh themselves with a pinch of snuff.

But it was as a major transport route rather than a tourist attraction that the Rhine has played such an important part in European history and culture. Scores of castles safeguarding passage along the Rhine or, alternatively, acting as strongholds of unscrupulous robber barons and thieves threatening river craft, testify to the river's strategic importance.

Its role as Europe's greatest commercial waterway has not diminished. The Rhine has its source in the Swiss Alps and enters the North Sea west of Rotterdam. It is joined below Mannheim by the Neckar, then by the Main and finally by the Mosel. Quite large craft can navigate the Rhine from Basle to Rotterdam. Koblenz, in Rheinland-Pfalz, lies in the middle of the 832 kilometre long inland shipping route. On an average of two weeks a year, barges can be delayed by ice round the Loreley rock. As the Rhine enters Rheinland-Pfalz it turns into the Rhine Gorge where there are a series of dangerous whirlpools and impressive escarpments. It is here that the Rhine has its succession of vineyards, woods, rocky outcrops and ruined fortresses – scenically magnificent, but needing a good deal of navigational skill to negotiate. The valley opens out at the Neuwied Basin where it is joined by the Mosel and Lahn and flows at the foot of the Siebengebirge to Bonn and Köln and then into the industrial landscape of Duisburg in Nordrhein-Westfalen.

Perhaps the most characteristic feature of the Rhine is the endless procession of huge motor barges many metres in length operating in tandem or with a tow, often used as a floating home for Rhine families as washing fluttering in the breeze and bicycles on deck indicate, and carrying freight such as Ruhr coal and hydrocarbons up to Switzerland. Increasingly freight is carried in containers. German imports include construction materials, fertilisers such as potash from Alsace and semi-finished industrial products. There is also substantial trade in oil and refined oil products. Such a form of freight transport is, of course, much more energy efficient and less polluting than comparable loads carried by diesel-guzzling lorries or even by relatively efficient electric or diesel freight trains.

But you will also see almost as many pleasure craft along the Rhine, many of them the familiar white Köln-Düsseldorf Deutsche Rheinschiffahrt cruisers that operate a regular river bus service calling at landing stages at all towns and villages between Mainz and Köln, as well as numerous package holiday cruise vessels from both the Netherlands and Germany.

Rheinland-Pfalz, as its name implies, covers much of the most dramatic central section of the Rhine, sharing the river with Baden-Württemberg and Nordrhein-Westfalen, and forms part of Germany's border with Belgium, Luxemburg and France. It also contains much of the important Rhine tributary the Mosel (Moselle). Both the Rhine and the Mosel areas are famed winegrowing regions. But also important are the Ahr with unusually for Germany an emphasis on red wine, the Nahe, the Saar and the Ruwer. Wine cultivation originated with the Romans and was developed with much expertise by the monks in the Middle

Ages. Uniquely in Germany Rheinland-Pfalz has a Weinbauminister, a Ministry of Viniculture.

The old Roman towns of **Mainz** (the state capital), **Koblenz, Trier** and **Worms** are old bishoprics retaining enormous historic interest. But modern industries such as mechanical engineering in **Kaiserslautern**, Mainz and Koblenz, shoe manufacturing at **Pirmasens** and jewelry making at Idar-Oberstein in the Hunsrück mountains give the region a wide industrial base.

The state of Rheinland-Pfalz was created as a result of the post-war restructuring of West Germany and involved bringing together areas with very different traditions that were originally parts of Bayern, Hessen and Prussia. The word 'Pfalz', from the Latin 'palantia' ('palatinate' in English) means the king's or emperor's residence, referring to the old Holy Roman emperors. The residence was of a temporary nature, used during visits for hunting in the forest or where the emperor stayed whilst journeying around his domains. But the region's central role in earlier history, reflected by its chains of castles, palaces, strongholds and imperial splendours, suffered a decline during more recent times when Prussia rose to power, when the area became known as 'Prussia's stepchild' and was therefore relatively marginalised.

Geologically, the wooded red sandstone mountains of Rheinland-Pfalz are a continuation of the northern Vosges in France and are broken by escarpments. The forested Wasgau with its hilltop ruins stretches between Alsace and the Pirmasens-Lindau road with villages lying in the hollows. The Pfälzerwald extends as an almost unbroken wooded massif in the south of the state, with relatively few inhabitants.

Much of this area is now part of the Pfälzerwald Naturpark south of Kaiserslautern, which has excellent facilities for both walkers and cyclists. There are direct rail services to Kaiserslautern whilst the line between Landau and **Saarbrücken** via Hinterwiedental and Pirmasens goes through the centre of the nature park. A preserved railway, the delightfully named Kuckucksbähnel – the little cuckoo railway – operates over the 13 kilometres from Lambrecht to Elmstein on summer weekends.

There are a number of superb waymarked paths through the whole of the West Pfalz, including the nature park and the Pfalzer Bergland to the north, with such exotic titles as the West Pfalz-Wanderweg (400 kilometres), the Musikantenland-Wanderweg, the Burgen Wanderweg and the Barbarossa Wanderweg. All are attractively packaged and marketed by the West Pfalz tourist office, using a variety of accommodation and luggage-carrying services, as walking holidays lasting between four and fifteen days.

There is no better way of exploring the Rhine itself than by boat. The KD services, shown in the DB Kursbuch, are frequent and DB rail passes and most rail tickets are valid on them. You can break your journey at numerous fascinating points. Alternatively, busy railway lines operate along each bank. InterCity and local services from Köln to Koblenz and Mainz on the left bank and local services along the right bank from Köln to Neuwied, Koblenz/Niederlahnstein and Wiesbaden. Ferries, both foot passenger and car, cross the river at various points. Package holidays are also available by boat, or boat and coach. Excellent value to discover the area is a Deutsche Bundesbahn Tourenkarte, valid in the region on trains, boats and many local buses.

The most beautiful stretch of the Rhine boat journey begins at **Mainz** with a view of Mainz cathedral with its spires and domes. In Roman times there was a 98 foot high aqueduct here, but today only some ruined stones mark what was undoubtedly a most impressive structure. The city itself lies in the fertile Mainz basin which is the most northerly point of the upper Rhine lowland plain. It was originally founded as an archbishopric by St. Boniface and from this beginning the city became the focal point of German Christianity. It is also the city where the famous Gutenberg Bible was first produced in 1450 when Johannes Gutenberg set up his printing press and transformed the world with multiple copies of books, which were now cheaper and more accessible to a much wider audience than the old hand-written and illuminated manuscripts. The Gutenberg Museum in the 'Zum römischen Kaiser' building deals with the history of printing. Among many lovely buildings in Mainz, one of the finest is the Renaissance electoral palace, which now houses the Römisch-Germanischen Zentralmuseum.

Although 80% of the old centre was damaged in the last war, there are still many very attractive parts of the city to wander through. Among many fine reliefs and sculptures in Mainz's churches, the Chagall windows in St. Stephan's church with their very penetrating blue colour are especially celebrated. Mainz is also the centre of the area's wine trade and is an important producer of Sekt, the champagne-style sparkling German wine.

On St. John's Eve there is a spectacular firework display where the Rhine flames with colour, a truly magical sight; and there is a long tradition of carnival festivities. The Hunsrück and Taunus mountains (see Hessen) are all within easy reach of Mainz by train as well as along the Rhine itself by boat.

As you continue downriver, you reach charming small wine towns like **Eltville** with its half-timbered buildings, **Ingelheim** with the twelfth century Saal church, and noted for its red wine and asparagus cultivation, **Bingen** with its Roman remains and caves – the Binger Loch – and

Rüdesheim with its cable railway to the Niederwald 'Germania' monument.

Rheinhessen, as this region is known, is Germany's oldest wine producing region with hectares of vineyards in such famous wine districts as Oppenheim, Nierstein, Nackenheim and Ingelheim, with countless large and small vineyards, wine cellars, wine festivals, wine tastings and wine tours available.

If you see the sign 'Früh Schoppen' outside a Gasthof in the area it means a morning glass of local wine is available, a Schoppen being the characteristic Rheinland thick-stemmed green wine glass. Most vintners are not allowed to have guesthouses on the premises, but for four months each year they can put out tables and chairs and sell their own wine for visitors' consumption – look for the sign 'Strausswirtschaft' which indicates this facility.

The St. Ursula Weinkellerei at Bingen is an example of a growing number of organic vineyards in Germany. Grapes are grown without the use of pesticides and nitrogenous, soluble phosphate and sludge fertilisers. A wide variety of permissible fertilisers used include stable manure, chicken manure, sea algae meal and extracts, crop residues, bark compost, and various mineral fertilisers provided there is no previous contamination. Regular soil analyses are made to check this. In the same way, care is taken that the vegetable and mineral preparations used will improve vine growth and promote disease resistant strains. The processing rules for the manufacture of juice, wine and sparkling wine are strictly adhered to and only grapes which are grown ecologically are processed.

The St. Ursula vineyard also aims to avoid using wasteful energy processes and care is taken that organic wastes from the grape processing do not pollute the environment. Processing, manufacture, bottling and storage must all take ecological factors into consideration and every effort is made for instance to use as little sulphuric acid in processing as possible. There is a stringent yearly inspection to see that these goals are being met and this includes operational reports on fertilisation, soil and plant cultivation, a site plan, a crop report and the submission of a cellar book.

A list of other organic vineyards in Rheinland-Pfalz and elsewhere in Germany is given in *Das Alternative Branchenbuch* (address on page 45).

The one-thousand-year-old castle of **Brömserburg** has a moat and houses Germany's oldest wine museum, including a collection of drinking vessels dating back over the last 2,000 years. The Brömserhof contains one of the largest collections of automatic musical instruments in the world and there is the chance to take the Winzer-express round the vineyards or to wander in a sheltered side valley of the Niederwald round the Rhein-Taunus Naturpark or continue along the river beneath steep cliffs and innumerable romantic castles and fortresses. In previous centuries not only was the Rhine an extremely difficult river to negotiate, but the cliff-tops and steep wooded slopes gave marauding robber bands plenty of cover. What is now seen as romantic scenery could, in times past, be threatening and dangerous terrain.

The Mäuseturm, originally a customs tower which stands on an island, is used today as a signalling tower, while the **Loreley Felsen** is a cliff rising steeply above the Rhine at a spot where the river is only 90 metres wide and at low water the dangerous reefs can be seen. The song 'Die Lorelei' describes a beautiful maiden combing her long flowing hair while perched on a rock, enticing sailors to their doom on those rocks as they listen to her singing. There are many other famous legends connected with the Rhine and among the best known are the Nibelungenlied, a great epic poem telling of priceless treasure hidden in the Rhine, passion, greed and betrayal. This is the legend which was transformed by Richard Wagner into his great operatic saga *Der Ring des Nibelungen*.

The wine town of **Boppard** is situated where six side valleys meet on the Rhine and was first a Roman, then a Frankish settlement. High above the Rhine and reached from Boppard by chairlift or steep footpath is a panoramic viewpoint, the Vierseenblick, where the river (owing to a series of bends and curves) looks like four separate lakes. There is a good choice of forest and riverside walks in this region, with no fewer than forty separate waymarked routes in the area. Ferries cross to Kamp and Filsen across the Rhine. **Bad Salzig** close by is an important cherry growing area, in the last century having a major export trade with England. A cherry festival is held in the village towards the end of June.

Marksburg, about 12 kilometres down river from Boppard, is another example of a fortress castle crowning a steep summit. It stands above the town of Braubach. It managed not surprisingly to withstand all attacks during its long history. This fact undoubtedly helped to make it the only example on the middle Rhine of an unblemished medieval castle. Annually, on the second Saturday in August, up to 500,000 people enjoy the sight of the Rhine lit up by the most fantastic firework display from Braubach to Ehrenbreitstein.

The old city of **Koblenz** is situated at a confluence where the Mosel flows into the Rhine close by the Deutsches Eck, which owes its name to the Deutschordensritter who founded a settlement at this point in 1216. An equestrian statue of Emperor Wilhelm I, erected in 1897 and recently replaced after war damage, marks the spot and symbolises German unity. A delightful Koblenz feature is the Augenroller, literally someone who rolls his eyes, which is the head and shoulders of a man with cap and beard, all sculpted in black and set under the clock of the old town hall. The clock mechanism causes the perpetual motion and on the hour he sticks out a red tongue. It is meant to symbolise the spirit of independence among Koblenz's citizens and was a way of defying the city's ancient clerical overlords. The Schängelbrunnen is a fountain with a figure of a boy who appears to spit at times at the unwary who linger too near. The city is dominated by Stolzenfels Schloß, the Prince Electors' palace and the magnificent hilltop Ehrenbreitstein castle, an object of attention for many painters including Turner, who captured it in a celebrated watercolour.

North and east of Koblenz is the **Westerwald**, including two nature parks. The 500 square kilometres of the Rhein-Westerwald Naturpark lie east of Bad Hönnigen and Bad Honnef, across gently forested hills and with something like 100 kilometres of waymarked paths. This area was known as Potter's Land because of excellent local clays, still worked, and it is possible to visit local potteries and even make your own earthenware pots. To the south is the slightly larger Nassau Naturpark around Bad Ems in the beautiful valley of the river Lahn, Lahnstein, Diez, Montabaur and Holzhausen. A short distance further up river and within easy walking distance of Lahn is the Premonstratensian abbey of Arnstein on a craggy, wooded rock above the valley. The Lahn valley is easily accessible from Koblenz along the Lahntalbahn via Bad Ems and Nassau to Wetzlar, and this line also serves the northern perimeter of the Taunus mountains (see Hessen), with a branch from Limburg to Montabaur on the edge of the nature park.

The **Mosel** river is 545 kilometres in length and is one of the Rhine's longest tributaries. It has its source in the Vosges mountains in France, but one half of its course runs through Germany. It winds its way through steeply wooded craggy banks, rather like the Rhine, and has an equally impressive series of ruined and restored castles overlooking its banks and vineyards. Again, the valley can easily be penetrated by both river and rail, with trains between Koblenz and Trier serving local stations and KD boats to Cochem and Trier via Bernkastel (winter months only to Cochem). The Mosel Wein Pfad is a popular footpath route alongside the Mosel between the picturesque old town of **Cochem** with its hilltop castle and the celebrated Mosel wine town of **Bernkastel**, with ample opportunities for wine tasting.

Vineyards were first introduced here by the Romans and the Neumager Weinschiff (wine boat) in the museum at **Trier** is an early example of the importance of winegrowing in the area. Trier is probably Germany's oldest town, with some superb Roman remains such as the Porta Nigra, the Roman city's northern exit. Other Roman remains include a basilica and the ruined baths with extensive underground channels. The splendid Roman amphitheatre was built in 100 AD and has room for 25,000 people. The town became a bishopric in the fourth century, the first north of the Alps, and was later upgraded to an archbishopric in the ninth century under Charlemagne. The city then became an electoral seat in the twelfth century. In the Dietrichstraße is a Frankenturm dating from the eleventh century and also one of the earliest fortified houses in Germany. The cathedral, one of Germany's oldest churches, has some superb interior stone carvings and a number of treasures. Half a kilometre southwest from the Hauptmark area is Karl Marx's birthplace.

About eight kilometres by rail from Trier is the town of **Konz** on the confluence of the Saar and Mosel, close to the border with Belgium, France and Luxemburg, with an open air museum at Roscheiderhof. The town tourist authority has put together some excellent cycling packages along minor roads through the upper Mosel area and Hunsrück and into Luxemburg. The cost of a four, five or seven day package includes overnight accommodation, cycle hire (optional) and all maps. An interesting regional speciality known as Häferschnapps or yeast brandy (also called Mosel whisky) is produced in the area from the waste products of the winemaking industry. Weincräwes is a regional dish composed of pork ribs and sauerkraut cooked with stock, Mosel wine, onions and a bay leaf. It is served on a bed of potato purée, with the pork ribs topped with lightly browned onions and pieces of bacon.

The **Hunsrück** region, a long line of hills lying between the Mosel and the Nahe, has achieved worldwide fame through Edgar Reitz's masterly film of rural life in Germany between the end of World War I and the 1980s, *Heimat*, seen through the eyes of local village people.

In former times many precious stones were mined in the region. Most veins have now been worked out, so that the stones cut and polished in Idar-Oberstein are generally imported from South Africa. However it is still sometimes possible for visitors to find their own stones and even to learn how to polish them themselves. A number of former mines are open to today's visitors – the Steinkaulenberg with its labyrinth of caves where gems were once mined, the Kupferberg mine in Fischbach with its traces of Celtic and Roman mining activity, the Herrenberg slate mine at Bundenbach and the quicksilver (mercury) mine Schmittenstollen at Niederhausen.

Idar-Oberstein, with a 500 year old church on a rock, makes a good centre to explore the Hunsrück, being rail served. There are still over a thousand precious stone cutters and gem dealers active in the town and there is a combined gem and diamond exchange with research centres of international rank. The Romantische Mühlenwanderung is a footpath route with luggage transfer and accommodation packages linking old watermills from Hoxel over Wenigerath, Gonzerath, Weiperath and returning to Hoxel. Riding holidays are also arranged, or you can take a Hunsrück-Safari in pioneer-style covered horse-drawn waggon, using your own sleeping bag for nights under the canvas.

The Saar-Hunsrück Naturpark covers much of the central part of this area, crossing into neighbouring Saarland. It is an area of gently rolling upland, open plains, woods and juniper heath. Geologically, the Hunsrück is composed of slate schists containing myriads of fossils. Celtic tribes mined the first mineral ores and built fortifications to protect them while their Roman conquerors built settlements with temples and villas. This is a relatively little known area, crossed by good networks of waymarked footpaths with many fine viewpoints, and is particularly rich in Roman and other remains.

The Nahe valley south of Boppard and Emmelshausen and fringing on the Hunsrück has a number of attractive spa towns, such as **Bad Münster am Stein-Ebernburg** where the huge Rotenfels cliff rises from the river, the highest crag north of the Alps. There are brine springs, Roman remains, villages with superb churches, vineyards, health spas, waymarked walking trails, and cycle routes. This is an area much less heavily visited than the main Rhine Valley, but easily accessible by train along the Mainz-Saarbrücken line via **Bad Kreuznach** and Idar-Oberstein, with a branch at Neunkirchen to Lebach in Saarland.

Emmelshausen is an attractive resort reached by a little scenic railway line from Boppard and lying in a countryside of wide fields and scattered villages. There are plenty of waymarked footpaths through extensive deciduous and coniferous woodland. Good walks lead to the romantic valleys of the Baybach with its ruined town of Waldeck or to the Ehrbachklamm with the castle Schloß Schöneck or the ruined Rauschenburg or the Ehrenburg.

Regional specialities of the Hunsrück are spit-roast and also Krumbierewurst, a sausage made of grated potatoes and belly of pork which is sometimes referred to as Kartoffelwurst.

The railway line which runs from Trier to Köln skirts the **Eifel** mountains, a long ridge of ancient and sometimes volcanic hills that forms the frontiers with both Luxemburg and the Belgian Ardennes.

The Ahr valley to the east is noted for its Burgundy-style wine. With its timber-framed houses on vine-covered slopes and over 500 hectares of vines under cultivation, the Ahr district is Germany's largest red wine producing region. A branch line from Remagen serves the Ahr valley, including Bad Neuenahr and Ahrweiler, noted for its narrow streets and half-timbered houses.

The South Eifel lies west of the old towns of **Prüm** and **Bitburg** – famous for its beer – and contains a cross-border European park, the Deutsch-Luxemburgische Naturpark, a superb area of thick forest, deep gorges, upland meadows and moorland. Walking opportunities of over 2,000 kilometres of waymarked trails include a number of special themed walks organised by the local tourist office, such as ecological rambles, night walks and rambles between local farmhouses offering accommodation.

The Schnee Eifel as its name implies is the wildest part of the Eifel, along the Belgian border, rising to the 698 metres summit of the Schwarzer Mann.

The central Eifel around **Gerolstein**, a town famous for its mineral water springs, is, because of its volcanic history, known as Vulkaneifel, the volcanic Eifel area. A notable feature of this popular holiday region are the deep lakes south of the town of **Daun** (bus rail links via Mayer or Gerolstein) formed by volcanic craters. Near **Kelberg** to the north are such remarkable geological phenomena as the Beilstein, an extraordinary basalt formation, whilst the Mosbrucher Weiher Naturschutzgebiet lies in an enormous basin shaped by volcanic activity.

At **Kasselburg** just north of Gerolstein is the Eifel Adler und Wolf Park, a reservation with major collections of these threatened species, eagles and wolves, whilst at **Hillesheim** there is a geological trail around the Hillesheim limestone basin. Walking packages in the Vulkaneifel include guided geological weekends and archaeological and natural history weeks.

Further information ———————————————————————

Fremdenverkehrsverband **Rheinland-Pfalz e.V.**, Postfach 1420, D-5400 Koblenz.
St. Ursula Weinkellerei GmbH, Postfach 1742, D-6530 Bingen 1.

Nordrhein-Westfalen _____

'Ein starkes Stück Deutschland' – a strong part of Germany – was the motto used in recent years by the government of Nordrhein-Westfalen in a regular series of full-page advertisements in the national press.

Conscious of the need to avoid a North-South divide, the state government of Nordrhein-Westfalen, Germany's most densely populated and heavily industrialised state with a population of over 17 million, is happy to spend money on well-placed propaganda to help change the image of the state, particularly of the Ruhr area. As they have convincingly argued, despite the enormous economic success of the southern states of Germany in attracting new computer-based industries, the real manufacturing wealth and economic power remains in the north. Germany has no intention of becoming a service and tourism led economy, and the state of Nordrhein-Westfalen has taken a high profile, interventionist role in helping to achieve the transformation of dying 'smokestack' industrial areas into modern high technology and quality engineering manufacture, wherever possible using old industrial land rather than greenfield sites. High upon the state's agenda has been the removal of some of the worst eyesores of the industrial past, cleaning up dereliction and 'renaturing' whole areas which a generation ago were amongst the filthiest and most industrially polluted in Europe. The soot which fell daily over the region, poisoning the soil and polluting the water, is now largely a memory, and though there is still much to be done, the advertisements with colour pictures of fish swimming in the clear waters of a once polluted industrial river are no mere boast.

Details that a visitor notices are the number of trees planted everywhere, the former slag heaps that now look like green natural hills, the dominance of cycleways in city and suburban areas, and simple mechanisms like concrete noise baffles built alongside motorways (and sometimes railways) which don't remain as blank concrete walls but are planted with trailing green plants to soften the effect and help soak up greenhouse gases.

There could be no greater demonstration of the effectiveness of a strong regional and federal government system than to see how, over recent years, environmentally, socially and above all economically, the region has improved. Nordrhein-Westfalen, which in more laissez-faire hands could have become one of the economic blackspots of Europe, enjoys renewed prosperity and an environment which is sometimes quite astonishingly green compared with the older industrial areas of other parts of Europe.

But Nordrhein-Westfalen is not just an industrial or former industrial Land. The state has always had a large rural hinterland including huge areas of superb countryside – forest, steep hills and attractive valleys, including a good section of the Rhine itself, as well as extremely charming old towns and villages.

The state was created after World War II from part of the old Rhineland and Westphalian provinces of Prussia, extending to the Dutch and Belgian borders, and also including the once independent state of Lippe to the north.

The core of the area is undoubtedly the **Ruhrgebiet**, which takes its name from the somewhat unpretentious river Ruhr, a tributary of the Rhine. The region forms the industrial heartland of Germany and indeed of northern Europe. It owes its origins to one of the richest bituminous coal seams in the world, around which grew huge mining, iron, steel and heavy engineering industries. Much but by no means all of this heavy industry has now been superseded by newer electronics, chemicals, synthetic fibres, paints, aluminium processing, consumer goods and petroleum refining industries. Between the towns of Köln and Bonn a large field of lignite or brown coal is mined.

Though the Germans were great pioneers of early industrial techniques, especially in areas such mining technology, the Industrial Revolution which was already transforming England in the late eighteenth and early nineteenth centuries, for a variety of social and political reasons, came relatively late to Germany. It took till 1838 before Franz Haniel, who lived near Borbeck on the Ruhr, was able to sink a mine shaft and to pump out its flood water with steam power before mining coal. British engineers supervised the building of the first railways and built the first locomotives from the late 1830s onwards.

But during the middle and late nineteenth century, expansion was rapid. By 1913 400,000 people worked the Ruhr coal mines and annually 130,000 immigrants arrived in the region from other areas. What were small Westphalian towns expanded into cities with populations of hundreds of thousands with breathtaking speed. Many of the workers who arrived were Polish and this Polish flood reached 30,000 per annum in 1890. By 1912 the mining office of **Dortmund** alone had registered 129,000 Poles. Other nearby areas had similar figures.

This vast expansion, the transformation of a largely rural economy into one of the world's leading industrial nations in a matter of decades, had to pay a price in terms of serious environmental degradation. For generations in the Ruhrgebiet the colour white hardly existed because of the sooty, dirty, gritty atmosphere. Living under the 'Dunstglocke' or permanent pall of smoke was a health as much as an environmental hazard.

Two Westfalen figures who became legends in their own lifetime perhaps illustrate this rapid transformation of Germany from a rural to an industrial economy most vividly. Alfred Krupp of Essen wanted 'workers and not thinkers' for his factories and laid down in extraordinary detail in a document the way his works were to be run and what was expected of his workforce. Krupp, a patriarchal figure, was also full of overweening pride, the 'Kannonenkönig' who sold cannons to friend and foe alike, was courted by kings, paid good wages, and organised health insurance plus pensions at an early stage for his workers. He built homes, hospitals and co-operative shops for them, but it was because he wanted his workforce, whom he saw very definitely as his inferiors, to consider the factory as their whole life. He made his fortune by manufacturing railway locomotives and his guns and weaponry were sold to whoever could pay for them immaterial of politics. So excellent was their manufacture, that possession of them could be a decisive factor in determining the outcome of late nineteenth century warfare. It is said with some justice that it was Krupp's guns that won the Franco-German war for the Germans.

Alfred Thyssen began work in **Duisburg** and then founded his industrial empire in 1871 in Mülheim on the Ruhr, producing coal, steel and heavy machinery. He pioneered a process of freezing the coal seams so that neither water nor the usual rush of soil and stone would interfere with mining the coal. He also originated a 50 kilometre high pressure pipeline from Hamborn to Barmen and used the superfluous gas from the cokeworks; this use of gas by remote control in 1906 was two decades ahead of its time and before the founding of what became Ruhrgas AG. He was again ahead of his time with his projects for super-national industrial and economic co-operation and such institutions as the Rheinisch-Westfälisches AG, the state's largest electricity works, arose out of his initiatives.

Essen is perhaps typical of the great Ruhr towns, which still had twenty-two working mines at the end of the 1950s before the great coal crisis. The Krupp factories moved after the war to **Bochum** and Rheinhausen, and only the Zollverein pit remains open today. Nowadays small and medium-sized industrial complexes use the former heavy industrial sites, and their products range from manufacturing machinery, precision technology and optics to synthetic fibres and much else.

Düsseldorf on the Rhine, the state capital, has an elegance reflecting its origins as an aristocratic residency. It is the state's financial and banking centre, with surviving parts of the old town around the remains of the castle overlooking the Rhine, scores of small restaurants and pubs full of character ('Alt' bier is particularly popular) and elegant shopping parades. It is also the region's cultural centre, with a number of important museums and galleries, opera, ballet and a symphony orchestra. Heinrich Heine lived here for some years and there is a small Heine Museum. But Düsseldorf is also famed for its splendid parks, with linking parks and gardens crossing the entire city.

Dortmund is another typical Ruhr city, an old Hansestadt and inland port on the Ruhr (and later the Dortmund-Ems Kanal), for many years Germany's main sugar and wheat market, and a major centre of both the steel and coal industry. It is also Germany's beer capital, having had brewing rights for over 500 years with such famous names as Dortmunder Union, DAB, Thier, and Kronen produced in vast quantities. There are also many smaller private breweries.

Like most Ruhr cities, it suffered massive war damage, and initial rebuilding was slow. But in recent years, modernisation and improvement – for example the building of a new underground system – has helped pull the city out of recession. It has a reputation of being one of the best and cheapest shopping centres in Germany. A former derelict steel works on the edge of the city was transformed, in 1959, into the site of Germany's first national garden show (an idea later imported to Britain), and is now the site of the impressive Westfalenpark around the television tower (with its inevitable tower-top restaurant), with more than 2,000 varieties of roses blooming in the landscaped gardens. Nearby are modern sports halls and congress centres, lakes and stadia. Many remains of once great industrial undertakings in the region have been kept as massive monuments. In otherwise green areas you will see pit-head wheels, water towers, cooling towers, chimneys, and other relics of earlier industrial technology which are not seen as shameful relics of the past but as part of a heritage to celebrate, stylish pieces of architecture with their own strange beauty. The finest of these, such as the machine hall entrance at the Zollern II mine, are now under state protection as national monuments.

Close to Dortmund and running along the valley of the river Emscher from Kamen and Lünen past Castrop Rauxel, Gelsenkirchen and Oberhausen to Duisburg, lies one of Germany's most ambitious urban renewal schemes. The Emscher Park scheme is an exciting and original concept which arose out of the Emscher Park building exhibition of 1988 and is an ambitious attempt to regenerate the natural landscape along the Emscher corridor and to create a new quality of life in urban areas over a ten year period. The Emscher river has suffered great pollution from industrial effluents, mining and even household waste. The Emscher Park's prime goals are to restore green areas in a landscape park, to improve the Emscher river and its banks in an ecological sense, to transform the Rhein-Herne Kanal which covers 46 kilometres from a shipping lane to a recreational waterway with habitats for fauna and flora and to protect industrial heritage sites. Workshop sites within the landscape park are to be attractive and well designed, in a green setting with good communications, while new forms of housing and flats and the creation of new social, cultural and sports amenities are seen as part of the essential pattern of the landscape park. A network of cyclepaths and footpaths is also being created within the area to a variety of scenic and industrial sites, which give positive incentives to leisure time within the perimeters of the park.

At **Hagen**, south of Dortmund, is the Westfälische Freilichtsmuseum Technischer Kulturdenkmal, an open air museum devoted to the evolution of industry where, along the old industrialised valley of the little Mackingerbach river with its millponds, almost every conceivable industrial technique in Nordrhein-Westfalen is demonstrated – wind- and watermills, manufacturing in iron, steel, non-ferrous metals, smithing, forging, papermaking, brewing, printing, dying, weaving and much besides.

Not that protection of the environment and pride in industrial heritage is new. In fact the Ruhr's huge population density already caused concern early this century and green spaces and recreation areas were created by the Ruhrsiedlungverband, an organisation established for this purpose in 1920 which in 1979 became the Kommunlareverband Ruhrgebiet. A variety of green recreational areas were established within the Ruhr area itself, on the Nieder-Rhein around Köln, in the Hohen Mark north of the Ruhr (now a nature park) and in other areas, all with carefully waymarked footpath networks through them.

More recently five local 'Revierparke' were created during the 1970s as a mixture of informal park and recreation area. These are actually organised at grassroots level by an Arbeitskreis or a working group of volunteers, so that each Revierpark can specialise in the facilities it would like to have, though there is no compulsion to do this and it can simply remain as a piece of ordinary parkland. There are also five reservoirs on the Ruhr used for recreation, which are favourite spots for rowing, canoeing and sailing, while anglers can fish for carp, trout and pike.

As in other older industrial areas pigeons are popular in the Ruhr. Between Duisburg and Hamm is the world's largest group of pigeon fanciers, 45,000 in all, who go to enormous lengths to care for and race their birds.

The Ruhrgebiet has one of the world's most sophisticated co-ordinated public transport networks, with interlinking mainline and S-Bahn trains, city Metros, light rapid transit and guided and conventional bus systems, trams and at **Wuppertal** a unique suspended overhead railway – the Wuppertalbahn. Common ticketing systems are available throughout, making travel anywhere in the Ruhr and in most of Nordrhein-Westfalen cheap and convenient. An interesting feature is that most local trains, trams and even some buses carry cycles outside peak hours – a cycle symbol denotes the places where cycles can be stored. There are also some fascinating schemes of rural bus networks where buses can carry cycles, for example in the Vestich area from Recklinghausen and around **Münster.**

The countryside is always extremely close in Nordrhein-Westfalen. The **Sauerland** (meaning 'south' land), immediately to the southeast of the Ruhrgebiet, together with the Rothaargebirge Naturpark and the Bergisches Land, forms a green lung for the nearby towns and cities and is easy to access by bus or train. It is an area of partially volcanic hills, rising to the 841 metre high Winterberg, penetrated by narrow valleys, with reservoirs, and with excellent networks of footpaths. **Lüdenscheid** is on the edge of the Sauerland, whilst two preserved railway lines known as Bürgerbahn operate to Halver and to Gummersbach and Valberf. A network of farmhouse holiday accommodation is available in the Rothaargebirge, whilst a variety of 'ohne Gepäck' walking packages are available in the Sauerland.

An even more delightful old railway – an electrified rack railway built in 1883 and the oldest rack railway in Germany – operates from the resort of **Königswinter**, upstream from Bonn on the Rhine, to the summit of the Drachenfels (dragon's rock) in the Siebengebirge Naturpark. This nature park includes one of the first areas in Europe to be protected (around the Drachenfels itself) for nature conservation, thanks to a 1830 Bürgerinitiative – a citizens' initiative – in the area. The nature park covers a series of seven impressive isolated peaks high above the Rhine, mostly capped with ruined castles. The dense woods are mainly oak and beech, with some hornbeam. The area is cut through with narrow valleys surrounded by alder and ash. Deer and wild boar, native to the area, are kept in enclosures so they can be seen by visitors and the park is rich in bird life, especially woodpeckers, with no less than eight species common in the area. Every spring there is a wine blossom festival in Oberdollendorf.

Bonn was a small, old university city on the Rhine, birthplace in 1770 of Beethoven, which in 1945 was chosen as the capital of the Federal Republic of West Germany. This resulted in the town expanding rapidly into an administrative centre, and it is assumed even when the main government functions are transferred to Berlin, certain administrative functions will remain in Bonn. The city, with more than 1,200 green open spaces and parks, and a 29 kilometre long 'Rhine promenade' claims to be Europe's 'greenest capital'. One or three day travel tickets for individuals and families are available on trams and buses in the Rhein-Stieg area.

Köln, one of Germany's great cities, was a major outpost of the Roman empire – its Roman name, Colonia, derived from the special status it received as birthplace of Agrippina, the wife of Emperor Claudius. In the fifteenth century, Köln was a free city, minting its own coins and raising its own army. Some of the outstanding Roman remains including the Dionysian pavement and the elaborate tomb of Lucius Publicius are in the fascinating Römisch-Germanische Museum. The gothic cathedral, one of the largest in Christendom, and only completed in 1880, is awesome in both size and architectural splendour.

Having been continuously occupied since Roman times, Köln's old town around the Schildergaße richly repays exploration. Older people in Köln have their own dialect. The distinctive 'kölsch' beer is to be found in most pubs. It is also the most celebrated town in Germany for its carnival in February, the seventh weekend before Easter, when the whole city closes down for non-stop merriment, culminating in Rosen Montag

(Rose Monday) with a massive carnival procession through the city centre.

Like most German cities, Köln takes environmental protection seriously, and a major project in recent years was to put a massive riverside inner urban motorway underground, to allow revitalisation of the riverside area. There is an excellent public transport network and a pedestrianised city centre. There are very good opportunities to get around the city by bus and tram. Recommended tram-and-walk trips are to the Rhein Park and Tanzbrunnen flower gardens, the Brück Wildpark, Groove Park in Zündorf, the Königsforst, or to Rodenkirchen by the Rhine.

Köln also lies close to superb countryside, including the Bergisches Land with direct trains to **Gummersbach** or into the nearby Eifel (see Rheinland-Pfalz), as well as frequent boat services along the Rhine to points as far as Mainz.

Kleve, on the lower Rhine, has a medieval castle known as the Schwanburg at the foot of which Lohengrin, hero of Wagner's opera, is reputed to have appeared. The town lies in an area of gentle countryside with a number of well worked out cycle routes linking local villages and rural attractions along the Dutch border.

South of Kleve and east of Mönchen-Gladbach, and accessible from both, is the Schalm-Nette Naturpark which forms part of the German-Dutch Maas-Schwalm-Nette cross-border park. A preserved railway line, the Selkantbahn, operates to the south of the park between Gilrath and Schierwaldenrath.

Aachen is barely an hour away from Köln by train and has an equally remarkable history, going back at least 2,000 years to when it was a Celtic settlement. 'Ahha' was actually the Frankish word for water. But the Romans enjoyed its health-giving waters many years before. Charlemagne held court here in 768 AD and brought craftsmen from many lands to build his chapel, which later became Aachen cathedral. His remains lie in the palace chapel. In 1166 Barbarossa declared it to be the centre of his empire. The cathedral with its superb palatinate chapel is now a UNESCO World Heritage site. The city flourished first of all as a pilgrimage centre and in later years, especially after the coming of the railway, as a major spa, a tradition which continues today.

Close by is the **Nordeifel Naturpark,** established in 1960 and united in 1971 with the Hautes Fagnes-Eifel (Hohes Venn) Naturpark to form a major cross-border (Belgium-German) nature park. The Eifel hills in this area are formed from some of Europe's most ancient sedimentary rocks – Cambrian, Silurian and Devonian, with some limestone and red sandstone. The hills are cut through with deep valleys, some of them holding reservoirs. Around 40% of Nordeifel forest is deciduous – beech, alder, birch, sycamore, oak and ash. It is also an area known for its rare flowers, which vary from Alpine plants on the moorland to Mediterranean species in the sheltered valleys, whilst broom makes such vivid colour in late spring, it is known as Eifel gold. Wild boar, red and roe deer are common and the mouflon have been introduced. **Kall,** served by railway, makes a useful starting point to explore the area, whilst the Rurtal branchline from Düren on the main line in the north serves **Heimbach** and **Abenden** on the river Rur, from where there are some delightful waymarked forest and riverside trails.

The Rursee is the largest manmade lake and dam in the west of Germany. Passenger boats operate on the lake and there are lakeside walks. Close to Monschau on the uplands are a series of enormous protective hedges, some 200 years old, built as windbreaks to protect exposed villages in an area 500-700 metres above sea level.

A fascinating initiative on the Belgian side of the Hohes Venn involves the reopening of part of the Vennbahn, an old railway line, between Raeren near Eupen and Büllingen on the border, for passenger use, forming part of what it is hoped may become a 'Ringbahn' to persuade visitors to the area to leave their cars and travel by public transport. Other parts of the route are to be developed as cycle trails. This Eifel-Ardennes park has already won a major international award for the quality of its landscape protection work which transcends national barriers.

The Naturschutz-Projekte der Stiftung Pflanzen is a voluntary project to protect endangered flora, in this case in the Oleftal near Hollerath, to the southwest of Hellenthal within the Nordeifel Naturpark, and not far from the German-Belgian border, where the wild daffodil reaches its most easterly distribution in Germany. Tree felling and other land use has caused the numbers of this attractive plant and many others to dwindle drastically. The Stiftung – a charitable trust – has started cross-border talks with colleagues in Belgium with a view to establishing a large cross-border nature reserve. It is hoped to get rid of dense fir trees by selling them as Christmas trees before they stifle all the daffodil plants. The organisation has already bought an area of land one hectare in size where the daffodil is particularly luxuriant, but was endangered by dense spruce. Uprooting the trees has been very successful and within two years up to 100,000 wild daffodils have now flowered there. A number of other interesting plants are being protected such as spignel, various orchids, wood anemone, cranesbill and heath milkwort.

East of Dortmund and Hamm on the railway to Paderborn is **Soest,** a medieval walled town that retains most of its walls and some superb buildings including half-timbered houses and inns, the Patroklidom dating from the eleventh century and the fourteenth century gothic

Wiesenkirch. The celebrated dark rye wholemeal Pumpernickel bread originated in this old market town.

The mainly flat Westphalian countryside of North Germany north of the Ruhr is dominated by the old town of **Münster,** with its castle, cathedral, fourteenth century town hall and superbly restored medieval town centre.

Münsterland, as the region is known, markets itself as a major cycling centre, taking advantage of the gently undulating countryside cut through by a network of quiet lanes and tracks. The '100 Schlösser Route' as it is known links a number of castles, palaces and grand country houses in the region. Promotional literature includes scores of places in the region where bikes can be hired. There are a number of extremely well organised cycle tour and accommodation packages on this and other routes, some of them with luggage-carrying facilities and many of them themed in appealing ways. You can take a week's cycling combined with a trip on a local preserved steam railway, the Teuto Express, that crosses Münsterland from Ibbenbüren to Gütersloh. Another trip is combined with the baking of bread (ingredients provided), a third takes in varieties of watermills. There is also a combined programme with nearby Osnabrück in Niedersachsen.

Kreis Lippe in the north of the state was a semi-independent principality, and a free state until 1947 before becoming part of Nordrhein-Westfalen. Lippe's symbol is a red rose – not unlike the rose of Lancaster – and it was noted for its enlightened rulers, including Prince Simon Augustus in the late eighteenth century who put together a number of reforms, many of which were continued by his remarkable daughter-in-law Pauline whose liberal ideas for social assistance and education were a century or more ahead of her time. Their castle in **Detmold** is now a museum.

Lemgo in Lippe, though well inland, was actually a Hansa town, thanks to extensive trade with both England and Flanders. It has some exceptionally fine, richly decorated buildings, reflecting its former importance and prosperity. Detmold, the old capital of Lippe, cannot quite equal Lemgo for architectural brilliance but is nevertheless a beautiful town, its centre car-free, claiming with justice to be a 'cycle friendly town'.

Close by is the **Teutoburger Wald,** near to the scene of a famous battle, one of the most significant events in early German history. Under the leadership of Arminius Hermann of the Cherusci, the Germanic tribes soundly defeated their Roman overlords. Varus, the Roman governor in Germany at the start of the first century, had introduced Roman jurisdiction and taxation methods far too hastily and took no account of the fact that the levying of taxes in Germany was then unknown. Not surprisingly there was great local bitterness, which culminated in the battle in the Teutoburger Wald in 9 AD. Of particular interest is the fact that Arminius Hermann had been previously loyal to Varus and had in fact been trained by the Roman army. It has never been fully established whether Arminius united the German tribes against the Romans to oust a foreign power or whether he was merely seeking personal aggrandisement. The great battle lasted three days and the Roman forces were totally destroyed; in all an army of over 30,000 men with only one Roman cavalry division escaping. Varus the Roman leader then committed suicide.

Centuries later, in 1875, a huge monument known as the Hermanns-denkmal was erected at the probable site of the battle, which was also seen as a symbol for the recently united German empire. The inauguration ceremony was in the presence of Kaiser Wilhelm I plus a great number of visitors and foreign dignitaries. The monument now provides a superb viewpoint across the surrounding countryside.

There is a bus from Detmold railway station to the monument or even better is to walk along the whole or part of the 165 kilometre Hermanns-weg from Rheine to Velmerstott, along the summit ridge of the Teu-toburger Wald. You can take five days over the whole route from Detmold to Hiddesen with a luggage-carrying package holiday from the Westfalen Landesverkehrsverband which also offers a choice of similar packages throughout the state.

Close to Detmold is the other branch of the Westfalen Freilichtsmuseum, with an exceptional collection of traditional rural buildings from the sixteenth century from all over Westfalen. At **Berlebeck** is the largest eagle sanctuary in Europe.

The Nordrhein-Westfalen (NRW) Stiftung was founded in 1986 as a semi-official charitable organisation devoted to conservation of the environment and also of cultural heritage in the whole of Nordrhein-Westfalen. It has a stork as its symbol. The original idea was inspired by the British National Trust and was to ensure the continuity of important heritage sites and objects in the widest sense of the word for the local citizens. The group's main workforce consists of volunteers who make themselves responsible for certain schemes they wish to further, so that though a good deal of cash is needed, there is also a potentially large workforce. Members pay the equivalent of at least £7 a year and families at least £10 and a good deal of the funding also comes from a lottery whose owners were keen to associate their profits with a worthwhile cause.

Already over two hundred schemes have been sponsored, which vary in size and style tremendously. One such scheme was originated by a couple who cleaned up an area of the Swisttal, a green oasis between Bonn and Euskirchen. They planted more than a thousand trees on their own initiative and they were rewarded by the return of such birds as the golden oriole, ducks, geese and kingfishers who were attracted by the cleared pond. The NRW-Stiftung ensures that their work will carry on in perpetuity. In contrast the Solingen Museum, set in the famous cutlery town, received a large grant to buy a princely eighteenth century complete table-setting. On the lower Rhine, in the swampy area called the **Hetter** between Rees and Emmerich, is the largest reserve of the endangered black godwit as well as a centre for other rare birds like the redshank and meadow pipit; again NRW was able to provide resources to help support the conservation work.

One of the largest projects is around the **Zwillbrocker Venn**, about a hundred metres from the Dutch border and originally one of the oldest nature reserves in Germany. The moor had dried out and the habitat of much of the fauna and flora was endangered. Now local people have formed an organisation which includes a laboratory where biologists, chemists, geographers and scientists work together analysing data in order to regenerate the area. In the Perlenbachtal the wild daffodil and many other flowers are free to bloom again helped by funds from the NRW so that appropriate sites can be bought or exchanged. The beautiful and famous Marienschrein at Aachen, regarded by UNESCO as of world heritage rank, covered with gilded silver, enamel and semi-precious stones and dating from 1220, was given substantial sums for its restoration. A Robert Schumann manuscript has been bought with NRW funds, while at the other end of the scale, a school in Paderborn has been helped to install small-scale biotopes in the school grounds for teaching purposes.

On a smaller scale the AKNV in the Lippe area, known as the 'Westdorfer Modell' after a successful scheme in 1985, encourages local conservation projects, whether it is simply providing precise directions for making suitable nesting boxes for swallows or encouraging the rooting up of bushes in the **Schnellental** so that the fringed gentian can multiply (with the flowering soon afterwards of 5,000 specimens, a successful outcome was achieved). At **Dalbke** a 400 metre fence for toads erected along a nearby trunk road has helped to protect and build up an otherwise endangered toad population. Help with nest building for dippers was similarly successful along the Wester and Osterkalle.

Farmers have been encouraged to lease fields surplus to their require-ments to the AKNV for a period of at least five years. Because the fields have been previously over-fertilised there is no quick solution to create botanical diversity apart from allowing the soil to return in time to a poorer condition so that a greater diversity of plant species will flourish. Other areas are planted with wild flowers and this has also improved the butterfly population.

Further information ————————————————————

Rheinland area: **Landesverkehrsverband Rheinland e.V.**, Bad Godesberg, Rheinallee 69, D-5300 Bonn 2.

Westfalen including the Ruhr, Münsterland and Lippe: **Landesverkehrsverband Westfalen e.V.**, Friedensplatz 3, D-4600 Dortmund 1.

NRW-Stiftung, Roßstraße 128, D-4000 Düsseldorf 30.

Saarland

Tucked into a corner of the southwest of Germany in the shadow of its larger neighbour Rheinland-Pfalz, and sharing a border with both France and Luxemburg, Saarland is, apart from the city-states, the smallest of the Bundesländer, with an area of only 2,571 square kilometres and a population of just a million.

It has had a remarkable history even by German standards. For a considerable time it was a 'Zankapfel' or 'bone of contention' between nations. Though actually only dating from 1957 as a federal German state, Saarland is proof today that it is possible to keep a strong regional identity both within the framework of a large nation-state and a greater European community.

The river Saar which gives its name to the state was called Savarus by the Romans. It has its source in the Vosges mountains in France and flows into the Mosel south of Trier. Saarland's major economic centres lie in the heavily populated Saar valley around Saarlouis, Neunkirchen and the state capital Saarbrücken, though a good third of the state is still forested and farming is still an important part of the economy.

But it is as a major industrial region that Saarland is best known. In 1514 the first iron pot was manufactured in Neunkirchen. The region's mineral wealth attracted the interest of neighbouring France. Saar coal from the rich Saarbrücken coalfield has traditionally been used to smelt the iron ore from neighbouring Lorraine in France. Inevitably the economic and political fortunes of the two regions became linked.

Not only iron and steel manufacture and metal processing developed in the twin regions, but mechanical and chemical engineering, and ceramic and glass production are also important elements in the economy. It was the European coal and steel community, the Montan-Union, founded in 1951, that ensured the free movement of coal and iron ore between the two countries, and this laid the initial foundations for the European Economic Community. The iron of Lorraine and the coal of the Saarland, in past decades a cause of strife, have thus become the seed of a united Europe.

Saarland did not exist politically, economically or culturally 150 years ago. The major part of what is now Saarland belonged to Prussian Rhineland and was governed from Trier. Part belonged to Bayern and the smallest section to Oldenburg. Up to 1834 there were substantial customs barriers between these regions and it was only in 1851 it was finally possible to cross into the Duchy of Oldenburg without such constraints. With the removal of such trade barriers the coalmines known as Saarland's 'black dowry', the ironworks and the glass furnaces could develop and expand.

Most people in the area, however, still lived by farming, but with the invention of steam power and the development of railways, it was possible to exploit the huge coalfields more thoroughly and export the coal to France and southern Germany. The ironworks also began to use steam power rather than water power, this having greater flexibility as regards location. New mines and glassworks were founded along the railway and industrial development received a further boost when the river Saar was canalised in 1866, linking it to the French canal system. Coke was produced for export.

Industrialisation brought workers, especially impoverished farmers and unemployed skilled manual workers to the area from other regions, some coming from northern Saarland, the nearby Hunsrück mountains or the Westpfalz area and staying as lodgers with local families during the week, returning home at weekends. Others were lodged in Schlafhäuser, special accommodation provided near the mines. In Maybach, in the Friedrichsthal, there are about thirty examples of Schlafhäuser, built at the beginning of the century. Everyone paid a monthly two mark rent and this included bed and bedlinen and the use of a cupboard. The houses were run more or less on military lines to keep order, with often an ex-soldier in charge, and the workers provided their own food, but they could buy a reasonably priced breakfast at the Kaffeeküche as it was called.

Quite a few miners walked each day along paths, still known as 'Bergmannspfad', to the mines, covering sometimes up to ten, twenty or even thirty kilometres from their lodgings to their place of work. As they passed by villages in their clumsy-looking footwear, they were mocked by locals as 'Hartfüßer' or 'hardfeet'. Mining colonies established themselves near the mines in such places as Altenkessel, Altenwald, Bildstock, Elversberg, Göttelborn, Heiligenwald and a number of other villages. In spite of the arduous nature of their work and often long journeys, many miners still kept a little patch of land which they and their families worked. They also often kept a goat for fresh milk which became known as 'the miner's cow'.

A 16 kilometre stretch of the Bergmannspfad, between Dudweiler and Merchweiler, can still be followed.

In the second half of the nineteenth century the Saar coalfields tripled in output with the local iron furnaces as their most important customers, though the quality of the coke was not as good as that of the Ruhr. After the Franco-Prussian War of 1870-1 a workers' movement arose in the area and by 1889 there was an actual union for the workforce with over two-thirds of the miners as members.

During the First World War the area was overrun by troops and was the site of many field hospitals. In 1915 it was bombarded from the air and to these sufferings for the civilian population was added near famine in 1916/17. As the war ended, the area was occupied by the French who were given Saarland as war reparation, but there were increasing problems between the French soldiers and the civilian population. The Saarlanders almost unanimously wished to return to Germany and this was achieved in 1935, providing Adolf Hitler with a major propaganda coup.

After the Second World War Saarland was again put under French rule, with France hoping to annexe the area permanently. A referendum made it abundantly clear that the Saarlanders themselves wished to remain German and Saarland was finally returned to Germany and became an integral part of the federal republic in 1957.

Like similar areas in Britain and France with a traditional 'smoke-stack' industrial heritage, Saarland has had to face the implications of industrial decline. There are only six coal mines currently working and only two steelworks survive, and a solitary glassworks.

Yet despite a century and a half of intensive industrialisation, Saarland is a surprisingly green state, both because of surviving areas of countryside – forest, vineyard and farmland – and as a result of both public and voluntary effort to return old industrial landscapes to natural beauty. Forests are now strictly protected, and opened up for walking with networks of waymarked routes. There are also a number of protected areas of countryside and natural features. Indeed it is often this contrast between industrial and rural that makes Saarland so attractive.

It is a densely populated area, with many industrial towns and villages, but culturally rich, with superb archaeological remains such as the great Gollenstein sandstone monolith near Bleikastel, the remarkable Celtic Hun Ring near Nonnweiler, and a menhir or large Celtic stone at Rentrisch known as the Spellenstein. At Nenning near Perl (served by rail) is one of the finest Roman mosaic pavements in Northern Europe. There are impressive medieval castles, fine churches and, inevitably, some fascinating pieces of industrial archaeology.

This is also an area rich in geological interest, with an impressive six kilometre long Felsenpfad at St. Ingbert near Saarbrücken which passes some immense weatherworn rocks. At the Schlossberghöhlen in Homburg are to be found the largest red sandstone caves in Europe.

The Saarwald Verein – the Saar forest club – has more than 12,000 members and has waymarked no less than 1,600 kilometres of footpaths, both linear and circular routes. The Verein also maintains ten Wanderheime (hostels) and works vigorously for nature and environmental protection in Saarland.

Particularly impressive among these routes is the 270 kilometre Saarland Rundwanderweg around the entire state, to and from Saarbrücken, taking in a huge variety of scenery in each of the state's six main Landkreise – Saarbrücken, Saarlouis, Merzig, St. Wendel, Neunkirchen and Homburg.

One especially impressive feature along the section of route between Petersberg and Bosen, some 25 kilometres from St. Wendel, is the Straße der Skulpturen where huge stone blocks of red or yellow sandstone, basalt or marble have been sculptured – though many still await an artist's shaping hand. They have been placed there in memory of the murdered Jewish sculptor Otto Freundlich.

A contrasting route is the 225 kilometre Saarwanderweg, marked with a blue St. Andrews cross, which follows the river Saar from its source at Saarquelle am Donon to its confluence with the Mosel at Konzerbrück. European Long Distance Footpath no 3 between the Atlantic coast and Czechoslovakia also crosses Saarland. For the budget conscious, another 175 kilometre waymarked route links youth hostels in Saarland.

One especially attractive feature about Saarland is that it is so compact, combining many typical features to be found elsewhere in Germany in one small area. It is extremely well served by rail, with a number of local lines radiating from Saarbrücken, and a good network of local bus services. It is also well away from the popular tourist areas.

Saarbrücken, the state capital, lies on the French border. As its name suggests, the city originated around a bridge over the river Saar at the foot of the Halberg. Little remains of its Roman foundations. The town received its charter in 1321. It suffered much from the effects of the Thirty Years War, achieved something of a revival under Fürst Wilhelm Heinrich in the eighteenth century with some fine neo-classical and baroque buildings, only to be demoted after the French Revolution to become a Prussian provincial town under the jurisdiction of Trier. But it grew rapidly into a major industrial centre during the last century.

The Deutsch-Französischer Garten in Saarbrücken was designed by landscape architects of both Germany and France as a symbol of increasing co-operation and unity. It contains Europe's largest Wasserorgel – an ornamental fountain feature operated like a gigantic organ. The nearby Aschbachtal has numerous footpaths and a deerpark. Other excellent walking areas within easy reach of the city centre include the Stadtwald and Fischweier, whilst the Treidelpfad is a popular cycle route.

The beautiful Warndt Wald in the Saargau near the steel and coal town of Völklingen was originally an aristocratic country estate and hunting reserve, where in later years Huguenots were invited to settle in nearby Ludweiler and build glassworks as the forest had such necessary raw materials as quartz sand and wood for making charcoal. The forest has 150 kilometres of footpaths and two wildlife parks.

The Merziger Becken in the northwest is known as the apple-barrel of the Saarland because of its many orchards producing an excellent local applewine known as 'Viez'. The main Saarland wine region lies mostly in the north around Merzig. The region boasts the oldest type of German grape, the Elbling. The Rivaner grape, also popular in the area, is similar to Riesling or Silvaner. A popular local dish to go with wine is 'Friture de la Moselle', small river fish crisply baked in hot fat.

The Schwarzwälder Hochwald, sometimes called the Errwald, runs across the north of Saarland, north of Lebach (served by branch railway) and includes the Teufelskopf north of Wieskirchenat, at 695 metres the highest mountain in Saarland. A preserved railway line operates on certain days in the summer months with steam traction between Merzig (on the main line to Trier) to Losheim and Wadern.

In Britten there is the largest holly plantation in Europe. A colourful local custom takes place in the town of Wadrill on Erbsensonntag, the second Sunday in Lent. A wheel is covered with straw, and decorated with a cross and two candles, and as darkness falls it is all set alight and two young people guide the burning wheel down the valley into the river Wadrill below. Round the Losheim-Stausee, which has bathing facilities, there are 100 kilometres of marked paths and more routes exist around the Prims-Stausee.

The hilly area to the north forms part of the Saar-Hunsrück Naturpark (see Rheinland-Pfalz). The 60 square kilometre Wadern Wald around the town of **Wadern** is included in this, and contains both commercial woodland and natural forest. Part of the forest is state forest, but increasingly the woodlands are being managed as natural forest with natural regeneration and native species being encouraged, in order to protect wildlife habitats and encourage diversification. Among features in the forest are prehistoric barrows, ancient boundary stones and direction posts, a section of the Roman Road to Trier, and numerous relics of early forest industry.

In the **Steinbachtal** west of Mettlach, a tributary valley of the Saar, is an interesting woodland conservation project known as the Modellprojekt Waldbiotope Steinbachtal. Its objectives reflect and clarify the many purposes that a forest serves. For example many animal, plant and insect species use a woodland as their natural habitat and the wood is also a provider of raw material in the shape of timber, and an energy source as regards wood burning. For many people it is either their workplace or indirectly their source of work as many industries such as furniture making or the paper industry are dependent on wood products. It also is an important recreation area and hunting ground.

The project believes it is important above all to encourage and protect mixed woodland which is appropriate for the area and to have a proportion of ancient trees in the woodland. Replanting takes place without damaging the woodland ecology. Some species like the wild boar, the pine marten, the kestrel, and the deer have proved adaptable and have managed to survive quite substantial changes to their terrain, while other species have found this much more difficult. The deer have become a great problem because there are no real predators to control their numbers, resulting in ten times the viable number for the area and leading to increased damage to trees. The project now removes spruce trees so that plants and animals which enjoy moist areas can thrive. Hideaways are constructed out of stones and brushwood so that birds, small mammals, and various other species can find hiding places. Water-loving plants such as iris and bulrushes are planted, fish ponds are restocked with local fish species and native flowering trees and bushes like bird cherry, elderberry and blackthorn are also planted. Dead trees still standing are conserved for various birds like doves or creatures like bats to make use of, while nesting boxes are provided for other bird species. The forests of Saarland are partcularly rich in fungi. There are at least 2,400 types recorded and they form an important part of the ecological system. However, 50% of fungi are now endangered, perhaps reflecting the increase in pollution in recent decades. Research has shown that on average, only half the number of fungi are present compared with fifteen years ago. As the regeneration of natural woodlands is dependent on fungi, this means that many ancient woods not just in Saarland, but the whole of Europe, could be at risk. An excess of nitrates also causes excessive growth of plants like nettle and wild garlic at the expense of other species.

Another fascinating scheme is the Naturfreunde Sanfter Tourismus im Saarland Projekt. This is a scheme, started in 1987 by the Saarland branch of the Naturfreunde, to provide a programme which introduces concepts of responsible tourism in particular to holiday providers and organisers. It readily advises any organisers who are interested in similar goals and produces detailed itineraries and routes for those interested in social history or the natural history of the Saarland region. It also undertakes 'green' journeys to areas such as the Alps and the Wattenmeer which particularly suffer the effects of pollution, and organises and advises school parties which may wish to run ecologically-orientated trips. It holds seminars to prepare teachers thoroughly for the task in hand and organises weekly trips for families who would like to explore Saarland on foot, by bike or by public transport taking in social, cultural, industrial, archaeological and culinary highlights. Cycle trips follow the Bliesgau, the Schwarzwälder Hochwald and the industrial Saartal, with stops at organic farms and similar places of interest. There are also photographic trips which seek not only natural beauty but also industrial themes.

Further information ────────────────────────────

Fremdenverkehrsverband Saarland e.V., St. Johanner Markt, Am Stiefl 2, D-6600 Saarbrücken 3.
Saarwald Verein e.V., Reichstraße 4, Postfach 401, D-6600 Saarbrücken.
Projekt Sanfter Tourismus, Naturfreunde Landesverband Saarland, Stadionstraße 10, D-6620 Völkingen.
Deutsche Bund für Vogelschutz (DBV), Landesverband Saarland e.V., Futterstraße 14, D-6600 Saarbrücken, publishes a five-times-a-year magazine *Naturschutz in Saarland*.

Baden-Württemberg _____

As its name suggests, Baden-Württemberg was formed by the combining of what were once two small independent German states, the archdukedom of Baden and the kingdom of Württemberg.

After World War II the Allies did in fact, initially create three federal Länder, but a referendum in 1951 established what has become in terms of per capita earnings, not only Germany's wealthiest state, but one of the richest provinces in the world.

It occupies the hilly southwest corner of Germany, its boundaries including the upper reaches of the Rhine valley between France and

Switzerland and the northern shores of the Bodensee (Lake Constance). Inland lies the Schwarzwald (Black Forest), the upper Danube and Neckar valleys, the rolling limestone ridges of the Schwäbische Alb (Swabian Jura), and to the northeast, the Schwäbisch-Fränkischer Wald. From the thirteenth century to the coming of Napoleon the southern part of the region was under Austrian rule, with the city of Freiburg as its capital. With Napoleon's victory, the Baden area became an arch-dukedom and Württemberg a kingdom instead of a loose collection of dukedoms.

The state's present prosperity owes much to many factors – among them a good climate and excellent communications both with the rest of Germany and with France. With companies like Mercedes-Benz, Por-sche, IBM, Leitz, numerous computer and software and electronic and optical equipment manufacturers, the Neckartal has become known as the 'golden valley' of Germany, with Stuttgart as its focal point.

Stuttgart lies in a great bowl along the Neckar between steep forested hills. The former capital of the old kingdom of Württemberg boasts that within 250 metres of the railway station grapes are gathered from city vineyards, to provide wine for the famous Ratskeller. Former royal palaces are used as the state parliamentary building and museum, whilst the palace gardens form a continuous stretch of green space in the heart of the city as far as the Rosensteinpark. Königstraße, the city's long pedestrianised main street with its intersecting arcades, is a fashionable shopping centre. The central areas are served by a modern underground light rapid transit system, with the vehicles becoming surface street cars once out of the largely traffic free city centre. They then curve their way up a steep hillside past a fiercely protected green belt of vineyards and birch woods which separates the city centre from outlying suburbs and satellite towns. Fast S-Bahn trains provide further links into such towns as Böblingen, Bad Cannstadt and Marbach, Schiller's birthplace and home of the National Schillermuseum. Prosperous, modern and success-ful, with many parks and green spaces, modern sculpture in every pedestrian area, a celebrated modern art gallery, a world famous ballet, a concert hall and an opera house, Stuttgart is the epitome of the contem-porary German city. It remains a busy inland port, barges from the Rhine reaching the city along the river Neckar.

The Neckar also runs past such famous old university towns as **Tübingen** and **Heidelberg** and, at its confluence with the Rhine, the city and port of **Mannheim**.

The Neckar valley provides some fine walking opportunities along waymarked paths. Many of the steep valley slopes are covered by terraces of vineyards. It's not entirely surprising that one particularly fine long distance walk is the Württembergischer Weinpfad (wine path) through vineyards and lovely old towns from **Esslingen** east of Stuttgart to **Aub** north of Bad Mergentheim. It is recommended you take three weeks for this meandering 300 kilometre route. A fit walker on the other hand could complete the 28 kilometre Neckartal-Odenwald Wanderbahn comfortably in a day. This old railway line from Mosbach to Mudau through the Naturpark Neckartal-Odenwald has been turned into a delightful footpath route. Cyclists have a choice of well promoted cycle routes, mainly using minor roads or farm or forest access roads, including the full 1150 kilometre Radwanderweg Baden-Württemberg!

The main Rhine valley has a series of famous and beautiful towns which fringe on the Schwarzwald – Karlsruhe, Offenburg, Freiburg and **Baden-Baden**, the latter one of Germany's most fashionable and elegant spa towns, first established by the Romans who discovered the health-giving value of its hot springs which can still be enjoyed to the present day, either as part of a 'cure' or simply as a fun experience in a modern themed pool.

Freiburg, a walled medieval city with a magnificent tall-spired cathedral overlooking the market place, is an outstanding example of rational transport planning, with the city centre only penetrated by taxis, delivery vehicles (at certain times) and trams which operate through the town walls on an east-west and a north-south axis along pedestrianised streets, served by feeder buses and outlying car parks to keep the centre traffic and pollution free. This is supplemented by an extensive series of cycleways from outlying suburbs. So successful are these, that many Freiburg business people commute to work by cycle.

About 40 kilometres north of Freiburg, along the Rhine, lies **Taubergiessen**, a Naturschutzgebiet along both banks of the Rhine which, to prove conservation respects no boundaries, lies partly in France and partly in Baden-Württemberg. This is one of the last surviving bits of unimproved riverside along the upper Rhine, consisting of old water meadows and reed banks, damp woods of white poplars, marshes and tributary becks, a superb habitat for water-loving plants and wading birds, for rare orchids, herons, cormorants, kingfishers, reed warblers.

SCHWARZWALD

The Schwarzwald is perhaps the most famous and long established holiday and walking region in Europe, criss-crossed as it is with a network of superbly waymarked footpaths, linking towns and villages with hotels and even with clinics providing various forms of health cure in the pure air and good climate of the region.

It isn't one single forest, but the name of a hilly region covered by a series of forests about 160 kilometres from north to south and between 60 to 80 kilometres east to west. The hills rise to around 1,500 metres with much of the land over 1,000 metres, in the form of long, thickly forested ridges. The area is bounded on the west and south by the Rhine, in the east by the valleys of the Neckar and the Nagold, and in the north by the Kraichgau region beyond Pforzheim.

The Schwarzwald has two distinct areas of contrasting landscape. The northern section has areas of moorland and heath as well as forest and vineyards, while the south has larger areas of forest and scattered farms and is the more scenically dramatic. Geologically the region was formed out of ancient rocks, granite and gneiss, but there are also areas of red sandstone which are sometimes dramatically exposed, and which give the forest paths a warm reddish tinge under carpets of pine needles. The higher reaches of the southern Schwarzwald are dominated by an immense granite massif through which deep river valleys carve their way.

More than half of the Schwarzwald is carpeted with dense fir, elm and pine woods, but there are equally large tracts of deciduous and mixed forest interspersed with open or semi-wooded areas. Much of the region has large areas of pasture, some arable farmland and orchards which in autumn hang heavy with fruit. This is also a region of unusually attractive towns and villages, such as Villingen, Rottweil, Triberg, Lenzkirch, Neustadt and Freudenstadt, many of them rich in historic features.

The sunny slopes of west and south overlooking the Rhine valley are covered by vine terraces that form geometrical patterns down the hillsides, and which provide many of the famous Baden wines, again with attractive wine villages linked by terraced and woodland footpaths and old castles on the ends of the long ridges.

The Schwarzwald isn't a national or nature park as such, though substantial areas of the region have been given special 'protected landscape' status by the state government. Many areas, such as the Wutachschlucht or the Blindensee, are also designated nature reserves where the wildlife has rigorous protection. There are also many areas of state or regional forest which are strictly protected.

It is an area rich in natural beauty. Though the forest may no longer be strictly natural, having been managed over generations, there is great variety of woodland and trees of different species and ages, permitting a rich undercover of ferns, grasses, fungi and wild flowers.

Forest verges are covered with wild flowers in spring and summer. There is also a profusion of butterflies; the Wutachschlucht for example boasts about 3,000 varieties. The woods also teem with wildlife such as foxes, squirrels, owls, small deer, wild boar, dormice, pine martens and lizards. In and around the woods and streams is a rich variety of bird life such as woodpeckers, nuthatch and dippers, with large birds of prey such as buzzards and other falcon in the open moorland areas.

Autumn is a particularly good time to visit the forest with leaves providing glorious colour. There are also masses of fungi of every shape, colour and size on rotting tree stumps. Winters in the Schwarzwald can however be long and severe, starting in November and continuing until May, with heavy snowfalls that block roads and tracks; the forest is used for cross-country skiing as the many pistes and route marks indicate.

The name 'Schwarzwald' reflects the legendary dark and inhospitable nature of the shadowy forest especially when covered with mist. For many centuries, before the coming of the railways and good roads, the central and more mountainous parts away from the Rhine and Neckar valleys were among the most inaccessible parts of Germany. Villages and farmsteads were scattered and so isolated, especially during the winter months, that it could often be a two days' journey to fetch a doctor.

In common with many upland areas of Europe, the farms were often not sufficiently economically viable to support an entire family unit, and other ways had to be sought. The wood production industry, with allied trades of papermaking and furniture manufacture, has always been important, while in times past huge pine trunks were fastened together into enormous rafts and floated down the rivers to sawmills to be made into ships' masts for sailing ships.

Over the centuries the Schwarzwald people became skilled wood-carvers, producing not only tools and utensils, but also beautiful carved figures, a tradition perpetuated by the simple carvings on many of the more modern little springs and fountains. This dexterity lead to the growth of the clockmaking industry.

Glassmaking started in the Middle Ages and was initiated by the monasteries and also by particular dukes and princes. It had a very definite effect on the landscape. Quartz was found in abundance, and wood was used in large quantities to make the charcoal to fire the furnaces. The result of this was that the original forest or wildwood became partially denuded and though constantly replaced, the species used tended to be the quicker growing firs and spruces. So stretches of dark, dense woodland in some areas, far from being natural, are the direct result of human activity. Though charcoal burning no longer survives in this form, the name 'Kohlenwald' for many areas of forest recalls this process. Mining for precious metals such as gold, silver, lead (galena) was also important in past centuries, and traces of these former industries can also be seen on the landscape.

Farming remains important, great clearances being made in the valley bottoms sheltered by the thickly wooded ridges to create fertile pasture-land, in which are characteristic farmhouses with their immense roofs. It is mostly dairy farming, with vast quantities of hay collected from the meadows stored in the great roof space above the house for feeding to cattle through the long winter. At the Vogtsbauernhof at Gutach, an open air museum, you can see a variety of examples of the different types of traditional Schwarzwald farmhouse complete with additional storehouses, bakehouses, a sawmill and watermill, and with displays of such traditional crafts as that of the blacksmith, straw basket weaving, charcoal burning and forestry.

The oldest type of Heidenhaus, as the earliest type of farmhouse is called, was made completely of wood and its vast roof nearly reaches the ground, with the hay loft over the cattle stalls and rooms for the farmhands reached by an outside walkway. Over the main living quarters is the threshing floor on the upper slopes so that hay carts can be conveniently driven straight in. Later forms of the Schwarzwald farmhouse still reveal many of these basic features.

The glassmaking industry was superseded by clockmaking, one of the Schwarzwald's most famous industries, which developed in the seventeenth century. From modest beginnings with wooden clocks, in two hundred years the industry grew to be a worldwide business with the annual production of 1.8 million clocks by 1870, supplying Europe and the rest of the world with robust, cheap, practical and reliable clocks.

Franz Ketterer of Schönwald is generally credited with producing the world's first cuckoo clock in the eighteenth century. Originally the cuckoo (whose 'call' was constructed on the bellows principle) popped out of an aperture from a simple tree painted on the face of the clock. Many decades later the cuckoo began to inhabit an elaborately carved home. The idea became a popular success, and cuckoo clocks were soon manufactured in vast numbers in Switzerland as well as the Schwarzwald. They are still made and sold in large quantities – **Triberg** is a major centre – mostly mass produced for the tourist market, but it is still possible to buy hand-crafted pieces of exceptional quality and charm.

Further developments were mechanical figures which did a number of ingenious things, mechanical musical boxes that could play a series of tunes and the elaborately engineered Orchestrion, a vast instrument which had the repertoire of an orchestra and had music specially composed for it. Sadly this brilliant technology, which reached its zenith before World War I, was rapidly made obsolete by the gramophone.

It was estimated that by 1840 some 5,000 people were occupied in some branch of the industry, with the addition of about a thousand clock dealers who actually sold the goods. By the mid nineteenth century competition, particularly from the United States, dealt a severe blow to the trade. In 1850 the Archduke of Baden founded the Fachhochschule (clock-making college) at Furtwangen which is still in existence and now

BADEN-WÜRTTEMBERG / **189**

the home of the famous Deutsches Uhrenmuseum (German national clock museum). Its first principal was Robert Gerwig, the brilliant railway engineer and builder of the Schwarzwaldbahn (Black Forest railway) through Triberg, who saw to it that youngsters learnt not only clockmaking, but also allied technology. He also arranged that additional materials needed for the industry apart from wood (available locally in abundance), should not be imported from abroad, but if possible from within Germany itself to encourage home industry.

The Schwarzwald clock trade also fought back by learning from the competition, particularly in the case of Junghans who adapted American mass production methods to German expertise so that his factory became the largest of its kind in Europe before the outbreak of the First World War.

This technical skill was again to be in demand during the Second World War, since so much sophisticated weaponry depended on the clockmaker's precision. Thankfully, since World War II the skills of Schwarzwald people have been put to use for the benefit of humankind – for medical equipment, optics, photographic and cinematic industries and above all the technology of computers and high-tech electronics.

A further important industry in the Schwarzwald and indeed the whole of Baden-Württemberg is winemaking. Winegrowing was probably introduced to the region by the Romans and developed by the Benedictine and Cistercian monks. Many vineyards have been in continuous use since this period. One pleasure of visiting the western side of the Schwarzwald and in walking through the winegrowing areas (for example along the Ortenauer Weinpfad) is that you can sit down in a small hotel or Gasthof after a day's walk through the vineyards and order a carafe or bottle of the excellent local wines for which you have seen the grapes ripening in the sun earlier in the day.

Baden is one of the few regions in Germany, along with Frankenland, allowed to bottle some wines, such as the Affentaler, in the famous triangular Bocksbeutel shape.

The whole of Baden-Württemberg has a particularly good winegrowing climate. One of the most beautiful winegrowing areas in Germany is to be found in the upper Rhine valley around the Ortenau, Breisgau, Kaiserstuhl and Tunnisberg areas with its fertile loess soils (volcanic in origin) and in the Markgräfenland in the southern Schwarzwald which has the Gutedel as a typical wine, light, delicate with a mild bouquet and often sold in Gasthäuser from the cask. The wine area from Freiburg to Offenburg has wine mainly for local use, whilst the Glottertal specialises in Spätburgunder and Weiße Herbst. Many local wine festivals take place in early autumn in towns and villages, which encourage guests to try the new wine at innumerable stalls where you buy your glass with your first drink and carry it round for further samplings. It is traditional to eat warm Zwiebelkuchen with new wine or 'Süsswein' or 'Weinmost' – the newly fermented (cloudy) grape juice of the wine harvest. Zwiebelkuchen is rather like French onion tart or quiche and can be delicious when the pastry is particularly light; chopped chives are sometimes added or even finely chopped bacon.

The Schwarzwald is justly famous for its food, reflecting cross-border influences from Austria, Switzerland and France. The famous Schwarzwalderkirschtorte (Black Forest gateau) in its original form and not the sticky imitation sold elsewhere is a multi-layered cake with cherries soaked in Kirschwasser and alternate layers of cream. Preiselbeertorte (red currant gateau) is a variation on the same theme, whilst fresh fruit tarts and cakes are invariably delicious.

Other specialities of the region include Spätzle, a particularly delicious form of fine pasta, Maultaschen which are square pockets of pastry filled with finely chopped meat, spinach and herbs, and Badische Schneckensuppe, a cream snail soup. Mushrooms are also served in great variety, often as a dish in their own right.

The Schwarzwald is also a region noted for its excellent beers, with a large number of small private breweries in many of the towns producing distinctive brews, some of them of a really special quality.

A good choice of accommodation together with superb scenery, good public transport and extremely friendly people – not always to be found in tourist areas – make the Schwarzwald an attractive area for a walking holiday. Another advantage is the waymarked footpath network. This is due to the work of the Schwarzwaldverein. Founded in 1864, it was created originally to help popularise the Schwarzwald for walking and tourism, and over the last hundred years it has created the world's oldest network of waymarked long distance recreational trails (the 281 kilometre Westweg between Pforzheim and Basle dates from 1900) through the Schwarzwald, together with a series of lookout towers to enable walkers to enjoy ridgetop views above the trees, and comfortable walkers' hostels. The Verein also co-operate with the state land survey office in publishing excellent 1:50,000 maps of their waymarked routes.

As the years have gone by, the society's role has changed increasingly to that of an environmental protection body. Major battles that the society has led in recent years include the saving of the Wutachschlucht from flooding by a huge hydro-electric scheme, the prevention of the building of new motorways across the heart of the Schwarzwald, the prevention of a scheme to widen and deepen the upper Rhine for huge container vessels, campaigning for the planting of more species of native trees rather than monoculture conifer afforestation, and wider political action against acid rain and Waldsterben (dying woodlands), now a serious threat to parts of the Schwarzwald.

The Verein now has over 92,000 members, with 237 district groups and 63 youth groups, many of whom are actively involved in practical countryside and footpath protection work on a voluntary basis. It has a total of 23,000 kilometres of waymarked footpaths under its care, from the famous Hohenwege to local link paths in different districts.

Perhaps the greatest single problem currently faced by the society is that caused by the private car, and the mass tourism effects of huge car parks and consequent environmental degradation, pollution and erosion in the countryside, which their president has described as 'an avalanche of tin' descending on the countryside.

But the Verein's concern does not confine itself to purely environmental issues. It is also dedicated to helping to maintain the way of life, customs and traditions of the area and to develop an awareness among young people of the natural world and pleasures of the countryside. It is particularly concerned with all aspects of environmental protection of the area. This also includes support for scientific investigation of threatened species, of the forest's ecological systems and related matters.

The Schwarzwaldverein's official trails provide the basis for a wide choice of self-guided walking holidays, many packaged with luggage-carrying facilities between Gasthöfe and hotels, varying in length from a score or so kilometres to a couple of hundred, and in duration from two or three days to a fortnight or more. You can of course do your own thing along any of the trails, backpacking and staying at local accommodation or hostels or even camping. But luggage-carrying services literally take the weight off your shoulders when long distance walking. Some packages are self-guided, others led by local leaders. Full details of available packages can be obtained from the Baden-Württemberg tourist office – address below.

The town of Freudenstadt is also developing a number of environmental initiatives linked to tourism, including self-guided walks in the forest linked to key environmental issues ('Waldspaziergänge') and themed activity programmes on conservation issues wherever possible using locally produced products and recycled materials. Specialist courses in green tourist practice are also offered for professionals working in tourism and travel.

If you are visiting the Schwarzwald without a car the excellent, well integrated public transport networks make it easy to get around. The main InterCity railway line from Köln to Basel runs along the Rhine valley via Karlsruhe, Offenburg and Freiburg, from where branch railways take you deep into the Schwarzwald; alternatively, good train services from Stuttgart link Pforzheim and Freudenstadt.

For rail enthusiasts, the region's railway system is a delight. The scenic Schwarzwaldbahn from Offenburg to Konstanz via Triberg and Villingen spirals to 832 metres above sea level through no less than thirty-six tunnels. Almost as fine is the steep Höllentalbahn between Freiburg and Neustadt, where powerful little electric locomotives ascend murderously steep gradients. This links to the Dreiseenbahn from Titisee to Seebrugg through the Bärental, at 937 metres Germany's highest standard gauge line. The 26 kilometre Wutachtalbahn between Zollhaus-Blumberg and Weizen is a preserved line only open on certain dates during the summer months, but a spectacular route with spirals in tunnels and magnificent viaducts, and sometimes operated by steam trains. There is also an excellent network of local buses between most of the towns and major villages, again working to an integrated timetable with rail services, several of the larger towns having their own local service networks. DB regional rail tickets (Tourenkarten) cover many of these local buses.

SCHWÄBISCHE ALB

A high Jurassic limestone ridge of hills rising some 1,000 metres above sea level, between the Neckar basin and the upper Danube valley, forms an area of rugged, mountainous countryside covered by scattered forests across the southeastern part of Baden-Württemberg – the Schwäbische Alb.

These steep ridges, isolated by often deeply eroded ravines, were exploited by medieval castle builders for their fortresses, including those of the Hohenstaufen and Hohenzollern. The Zollern were originally lords of Schwaben who eventually changed their name to Hohenzollern and became kings of Prussia and eventually emperors of all Germany. Their castle near Hechingen is one of the most famous and romantically situated in Germany. The Staufen were the family of Emperor Friedrich Barbarossa. These and other castles on the white limestone bluffs above dark green forest above the Neckar or the Danube valleys make dramatic features.

Like the Schwarzwald, this was a region where local people always had to struggle against the difficulties of a harsh terrain, this time compounded by lack of water on the high limestone uplands. Again they responded with the development of many ingenious industries, such as the making of toys and harmonicas, which led eventually to the manufacture of textiles, turbines, hydraulic transmission systems, cutlery and precision balance instruments.

The Schwäbische Alb is perhaps known to modern travellers who cross southern Germany by railway as the spectacular range of hills between Stuttgart and **Ulm** where even InterCity trains often have to be double-headed with two locomotives, to cope with steep gradients near Geislingen.

This is an extremely popular walking area, rich in geological and botanical interest, perhaps not as heavily used as the Schwarzwald, nor as well known outside Germany. The Schwäbischer Albverein, which has an even larger membership than the Schwarzwaldverein, takes an active role in the protection and the waymarking of paths and the environment. It also has a chain of Wanderheime (walkers' hostels) open to members and non-members alike, and maintains and waymarks footpaths in the adjacent Schwäbische Wald and the Neckar valley as well.

Good rail-based centres to explore this region would be **Geislingen, Göppingen, Schwäbisch Gmund**, Gerstetten on the branch railway from Amstetten (no Sunday trains), Albstadt, Aalen, Balingen, **Reutlingen** or even the picturesque old city of Ulm itself. As in the Schwarzwald there are also a number of scenic and historic railway lines which can be used to take advantage of excellent walking opportunities. These include the 108 kilometre Hohenzollerischen Landesbahn from Kleinenstingen to Gammertingen to Hagerloch, Sigmaringen and Sigmaringendorf, and the 18 kilometre line to the north from Gaildorf to Untergröningen in the Kocher valley operated by the Württembergische Eisenbahn Gesellschaft.

If you are visiting the area for the first time for a walking holiday, it might make sense to take advantage of one of the pre-planned waymarked walking routes in the region organised on the 'ohne Gepäck' principle of having your luggage carried between overnight stops.

Cyclists are catered for with forty recommended cycling routes in the region, which are described in a leaflet available from the Schwäbische Alb tourist office, whilst another leaflet suggests twelve linking cycle tours 'on the trail of the Staufen' around Göppingen.

SCHWÄBISCH-FRANKISCHER WALD and HOHENLOHE FRANKEN

Though not perhaps as dramatically impressive as the Schwarzwald or Schwäbische Alb, this area of old villages, pastureland, vineyards and medium-sized hills and forests, now a nature park, offers fine walking opportunities within easy reach of the cities of Stuttgart and Mannheim, with centres at **Waldenburg, Bad Mergentheim, Rudersberg** and **Murrhardt** all being served by rail. An interesting feature is the surviving remnants of the 550 kilometre long Roman boundary wall in Germany, the Limes, built 148-161 AD, which runs through this area and now forms part of a long distance walk. A Roman watchtower has been restored near Lorch Abtei. The area around the Bleichsee, near the Löwenstein, forms an important landscape conservation zone.

There is a good choice of waymarked walking routes through the Schwäbisch-Fränkischer Wald and its nature park, including luggage-transport walking and accommodation packages bookable through the local tourist office.

Hohenlohe Franken, around the Kocher and Jagst valleys and the towns of **Crailsheim** and **Schwäbisch Hall,** was once a region of little independent free cities in a similar area of rolling countryside and attractive woodland. Schwäbisch Hall was an old salt mining town, and its brine springs were later much valued for saltwater bathing as a health cure. At **Langenburg,** a delightful small town on the river Jagst, a court pastrycook created the little fingernail-sized biscuit known as the Langenburg Wibele, now a Baden-Württemberg speciality known all over the region.

BODENSEE

Bodensee (Lake Constance) is a vast inland lake the surface and shores of which are shared between three countries, Germany, Austria and Switzerland, and between two Länder, Baden-Württemberg and Bayern. With an area of 53,800 hectares (208 square miles) the Bodensee is the second largest of the Alpine lakes.

Konstanz, the town that gives its anglicised name to the lake, is the largest settlement on the lake. Its suburbs cross the border into Switzerland. The main part of the lake is known as Obersee; the two arms to the west are known as the Überlingersee and the Untersee, and these provide some of the lake's most impressive scenery. There are a number of nature reserves in the area.

The Bodensee creates its own, almost Mediterranean microclimate, generally free of frosts, where tender plants and fruits can flourish along its shoreline. There are vineyards, orchards and superb lakeside villages linked by walkways. The area can be explored by using the frequent boat services which link attractive resorts along the shores of the lake or along the upper Rhine – from Konstanz to Radolfzell or along the Rhine to Reichenau, from Konstanz to Überlingen and Bodman, or across the Obersee to **Friedrichshafen** to **Lindau** and Bregenz in Austria. A network of trains and buses penetrate into a hinterland – Schwäbisch

Allgau – an area noted for its attractive villages, small resorts and baroque palaces with a distinct Bavarian flavour.

There are a number of nature reserves around the Bodensee, particularly around the Untersee and Zellersee near **Radolfzell** west of Konstanz. Peat bogs and low lying meadows around the lake are a habitat for bird's eye primrose, Siberian iris, bug orchids and marsh gladiolus, with pasque flowers and field gentians in the drier areas. The lake is also an important moulting area for common and red-crested pochards, whilst an estimated 200,000 duck and geese winter on the lake.

Cyclists can reach the Bodensee from Ulm railway station along the Radwanderweg Donau-Bodensee. A choice of three routes – 160 kilometres (Hauptroute), 170 kilometres (Ostroute) and 160 kilometres (Westroute), marked with distinctive blue-and-white waymarks, plus linking routes including one along the edge of the Bodensee to Lindau, enables several days' touring to be planned. The Baden-Württemberg state tourist office issues a comprehensive free leaflet with route, cycle hire and accommodation details and in typical German style details of the appropriate bronze, silver or gold badges, depending on how many of the three routes you have completed.

Further information

Fremdenverkehrsamt Baden-Württemberg, Esslinger Straße 8, D-7000 Stuttgart 1.

Schwarzwald Fremdenverkehrsverband, Bertoldstraße 45, Postfach 1660, D-7800 Freiburg.

Umweltinitiativen Freudenstadt, Kurverwaltung Freudenstadt, Am Promenade-Platz 1, D-7290 Freudenstadt.

Touristik-Gemeinschaft Schwäbische Alb, Korhaustraße 14, D-7070 Schwäbisch Gmünd.

Fremdenverkehrsverband Neckarland-Schwaben, Lohtorstraße 21, D-7100 Heilbronn.

Schwarzwaldverein, e.V., Hauptgeschäftsstelle, Rathausgasse 33, D-7800 Freiburg.

Schwäbischer Albverein, Hauptgeschäftsstelle, Hospitalstraße 21b, D-7000 Stuttgart 1.

Fleur and Colin Speakman, *Walking in the Black Forest* (Cicerone Press, 1990).

Bayern

The blue and white chequered flag of Bayern (Bavaria) is to be found throughout Germany's largest federal state. In fact, you'll see it far more often than the black, red and gold of the federal flag, and when you cross the border even from another Land within Germany, roadside signs will proclaim you are entering Frei Staat Bayern – the Bavarian free state.

Bavarians feel themselves to be different from other Germans. The Bavarians are an ancient people. After all their land was an independent dukedom and kingdom occupying what is now southeast Germany and part of what is now Austria, ruled by a single royal dynasty, the Wittelsbachs, for three quarters of a millenium. Even today you'll see in shops and restaurants, and indeed in private homes, photographs and paintings, like icons, of the penultimate Wittelsbach monarch, the tragic young Ludwig II.

And Bayern is different. The similarities with neighbouring Austria are sometimes startling, and not just in the Alpine regions. Little onion dome baroque churches grace every village. Local people will say 'Grüß Gott' to you rather than the more formal 'Guten Tag'. Many common dialect words are similar to those used in Austria. Like Austria, this is predominantly a Catholic country.

But paradoxically it is the larger-than-life-size Bavarian in Lederhosen, with a ridiculous 'shaving brush' Gamsbart, wearing a hunting hat and clutching a foaming tankard of beer, who has become the stereotype of a German!

You will however see people wearing Bavarian national costume on every conceivable occasion, women a form of the attractive dirndl (also Austrian), men the grey suit with a green lined collar or, indeed, the celebrated Lederhosen. And you will also see people enjoying superb Bavarian beer from those massive litre-sized tankards known as a Maas, in any Bierkeller or Fest.

There is even a special Bavarian political party, the CSU, a slightly more conservative form and close ally of the CDU. The CSU has held power continuously in Bayern for thirty years; the late Franz Joseph Strauss was its leader who, during his lifetime, became almost a folk hero for Bavarians.

'A land of farmers, priests and artists' is how Bayern has been typified, but this time with a real grain of truth. North Germans occasionally resent and even mock the folksiness and sometimes deep conservatism of the Bavarians. Yet the state's strong sense of identity has helped create not only a thriving tourist industry, but overall economic prosperity compared with the rural poverty of times past, which is yet further evidence of the value of decentralised government.

Significantly enough, the state takes a high profile in environmental protection, particularly over such matters as nature conservation, protection of water sources and water purification, dealing with rubbish and noise pollution.

Tourism policies have done a great deal to integrate farming and tourism, with opportunities for farm holidays and, unique in Germany, a scheme of 'Einkaufen auf dem Bauernhof' (shopping at the farm) whereby people are encouraged to call in at farms for fish, fruit, meat, poultry, eggs, milk produce, honey, wine. The Bayerische Bauernverband, the Bavarian equivalent of the National Farmers' Union, publish an annual booklet which lists addresses and phone numbers of farms, including organic farms, where you can ring up beforehand before calling in for the produce you want.

The river Danube – the Donau – cuts across the central part of this vast state, and makes a useful dividing line. The area to the north, between the Danube and the Main, is dominated by a single region – Franken – whilst in Ost Bayern (East Bavaria), running along the Czech border, lie the Oberpfalzer Wald and the Bayerische Wald.

The Danube, Isar and Inn valleys cross an area of relatively low-lying, richly agricultural countryside, usually known as Niederbayern or Lower Bavaria.

To the south of München (Munich) is Oberbayern – Upper Bavaria, first of all the Alpine foreland, an area of lakes and beautiful rolling countryside, and then in a narrow bank along the Austrian frontier the Alps themselves, from the Bodensee through the Allgäu and across via the Zugspitze, Germany's highest peak, to the Salzburger Alpen and, in the extreme southeast corner, spectacular Berchtesgadiner Land.

FRANKEN

Historically, Franken is the relic of a great East Frankish kingdom of Germanic tribes, which by medieval times was a much reduced but nevertheless independent dukedom.

It is an especially attractive and varied region of countryside, with superb old towns and villages, much of it extremely hilly, including much limestone, the valleys cut through with rivers and dotted with small lakes. It's an area which still has a strong medieval feel to it, not just the towns, but in the patterns of agriculture which in many respects reflect an age-old tradition. It is famous for its beer, with numerous small independent breweries producing a variety of specialist beers, for its excellent sausages, and for the superb Franken wine.

The city of **Nürnberg** (Nuremberg) on the Danube is the region's capital and focal point. Despite war damage which destroyed much of its medieval heart, and its modern industrial expansion, Nürnberg remains a remarkable historic centre. It was here that the Meistersinger Gilde (Mastersingers Guild) worked in the fourteenth and fifteenth centuries, including Hans Sachs, celebrated in Wagner's great opera. It was a great centre of the visual arts. Albrecht Dürer (1471-1528) was only one of scores of artists working in the city; Dürer's house survives as a museum. The city's medieval ramparts have survived, as has the elaborately decorated gothic fourteenth century fountain, the Schönner Brunnen and a number of fine churches. Also of national importance are the Germanische Nationalmuseum (of arts and craftmanship) in a Carthusian monastery and the Verkehrsmuseum (national transport museum) containing a splendid collection of early and later steam locomotives.

Bamberg to the north suffered less war damage and is a superb cathedral city with a magnificent medieval town centre. The poet and storyteller E.T.A. Hoffmann lived for a time in a tiny house in the city, using his home as the setting for one of his most famous tales – *The Golden Pot*. Over to the east lies **Bayreuth**, an old Franconian town and residence of the Margraves of Brandenburg. The town's name is now inexorably linked with that of Richard Wagner and also with Franz Liszt (Wagner married Liszt's daughter, Cosima). Thanks to help from King Ludwig II, the famous Wagner Festspielhaus was built there in 1876 and inaugurated with a performance of the epic *Der Ring des Nibelungen*. Wagner festivals have been held there ever since.

Between Nürnberg, Bamberg and Bayreuth lies the Fränkische Schweiz-Veldensteiner Naturpark, a huge area of almost a quarter of a million hectares, consisting of Jurassic limestone and dolomite formed into rocky crags and pinnacles and peaks, with steep-sided valleys through which streams flow, and what are called 'dolines' – hollows created when underground watercourses collapse, as well as numerous caves. The Teufelshöhle has the largest entrance to any cave in Germany and the remains of a huge Ice Age cave bear were found there. The limestone produces an extraordinarily rich flora, including gentians, aquilegias, orchids and lilies. Forest cover is mainly beech and spruce.

The railway line from Nürnberg to Bayreuth serves the area at Pagnitz whilst a branch railway from Forcheim on the Nürnberg-Bamberg line links Ebermannstadt. This is extended on summer Sundays with a Museumbahn (preserved railway, steam in high summer) to the delightful hilltop village of Gössweinstein and on to Behringsmühle. DB and local bus companies offer an excellent value 'Bus und Bahn' Fränkische Schweiz Gästekarte (guest card) which covers all buses and trains in the area for a one or two week period. This is available at local tourist offices. Over 4,000 kilometres of waymarked paths await the keen walker in the area.

South and east of Nürnberg lie the great rolling limestone hills of the Franken Alb, a continuation of the limestone Schwäbische Alb and very similar in character (see Baden-Württemberg), though greener.

Further west lies the Steigerwald, its name literally meaning climbing forest, which ascends the hillsides in great steps. Again, this contains a nature park, noted for its magnificent flora and its red deer. Close by, south of **Ansbach** and overlooking the Sulzach valley, is Frankenhohe, the Franconian Heights, another nature park, noted for its richly varied countryside, deciduous woods, superb villages, winding valleys, small lakes, and network of footpaths.

A popular long distance footpath, the Main-Donau Weg, runs to the immediate east of the area and connects such superb towns and villages as

Detwang, Rothenburg ob der Tauber (considered to be Germany's finest unspoiled medieval township), Schillingfurst, Feuchtwangen, Dinkelsbühl and Oettingen. **Nördlingen** to the south is a former imperial free city and has the only complete city wall around any town in Germany. All these towns are, incidentally, rail served or rail and bus served, albeit between Nördlingen and Dinkelsbühl by a steam powered museum railway – could there be a more delightful way of linking two medieval German towns?

A particularly interesting project in the **Feuchtwangen** area undertaken jointly by naturalists (Bund Naturschutz in Bayern), shooting interests (Jägervereinigung) and the local authority (Bezirk Mittelfranken) is a scheme to support the reintroduction of the partridge by encouraging local farmers to leave generous wild flower areas around the edge of fields, many of which have lost their hedges. The return of the partridge is seen as a symbol of an enrichment of species variety, including wild flowers, in the area. Especially significant is the philosophy of working closely with farmers to achieve these common aims, and the degree of co-operation between sporting and conservation interests which can be achieved.

Another imaginative project in the same region, this time around Neustadt/Aisch-Bad Windsheim, is utilising disused brewery cellars, of which there are many in Franken, to provide badly needed overwintering quarters for bats, another threatened species.

The Altmühltal, which lies at the confluence of the Danube and the Altmühl river, dominated by the 90 kilometre long winding Altmühl valley and the 600 metre high Hahnenkamm, is the largest nature park in Germany, covering around 3,000 square kilometres. This is an area as attractive for its nature conservation interest as its culture and history, with castles, ancient forts, medieval buildings and old villages, as well as being particularly rich in Jurassic fossils. It was here that the first archaeopterix or fossil flying bird was discovered, which provided the crucial evidence that birds evolved from reptiles.

This is also an area where the Naturpark is carrying out a fascinating project to create a 'synthesis' between tourism and nature protection, to involve visitors in the conservation process using a variety of educational means, focused around a Naturparkzentrum in a former monastery at Eichstätt. The philosophy is to create sustainable recreation opportunities as a means of reducing pressure on more sensitive areas. There are 3,000 kilometres of waymarked paths, twenty-two themed trails, around 500 kilometres of cycle paths, 150 kilometres of river open to boating (with ecologically 'sensible' resting points along the banks), as well as areas for climbing. The area is easily accessible by train, with a short and well served branch line to Eichstätt off the München-Treuchtlingen-Würzburg main line.

Franken's main winegrowing area lies around the beautiful old city of **Würzburg** on the Main. Franken wine is stronger and drier than most other German wines, and comes in the celebrated Bocksbeutel, the triangular-shaped bottle which Franken people claim has a 3,000 year old history, its shape being based on a stitched leather bottle that could be carried like a hip flask. It is one of the great European wines, celebrated in history as being the wine drunk by Barbarossa at his wedding, and in more recent times at the coronations of German Kaisers and of Queen Elizabeth II of England.

The Fränkische Weinland, around Würzburg, is also fine countryside, with its own nature park, and wine terraces and villages to explore.

To the northwest, and extending across the border with Hessen, above the Main valley around **Lohr** and **Aschaffenburg**, is the Bayerische Spessart Naturpark, 70,000 acres of deciduous forest noted for its 700-year-old oak trees. Deciduous trees are now being planted to maintain the balance between oak, beech, spruce and pine. It is an area important for its archaeology, including Stone and Bronze Age remains. Of particular interest is the Eselweg, a medieval donkey track used for carrying salt between Schlüchtern and Englesberg.

The Rhön Naturpark, southeast of Fulda in Hessen, with popular tourist centres at **Bad Brückenau** and **Gersfeld** (the latter rail served), lies around the vestiges of a huge, extinct volcano and is an area of high moorland, with a number of impressive peaks all excellent for walking, such as the Wasserkuppe (950 metres), just over the border in Hessen, and the Kreuzberg (932 metres), both notable viewpoints. The region, which reaches into both Thüringen and Hessen, is now a biosphere reserve – see these sections for further details.

A further series of beautiful areas form the boundary with Thüringen. The **Haßberge** is considered to be one of the quieter holiday areas, whilst the upper Main valley, famous for its monasteries and palaces, includes the old town of **Coburg**.

The **Frankenwald**, northeast of Kronach and north of Kulmbach, is another Naturpark, a magnificent area of forest, cut through with deep, winding valleys and honeycombed with waymarked walking routes that link small towns and resorts. These include such named routes as the Alexander von Humboldt Weg and the Burgen (castles) Weg. The Frankenwald forms a continuous forest area with the adjacent Thüringer Wald.

The **Fichtelgebirge** is often described as the roof of Germany, the meeting of such hills and forest ranges as the Frankenwald, the

Thüringer Wald, the Erzgebirge, and a major watershed with sources of tributary rivers that lead to the Rhine, the Saale, the Danube and the Elbe. The area has mixed forests, craggy rock formations and broad, lush valleys with a choice of spa towns and 'Luftkurorten' – an untranslatable term, but basically moorland or mountain resorts known for their good air and healthy climate.

OST BAYERN

In this region the line of thickly forested hills continues and, to the east, forms the border with Czechoslovakia. The Oberfalzer Wald is a popular holiday area of forest, lakes, open farmland and meadowland, and scattered villages, much of it a fairly gentle landscape but with areas of granite crags capped by ruined castles. Traditional farming is considered an important influence on the landscape and it is also an area known for glassmaking.

Further south, and northeast of Regensburg, is the **Bayerische Wald**. It falls into two distinct areas, the area south of Furth im Wald and around the towns of Cham and Lam is a Naturpark, whilst the area south of Bayerisch Eisenstein and Zweisel is a Nationalpark.

The Oberer Bayerische Wald extends over medium-height hills where mixed forests and woods divide shallow valleys with streams, pastureland, small towns and holiday resorts. At **Furth im Wald** each August a festival takes place which includes one of Germany's oldest folk theatre pieces, the Drachenstich – the slaying of the dragon by the knight Udo, a brilliant costume piece dating from the fifteenth century.

Craggy outcrops give drama to a variety of walking routes through the Naturpark, including the 160 kilometre Pandurensteig which crosses the whole of the Bayerische Wald from Waldmünchen, taking in some impressive scenery north of **Cham** through the edge of the Nationalpark, to **Passau** on the Danube. The Panduren were a group of ruthless mercenary soldiers, mainly Slavs, Hungarians and Rumanians, hired by the Austrians, who in the eighteenth century plundered the Bavarian border regions. Their exotic uniforms and curved swords made them particularly feared; rucksacks and walking sticks replace curved scimitars along a trail which can be done in stages of around 20-25 kilometres per day with an accommodation and luggage-carrying service.

The **Nationalpark Bayerischer Wald** covers part of the western side of Central Europe's most extensive area of forest stretching across into Bohemia. This is a superb, strictly protected area of natural and semi-natural woodland, rising on ancient hills of granite and gneiss to over 1,400 metres above sea level. Remnants of ancient woodland include spruce, silver fir, maple, elm, aspen, alder, willow yew and bird cherry. Rich ground vegetation includes a variety of mosses, ferns, herb Paris, cyclamen, May lily and the rare Hungarian gentian, otherwise unknown outside the Alps. Streams flow into wetlands and bogs, which again carry a variety of rare species including mountain pine, bilberry, cranberry, and orchids. A particular feature are areas of raised bog or Filze, consisting of moss and plant remains rising several metres above surrounding land.

Woodland management aims to remove some of the effects of previous commercial afforestation by allowing artificial drainage channels to become blocked to allow boggy areas to recuperate, and letting fallen trees lie to rot to allow natural processes of regeneration to occur. Natural woodland of differing age and species is less vulnerable to Waldsterben, to wind and to insect damage, then monocultured plantations are. Bird life to be seen includes goshawks, honey buzzard, black grouse, hazel hen, ring ouzels, a variety of owls, woodpeckers, flycatchers. Red and roe deer are now becoming a problem because of their numbers and may have to be culled.

What is exciting about the national park is how the needs of visitors and of visitor education is balanced with conservation needs. Strict zoning, including suspension of the Betretungsrecht (except for footpaths) at certain times of the year in the central core zone protects wildlife habitats and vulnerable areas, but the emphasis is on positive visitor involvement rather than negative exhortation.

Near **Neuschönau** is the Hans-Eisenmann Nationalpark Haus (served by bus from Grafenau and Spielgelau), a beautifully designed purpose-built centre with excellent interpretive displays of forest life, which also emphasises wider ecological issues such as the causes of Waldsterben. Close by is the Tier-Freigelände, a 200 hectare reservation where visitors can see native and now locally extinct species of animals and birds in as near as possible natural surroundings. Species include bison, bear, wolf, lynx, deer, otter, wild pig, badger, eagle, owl, capercaillie, species that people could not normally see even where they still exist. At **Sankt Oswald**, outside the park boundary, is a Waldgeschichtliches Museum which focuses on the cultural life of the old foresters and glassworkers (the traditional industry in the area, using forest charcoal) in some 'hands on' exhibits which seek to involve visitors in the experience. There is a woodland play area for children and areas devoted to forest history where you can wander freely and even scramble among rocks. By concentrating the largest number of visitors into robust areas, pressure is reduced in the more vulnerable hinterland.

Significantly, the national park authority co-operates closely with local villages in remarkable green tourism initiatives whereby visitors

204 / GERMANY BY LÄNDER

stay in local accommodation outside the park, thus benefitting the local economy, while taking part in Nationalpark walks. Beautifully way-marked themed trails, many of which go outside the park, also help to raise awareness of ecological issues. However, it is also possible to follow waymarked paths deep into the heart of the forest. Of outstanding quality is the walk from **Spiegelau** to the summit of the Großer Rachel (1,453 metres), past the Rachelsee with its much photographed wooden-tiled chapel by the lake. Part of the route crosses an area of bog by an elevated wooden pavement known as the Ochsenklavier (ox piano, as it resembles giant piano keys) where the walker can look down at dwarf pine and willow without damaging a fragile system.

Both Grafenau and Spiegelau are excellent centres from which to explore the national park, with a choice of reasonably priced accommodation. Both are served by train on the little 'Waldbahn' branch railway which runs from Zwiesel, itself on a branch railway from Plattling on the Regensburg-Passau main line, and there is a bus service from Passau. Packages of accommodation and national park activities can be purchased through the local tourist office. Local buses from both these centres penetrate deep into the national park.

It's also worth visiting at least one of the glassworks in the area to see craftsmen at work using age-old techniques (albeit with modern gas-fired heating rather than charcoal) to create superb hand-blown glass in traditional styles. Bavarian glasswork rivals Bohemian for its beauty. The works at **Frauenau**, on the Waldbahn railway, are the oldest in Germany and some of the Jugendstil styles still being created are true works of art.

The local tourist office at Freyung-Grafenau also publishes a 64.5 kilometre recommended 'historic cycle trail' around the edge of and into the national park.

The Danube valley itself richly repays exploration. Boat services and cycleways link Nürnberg, Regensburg and Passau. **Regensburg** is an especially lovely city, with a surviving Roman tower and some superb architecture. The café on the riverside selling bratwurst, sauerkraut and beer is one of the oldest in Germany. **Passau** is spectacularly beautiful. It stands on the confluence of three rivers, the Danube, the Inn and the Ilz, the main part of the old town including its magnificent cathedral crowded onto the narrow peninsula between the Inn and the Donau. You can walk or cycle from here into Austria, the Danube cycle train going as far as Vienna. If Passau itself now suffers from too much tourist pressure (coaches arrive here in large numbers from both Germany and Austria), there is a lovely quiet hinterland of rolling farmland and scattered villages for farm holidays or bed and breakfast accommodation away from the main tourist pressures. Its gentle gradients make it a particularly good area for cycling.

MÜNCHEN AND OBER BAYERN

Augsburg shares with München the distinction of being one of the most impressive cities of southern Bayern. Originally a Roman city, it flourished as a great cultural, financial and religious centre in the fifteenth century, and has an impressive cathedral, some superb late Renaissance architecture and, around the Fuggerei, an amazing area of early sixteenth century workers' dwellings – probably the first example of municipal housing in the world.

The city of **München**, fashionable, elegant, with its massive palaces, public buildings, squares, boulevards, reflects a regal past – the later Wittelsbach era, especially the reign of Ludwig I (1825-48) who tried to make the city one of the most impressive royal capitals in Europe. The present day city also contradicts any notion of Bavarian provincialism, being a major European cultural and artistic centre, known for its liberal and progressive views, and sometimes referred to as Germany's 'other' capital. It shares the prosperity of southern Germany, being a centre of the electronics industry, precision engineering, machine tools, optics, chemicals, printing and publishing, and of course brewing, with the world famous Oktober Bierfest as a celebration of the glory of its brewers' art. It isn't entirely surprising that a Wittelsbach, a descendant of the last Ludwigs, should own one of the many excellent local breweries.

München's pedestrianised central streets, around the handsome Frauenkirche and Marien Platz, and along Neuhause and Kaufingerstraße, are in the summer months and on warm summer evenings taken over by young people, with cafés and pubs spilling out onto the pavements, and music of every type – Mozart, heavy metal, rock, jazz, blues, delighting crowds of bystanders, accompanied by recitations, street theatre, cabaret, political statement.

A short walk away is the famous Englischer Garten, an English-style garden with lakes and pavilions, laid out in the eighteenth century, whilst the Nymphenburg Schloß, served by tram, has fine parkland, ornamental canals and botanic gardens. Like all major German cities, München has an excellent integrated public transport system – S-Bahn, tram and bus – to make travel round the city and out into the adjacent countryside cheap and simple. Cars are increasingly being restrained in the city centre.

About 5 kilometres northeast of München, alongside the Mittlere Isar Kanal, reached by München S-Bahn line S3, is a series of around thirty fish ponds and a reservoir – the Speichersee – with fringed reedbeds and riverine forest, which form the Ismaniger Teichgebiet which was originally created as a biological purification system to deal with the effluents of the city. But the ponds, rich in nutrients and consequently aquatic fauna, have also become a bird reserve of international importance, designated a 'Europa-Reserve' by the International Council of Bird Protection. As many as 85,000 wintering waterfowl are recorded there each year, and feeding species include tufted duck, pochard, night heron and gadwall as well as gulls and terns in abundance. It is, however, feared that industrial and motorway development could damage the area.

A short S-Bahn ride on line S5 from München leads to the Starnbergsee, one of the five attractive lakes which make up what is now being marketed as the Fünfseenland (five lakes country) in the Alpine foreland. **Starnberg** itself is a small, yet elegant resort on the northern end of the lake, from where motor launches go clockwise and anti-clockwise around the lake to a regular timetable.

At **Berg**, some 5 kilometres from Starnberg and reached by a lakeside path or by ferry, is a small Votivkapelle or chapel opposite a cross in the lake where Ludwig II died in mysterious circumstances in 1886. The king's body and that of his doctor were found floating in the lake. To this day it is not known if the 41-year-old monarch and his companion were murdered or died accidentally. Whether or not Ludwig was 'mad' is also open to debate. For certain he was no politician. His love of natural beauty, of great music and fine architecture are, in fact, for many people the marks of sanity. His patronage of Wagner probably saved the composer's life and enabled such later masterpieces as *Tristan* and *Parsifal* to be completed. His celebrated castles at Linderhof, near Oberammergau, at Herrenchiemsee on the Chiemsee and at Neuschwanstein near Füssen, almost bankrupted the state when they were built, using the talents of hundreds of architects and leading craftsmen in their building and decoration and were a major cause of Ludwig's downfall. But they now bring in millions of marks in foreign currency.

A group of local authorities in the area, the Arbeitsgemeinschaft Fernwanderwege in Voralpenland, have co-operated to develop the König Ludwig Fernwanderweg, a 120 kilometre superbly waymarked route from Starnberg to Ludwig's fairytale castle of Neuschwanstein at **Füssen**. The route, waymarked through forest and meadow with a little blue 'K', exploits the gentle rolling countryside of southern Bayern, always with the Alps in the background, the snowy topped mountains getting closer and the scenery more dramatic as you walk towards them. The route takes in such wonderful features as Dießen on the Ammersee with its baroque church designed by Michael Fisher, the monastery at Wessobrun where the first German written script was recorded and where there is also a magnificent abbey church, the Ammerschlucht gorge, and the breathtakingly beautiful Wieskirche, designed by the Zimmerman brothers, a masterpiece of baroque. The climax is Ludwig's castle of Neuschwanstein, in its perfect setting on a rocky outcrop which can be reached by ascending the Pöllat gorge, and the less dramatic but almost as impressive Hohenschwangau palace, with its Lohengrin association. Inevitably Neuschwanstein suffers from all the effects of hard tourism, with over two million visitors, mainly by coach and car, every year, and vast queues of tourists and multilingual guides to take you round the superbly decorated art nouveau state rooms.

The walk ends at Füssen on the edge of the Alps and close to the Austrian border, from where local trains link with express services to München via Buchloe. The organisers, the AFV, provide an excellent pre-arranged six day accommodation and luggage-carrying package using local hotels, Gasthöfe and even farmhouses along the route, usually with good opportunities to meet other walkers sharing the route, but not in an organised party as such. One real delight for connoisseurs of Bavarian beer are the excellent opportunities to visit some of the small brewery Biergartens attached to monasteries, with superb beers brewed by monks on offer, including the famous strong dark 'Bock' beers.

Other walking packages organised by the AFV include the Lech Hohenweg along the upper Lech valley, and the Prelätenweg which traces routes used by clergymen and clerics through the area in former times.

Cyclists are catered for by an excellent, largely traffic-free network of waymarked cycle routes. A six night 'Super 8' package, suitable for families with children, is arranged for visitors, including cycle hire, by the Ammersee tourist office.

Cycling is also promoted heavily in the region to the west of the Lech known as Allgäu Bayerisch Schwaben, which includes the Forggensee, the top of the Iller valley and across to the Bodensee and the curious, but delightful lake island town of Lindau with magnificent views of the lake and snow-covered Alps in the background.

The Bayerische Alpen are a treasured place for most Germans, particularly for walking and skiing. **Garmisch Partenkirchen**, where composer Richard Strauss lived for much of his life, is perhaps the most popular of several resorts and huge luxury hotels and holiday apartment complexes crowd the valley bottom. From Garmisch you can take the electric rack railway through a 4.5 kilometre tunnel almost to the summit of the Zugspitze (2,963 metres above sea level), in clear weather one of the finest viewpoints of the Alps on the border with Austria. There are also cable car services to other peaks, and chair lifts. **Mittenwald**, the next station down the line and closer to the Austrian border, has less glamour but also less expensive accommodation, and offers just as excellent mountain walking.

If mass tourism is not to your taste, few areas in the Alps can compare with **Berchtesgaden Nationalpark**. Berchtesgaden itself is tourist Germany, the village centre admittedly being nicer than the brash and noisy crossroads. It is easily reached on the branch railway line from Freilassing via the attractive old salt town and spa of Bad Reichenhall. All this 'outer' area forms part of a wider Berchtesgaden Alpenpark where recreational activity, including skiing (with chair lifts and cable cars), walking, cycling and car touring flourish, though with a reasonable measure of landscape protection. In this respect it is not dissimilar to an English or Welsh National Park.

Tourists in their thousands make their way via Schönau to the shores of the Königsee (bus or 4 kilometre footpath route from Berchtesgaden), where by the usual lakeside bric-a-brac (but including a good national park centre), you must wait for the quiet and pollution-free electric-powered boat to take you across the clear green waters between vast walls of rock, the snow-capped summit of the Watzman above you. You are now in a near silent world away from the noise of motor traffic. The landscape has an overwhelming, awesome beauty. The Königsee is the purest lake in Germany and you can see fish swimming deep below the boat as it cuts across the surface. Halfway across the lake the boatman, if there are enough visitors, will probably perform his party trick, the blowing of a bugle to hear the returning echo, like a Mahler symphony, with a second or so time gap from across the lake.

Most visitors alight at the little red-domed pilgrimage church of St. Bartholomä to have coffee or a meal in the nearby restaurant. Some will make their way along the rocky footpath to view the Eiskapelle at the bottom of the glacier from the Watzman. Others continue the boat journey to the head of the lake and walk across the headland to the magically lovely Obersee at the head of which is the Fischunkel Alm, a little traditional and carefully restored Alpine farm in the meadow, selling homemade cheese and black bread with buttermilk to provide a delightful – and delicious — touch.

Beyond this point, only a small number of well equipped mountaineers penetrate into the great ring of high and formidable mountains that form the border with Austria. A similar situation occurs along the adjacent Wimbachtal, where beyond the Wimbachklamm the walker follows a broad, dry, stony valley towards what is known as the Steinernes Meer, the stony sea, an astonishing feature. Another fine walk is along the Klausbach valley to the Bind Alm, though this valley is shared with a motor road over the border. All the roads and tracks into the central areas of the national park are totally closed to cars and motorised vehicles, and whilst you can reach the edge of the area by for example car or bus, the only way to penetrate into the national park is on foot. There are however over 190 kilometres of footpaths within the relatively small area of the national park.

Berchtesgaden Nationalpark, by accident or design, demonstrates the value of the concept of a 'long walk in' to a protected area.

In fact the park has a long history as a protected area, going back to the time of the Bavarian kings when it was a hunting reserve, which became a protected area for plants as early as 1910. Plans to expand the inn at St. Bartholomä and to open up the area for tourists led in stages to a Naturschutzgebiet in 1960. Further impetus for even higher national status came when in the 1960s there were plans for a cable railway up the Watzman. This was opposed by the German Alpine Club and many other nature protection bodies and finally led to the creation of the Berchtesgaden Nationalpark in 1978, covering 21,000 hectares of the southern portion of the Berchtesgaden Alpenpark, in effect dividing the area of the Alpine park into two – a northern 'recreation zone' including all the busy tourist towns and villages, and a strictly protected quiet zone.

The national park's main purpose is threefold – to protect natural habitats, to research into habitats and ecological communities and to provide education and suitable recreation facilities for visitors. Anything which damages or destroys the park is therefore illegal.

Special features of the park include the most northerly glacier of the Alps, superb natural deciduous woodlands, herb-rich Alpine meadows, the Königsee itself, one of the deepest of Alpine lakes, and dramatic geological features, including caves, limestone pavements, screes, fossils, and limestone formation of Ramsau dolomite. The flora includes dwarf mountain pines, juniper, dwarf Alpine roses, white Alpine poppies, globeflowers, columbine, orchids, saxifrage, wild crocus, rockrose, and dwarf box. Animals to be seen include red deer, chamois (both now increasing in number because of their protected status to a point where the numbers could cause damage to the forest), ibex, marmots, snow hare and snow mice, the Alpine salamander, whilst rare bird life includes the golden eagle, Alpine chough and the ptarmigan.

Current plans, being discussed with neighbouring authorities in Austria, are to re-introduce the lynx to this part of the Alps, to allow this shy creature of the high Alps to take its place once again in the region's ecological system.

Further information

LFVV Bayern, Prinzregent Straße 18, D-8000 München 22.
Fremdenverkehr Franken e.V., Am Plärrer 14, D-8500 Nürnberg 80.
Naturpark Altmühltal, Notre Dame 1, D-8070 Eichstätt.
FVV Ost Bayern, Landshuter Straße 13, D-8400 Regensburg.

FVV München-Oberbayern, Sonnenstraße 10, D-8000 München 2.

Arbeitsgemeinschaft Fernwanderungen in Voralpenland, Von Kühlmann Straße 15, D-8910 Landsberg Lech.

Nationalpark Berchtesgaden, Doktorberg 6, D-8240 Schönau a. Königsee.

Nationalpark Bayerischer Wald, Freyungerstraße 2, D-8352 Grafenau.

Fleur and Colin Speakman, *King Ludwig Way* (Cicerone Press, 1987).

Einkaufen auf dem Bauernhof in Bayern – available from Bayerischer Bauernverband, Max-Joseph Straße 9, D-8000 München (price around DM4.00).

NOTES

NOTES

NOTES

NOTES

NOTES

NOTES